ESSAYS IN THEORY AND HISTORY

ESSAYS IN
THEORY AND HISTORY

An Approach to the Social Sciences

Edited by

Melvin Richter

Harvard University Press
Cambridge, Massachusetts
1970

In memory of
Klaus Epstein and Michael Olmsted

PREFACE

The papers in this volume by Professors James, Richter, Tilly, and Walzer were delivered at a meeting held in Cambridge, Massachusetts, in April 1967. As for the others, I should like to thank the Princeton University Press for permission to reprint the late Klaus Epstein's introduction to his *Genesis of German Conservatism* (Princeton, 1966) and the Wayne State University Press for permission to reprint Walter Dean Burnham's "American Voting Behavior and the 1964 Election," from the *Midwest Journal of Political Science* XII (February 1968). An earlier version of Professor Beer's paper was presented at the 1967 Annual Meeting of the American Political Science Association, and Professor Thernstrom's contribution was first prepared for the Anglo-American Colloquium of the Society for the Study of Labour History, held in London during June 1968. My paper was revised and extended during my tenure as Senior Fellow, National Endowment for the Humanities, 1967–68.

The Introduction to this volume owes much to memoranda and materials supplied by Mr. Edward T. Wilcox, Director of General Education and the Freshman Seminar Program, Harvard College, and by Professor Beer. Mr. John Hoffman's detailed criticism of an earlier draft helped correct errors.

Thanks are due to my research assistant, Mrs. Binnaz Bingöllü Sayari, a Ph.D. candidate in Political Science, City University of New York, who helped type and prepare the manuscript; to the staffs of the New York Public Library and the John Jermain Library, Sag Harbor, Long Island; and to the Carnegie Corporation of New York, which made it possible to hold the meeting where most of these papers were given and to publish this book.

Melvin Richter

November 1969
New York City

vii

CONTENTS

Introduction   1

THEORY

1. Samuel H. Beer *Political Science and History*   41
2. Melvin Richter *The Uses of Theory: Tocqueville's Adaptation of Montesquieu*   74
3. Klaus Epstein *Three Types of Conservatism*   103
4. Michael Walzer *The Revolutionary Uses of Repression*   122

HISTORY

5. Charles Tilly *The Changing Place of Collective Violence*   139
6. Sydney V. James *Colonial Rhode Island and the Beginnings of the Liberal Rationalized State*   165
7. Walter Dean Burnham *American Voting Behavior and the 1964 Election*   186
8. Stephan Thernstrom *Working Class Social Mobility in Industrial America*   221

Appendix A. Reading Lists and Examinations. 1951–1952, 1968–1969   241

Appendix B. Teaching Staff, Social Sciences 2 (1946–1970)   255

Notes on Contributors   256

Notes   258

Index   287

ESSAYS IN THEORY AND HISTORY

INTRODUCTION

This collection is the work of some who have taught in Social Sciences 2, a General Education course given at Harvard since 1946 by Professor Samuel H. Beer. All the authors have shared in an unusual intellectual relationship, both with their colleagues at the time they served together as staff and in the subsequent meetings that have brought together those who have taught in different years. Under the influence of this association have come not only these papers, but a number of books. Many of them have provoked critical attention, but as yet no one has remarked their common provenience. This volume is meant to perform that function, to affirm the solidarity of the work done recently, or in progress by members of this group, which is united by its belief in the value of developing comparative social and political theory of a sort that may be applied to historical materials.

A further purpose of the book is to shed some light upon how the social sciences may be taught in a genuinely interdisciplinary form and to outline one successful method of training graduate students to teach in this way. This course has developed its own distinctive style of putting questions and has gone some way toward developing answers to them. As an approach to general education it has had a profound effect upon those teaching in it, an experience that suggests rather less incompatibility between teaching and research than is sometimes supposed. Much has been said on the topic of how difficult it is to persuade graduate students to teach general education courses. Indeed the absence of connection between such instruction and the professional concerns of the departments within which young instructors must make their way has been cited as among the most important reasons for the decline of general education in even those universities most committed to its maintenance. Those who have taught in this course would like to stress its professional value to them, and although its worth will occasionally be argued on the basis of benefit to undergraduates, the emphasis will fall upon what it has done for professional researchers and teachers. This is done not because there is little to be said about the course's appeal to undergraduates (it was the largest in the college until Professor Beer decided to limit enrollment), but rather because each of the contributors feels that he can best speak in his own voice and testify most directly through his own work.

It may be that the time has passed for well-intended calls for interdisciplinary work. After two decades of such invocations the social and behavioral sciences remain, with certain exceptions, isolated from historical studies. And although historians seek increasingly to utilize the hypotheses and techniques of their colleagues, what is borrowed is not always suitable to the nature of their tasks. This gap between social science and history derives in large part from two sources: the vested interests of the separate disciplines and the training of graduate students. These students generally learn only the research techniques and intellectual operations practiced by the department that grants them their degrees. Almost no professional priority is given to work that bridges departments. Even in those few programs with a genuinely interdisciplinary intent, the merger of theory with history tends to remain programmatic. This outcome has been quite reversed by those who have taught in Social Sciences 2. Trained to apply theory to history, they have assimilated the operative methods and critical standards of both the professional historian and the social scientist. In the papers that follow, it is difficult to determine the writer's discipline, although the authors are formally historians, political scientists, and sociologists. What they offer here are examples of a method based upon mastery of more than one departmental discipline.

This is not to say that all the contributors to this volume belong to the same school, if that term is understood to denote a precise set of dogmas about research procedures or a narrow consensus about matter worth investigating. Their techniques vary from archival research in public records, the use of personal documents, and the textual analysis characteristic of intellectual history to survey research and the analysis of aggregate data and its processing by computer. On their face, the subjects treated may appear to diverge. But it will be argued below that these contributions are united by a style of comparative and historical analysis. And though there are marked differences among these applications of this method, such individuality is itself encouraged by experience in teaching this course.

II

The beginnings and subsequent development of Social Sciences 2 cannot be separated from the original assumptions of the Harvard General Education Report of 1945, more familiarly known on its native grounds as the "Redbook." [1] Professor Beer's original design was to realize the objectives of a course described in the Report as an example of what general education in the social sciences might become.[2] Yet in the twenty-five years since its publication, this course has responded to influences and evolved a mode of proceeding quite unforeseen either by the committee responsible for the Report or by Professor Beer when he first gave Social Sciences 2. Such innovations have stemmed from the drastic changes that have transformed the social sciences, the composition and abilities of the undergraduate and graduate student bodies, and the political situation at home and abroad. Not the least striking development has been an increasing specialization and professionalism in a course that was originally designed in reaction to precisely these aspects of modern knowledge. Yet in so doing, it has not altogether lost the generality sought in its initial conception. But now this is attained by comparing whole societies and political systems in a number of ways that presuppose technical training.

General Education in a Free Society appeared in 1945. It was the product of nearly three years of work by a Harvard committee established by President James Bryant Conant, who himself contributed the introduction. Its subsequent effects, which were considerable outside of Harvard as well as within, derived as much from its timing and circumstances as from its premises, many of which were shared by Americans determined to make something better of the postwar world than what had existed before. It was such aspiration rather than any genuine novelty of program that distinguished the Report. In fact, it added little to the theory and practice of general education as known at Columbia University and, to a lesser degree, at the University of Chicago. Beneath the call to a rededication of the university to the purposes of a liberal democratic society could be detected the tacit recognition that Harvard had adhered too long to the great latitude in choice of courses allowed undergraduates by President Eliot. At both Columbia and Chicago the elective system in its full purity had long been abandoned.

General education at all three universities shared certain assumptions, which have been summarized admirably by Professor Daniel Bell:

1. It was felt that American society was such that students had to acquire, if not a single purpose, at least a sense of common tasks confronting them as citizens.

2. The history of Western civilization must be emphasized so as to broaden the student's perspective beyond that of purely American experience, to make him aware of these recurrent problems confronting man in society and politics, and to confront him with the history and conditions of that freedom Americans tend to accept as their birthright. "If there is a single conclusion to which the programs point, it would be instilling the idea of civility."

3. As against that specialized research that had come to dominate even the most traditional studies, there was asserted the need on the part of all students to acquire that humanism deemed essential to any educated man.

4. An interdisciplinary approach is wanted to overcome the fragmentation of knowledge. "The multiplication of knowledge, the rise of many new subfields and subspecialties, the cross-cutting of fields all led to a desire for courses that emphasized the broad relationships of knowledge, rather than the single discipline. This integration was to be achieved through a survey of fields, the elucidation of fundamental principles of disciplines, the centrality of method or a combination of all of these." [3]

In his charge to the Committee on the Objectives of a General Education in a Free Society, President Conant had declared that "the heart of the problem of a general education is the continuance of the liberal and humane tradition." [4] These terms defined the committee's point of departure. Such esteem for the notion of a distinctively Western heritage, liberal and humane, managed to unite both those who thought of themselves as conservative and elitist and others whose views were progressive and egalitarian.

Unlike T. S. Eliot's theory of tradition, this Harvard version could easily be connected to Americans' image of themselves and their society. President Conant wrote of "the broad basis of understanding which is essential if our civilization is to be preserved," of what was required for "the sufficient educational background for citizens of a free nation." [5] In this view scholarship must be made relevant to the participating citizen. Such a civic emphasis may be contrasted to the preoccupation, omnipresent some fifteen years later, with "education for excellence," a slogan not unconnected to the first Soviet Sputnik. In the late 1960's a trend can be discerned toward a rewriting of the American experience in a way "usable" to present demands for remaking the society and polity on a pattern at once more just at home and less interventionist abroad. Such pragmatic objectives do not differ in kind from those of 1945. Then the past had to be connected with a retrospective rationale for the American effort in the Second World War, as well as with the generating of enthusiasm for coping with the host of new problems and further responsibilities growing out of the postwar settlement. If history bulked large in such a program, it was not history for its own sake, but rather for that of elucidating the Western tradition or those elements of it still alive and nourishing civic action. Notwithstanding ostensible differences, American attitudes toward higher education have remained highly instrumental, reflecting what has been understood to be national needs, whether in the postwar period or in the present movement toward racial justice and the reduction of the United States' role abroad.

In 1945 the stress upon citizenship was strong, so much so that even one who responded favorably to the Report when it appeared now finds it difficult to reconstruct the emotional springs of this motif, which has largely lost its power to stir readers. Some may seek an explanation in the theory that an ideology was needed for the impending cold war that would begin just as soon as it was safe to attack the Soviet Union, once it had completed its major part in defeating Nazi Germany. Another hypothesis has been suggested to explain the ideas and feelings that supported the general education movement.[6] In this view nothing was more crucial than the conditions proper to the Second World War and the great depression preceding it. It is sometimes forgotten that during the depression and the New Deal many intellectuals had celebrated social conflict as fruitful, indeed as the precondition of change for the better. Although this position is in many ways persuasive when properly argued, its statement during the New Deal tended to be superficial, resting as it usually did on a facile pragmatism modified for the occasion by doses of progressivism such as Charles Beard's and eclectic borrowings from Marxism. All at once, with the American entry into the war and the Nazi attack upon the Soviet Union, consensus and solidarity became the supreme political values. How were these newly discovered virtues to be justified? What was it that was being defended against Hitler?

The possibilities were not unlimited. As a slogan, "Democracy" suffered from its earlier abuse by Woodrow Wilson. Race had been appropriated by the other side. Given American pluralism, no particular religion could be pressed into service. Yet a cause and a creed were necessary. Nor did this come about simply because leaders were cynically seeking symbols by which to manipulate the masses. No American elite was prepared by anything in its intellectual training or political experience for the rise of Hitler. Pragmatic, Lockean, and ahistorical, the American stock of ideas was inadequate to confront so formidable a threat to its values. In view of the Nazi threat to liberal humanism, it was not unreasonable to assert that what was to be defended was the "Western," or as religious spokesmen tended to put it, the Judeo-Christian tradition. Yet American higher education had become so specialized, had so taken for granted precisely those premises attacked root and branch by the Nazis, that no other theoretical rationale was available. In retrospect it now appears that American political philosophy and political science were at once excessively empirical and self-centered. As late as 1938, no one had yet felt the need to revise previous statements and defenses of American values in the light of the totalitarian attack upon them. In the elementary course in government at Harvard in that year the only work of theory was a set of selections from Blackstone. Thus the university system was vulnerable to the charge that its instruction was at once so specialized and haphazard that both students and their teachers were intellectually ill-equipped to deal with threats to their liberties.

Although Stalinism appeared preferable to Nazism, it too brought into question the unreasoned consensus supporting American institutions. Of course the depression had brought many to uncertainty or to outright rejection of what then passed for American political philosophy. But Communism did not hold very many of those who joined the party. The tortuous course followed by Stalin alienated many who debated passionately the Moscow trials, the Soviet-Nazi pact, the attack on Finland, the denunciation of Britain and France as imperialist powers in 1940, and the quick change in tune once the Soviet Union was itself invaded. Thus Communism in its Stalinist mode had already been diagnosed as a threat when events in 1941 made the United States and the Soviet Union reluctant allies. For the next four years most differences on the level of ideas were muted. This was due to a number of reasons ranging from pure expediency to a hope that the Soviet Union, once freed from the Nazi danger, would forsake its former practices. The settling of accounts with Marxist theory was therefore deferred. And again it could be seen how impoverished the American stock of ideas had been left by the principal trends of specialized education. At Harvard as elsewhere, many scholars had identified themselves with the ideals of a disinterested science that had the unique objective of advancing knowledge. When combined with an undergraduate scheme of education that permitted virtually free choice, the result was a curriculum not easily defended. Although an excellent education was available to those who cared to seek it, many undergraduates acquired degrees merely by the accumulation of miscellaneous credits. Such a system did not require students to consider their basic assumptions or those of their society.

Thus the Report stressed the part value judgments should play in general education. "Unless the educational process contains at each *level of maturity* some continuing contact with these fields in which value judgments are of prime importance, it must fall short of the ideal." [7] If history is to be studied, for example, it can contribute to general education only if its subject and aims go beyond that of establishing what in fact happened. One way of avoiding a concern with the past for its own sake is to stress the importance of ideas. Unless the student "feels the import of those general ideas and aspirations which have been a deep moving force in the lives of men, he runs the risk of partial blindness." [8] The basis for this assertion was philosophical, or perhaps ideological. It rested upon the belief that men, even among events of extraordinary magnitude, may decide their destiny by reason and will. It need scarcely be said that such a position was meant to counter both the irrationalism of the Nazis and the materialistic determinism that has always been a significant component of Marxism, if not Leninism. Composed in equal parts of pragmatism and an attenuated idealism, this was a peculiarly American faith. Its pragmatism took the form of a belief that in principle all problems are capable of resolution; its idealism rested upon the belief that nothing counts for more in human action than men's orientations through ideas and values. The Report took the position that in the universities of a democratic society, students cannot be left to themselves to learn or not to learn the basis of the consensus that holds their political system together. Such a con-

7

nection between the potential capacity of citizens to understand and take appropriate action on the one hand, and their education on the other, had long been perceived by political philosophers. Now it became an essential part of the theory of general education in a free and democratic society.

III

In the spring of 1946 Professor Beer was invited to teach one of the new courses to be offered for the first time on an experimental basis in the General Education program. It had been decided that there should be a number of courses offered on the intellectual level in each area, rather than having but one course, as was the practice at Columbia and Chicago, where the notion that all students should share a knowledge of the Western heritage has been interpreted to mean that they should do so within the same format. This never became a principle of general education at Harvard.

Although the faculty of Harvard College approved the introduction of general education in 1945, it was not until 1949 that the program was made compulsory. By that time certain concepts of the Redbook could not be applied. For not only were there a number of courses satisfying the general education requirement in each area, but with a few notable exceptions, they had been limited to the introductory level. Yet compulsory general education courses for more advanced students had figured in the program as originally conceived. Thus by practice, rather than by deliberate choice, elementary courses came to assume a dominating position in general education at Harvard. Professor Beer has taught his course from the beginning to the present day.

Social Sciences 2 has now passed through three distinct phases, the first of which lasted from 1946 through 1950. During this time the notion of heritage dominated the concerns of the course, although much was made of such moral and political values as liberty and democracy. Perhaps the single most important assumption was that general education was to consist of a dialogue between teacher and student about "great issues," all of them rooted in the human situation, and hence incapable of definitive solution. This approach was somewhat loosely linked to the use of such social science theories as might explain what the General Education Report had called "The Evolution of Free Society," its paraphrase of Benedetto Croce's *History as the Story of*

Liberty. History was to be treated purposively, with periods and places chosen for what they might contribute to an understanding of the grand theme. Certainly such a course resembled neither what was being done by historians nor by social scientists. But it also ran the risk of being repudiated by them as nothing more than vague debate about issues better treated by philosophers. In fact since the demise of idealism professional philosophers no longer addressed themselves to history or politics in this style.

As might have been expected, the course when first taught suffered from this assortment of divided aims and from the absence of any body of organized concepts that might order its historical materials. The ideal of interdisciplinary treatment was vivid; the means of attaining it, obscure. Put otherwise, the sentiment of opposition to specialization in the social sciences was not in itself enough to produce an adequate conceptual scheme. In part the difficulties stemmed from the social sciences themselves, as then practiced in the United States. Professor Beer, in his initial version of the course, made use of Ruth Benedict's *Patterns of Culture* to illuminate the Dark Ages, described in his outline as a "barbarian society." Walter Bagehot's *Physics and Politics* served as an introduction to a theory of the development of human communities. It hardly needs saying that anyone attempting a similar course today would begin with incomparably greater intellectual advantages: the study of development and modernization has become one of the chief foci of social theory. Yet by beginning in a way that abandoned the strict chronology of the history courses for the alternative procedure of the theoretical treatment of significant cases, an important step had been taken. Although the case method now scarcely creates the impression of intellectual adventure, its application to historical materials in 1946 constituted an innovation at Harvard. And almost as novel was the deliberate resort to theorists from the other social sciences, together with the search for a pattern that might fit together societies widely separated in space and time. In the hands of an investigator sufficiently open-minded to take advantage of the transformations about to take place in social theory, such an approach could lead to another, rather more solidly based on both comparative analysis and historical research.

In its first phase the course studied eight topics, beginning with England prior to the Norman Conquest and ending with Marxian Socialism. The choice of this starting point, rather than classical Greece and Rome, in part was determined by the criterion of relevance to the Anglo-

American style of citizenship and political liberty; in part by the nature of Professor Beer's own historical training. In new enterprises men must take advantage of such resources as they possess, for even with them an extraordinary effort in both theory and history is required if a course such as this is to be something more than reshuffling of old labels. The conditions and development of freedom were studied in relation to: 1) Anglo-Saxon Society; 2) Innocent III; 3) Edward I; 4) The Puritan Revolution; 5) Louis XIV; 6) British Reforms in the Nineteenth Century; 7) Germany under Bismarck; 8) Marxian Socialism. As for what was done with these topics, one not unfriendly critic has remarked that at this time, the course presented simultaneously the historiography, political philosophy, and use of social science characteristic of liberalism. All of these strands converged in what some construed to be the implicit teaching which a well-informed student might carry away, that is, that the study of previous crises of liberty leads to political wisdom, perhaps even political virtue.

This array of problems and periods proved to be less durable than certain other aspects of the course. These have continued with little modification from the beginning to the present day. Every week there are two formal lectures by Professor Beer and a discussion meeting of undergraduates with one of the graduate teaching fellows who assist him. For every topic there is a paper of 1,500 to 2,000 words on a subject set by the section man. These papers are in lieu of the quizzes and midterm examinations once universal in Harvard courses restricted to freshmen and sophomores. At the end of each term there is, however, a final examination, once based wholly, but now only partially on questions given in advance to the students.

As a matter of principle the graduate students teaching in the course are recruited from several disciplines, among which history and political science predominate, although there have been some sociologists, and more exceptionally, philosophers, economists, anthropologists, and law students. Once a week the section men meet with Professor Beer, who discusses with them the substantive issues that he and they will be taking up the next week. Most of the participants remember these staff meetings as among the high points of their graduate life at Harvard. My own experience was in the two years from 1951 to 1953. Unlike most other occasions of this sort, Social Sciences 2 staff meetings had an intellectual rather than an administrative focus. In the sustained arguments that characterized them, no quarter was asked or given, although there was a remarkable absence of personal animosity or stubborn adherence to individual views. Dialectic and vigorous criticism extended to Professor Beer's lectures as well as to glosses by others of what he had said. Most valuable in these discussions among men trained in different disciplines was the fact that everyone participating had read the same materials which had to be taught and explained. In this context it became possible to assess explanations offered from the vantage points of the respective disciplines of those making them. General theories were wanted, but when supplied, had to be defended against alternative statements. Thus meaningful conversions to other disciplines took place, just as overambitious explanations were brought up short by confrontations with inconvenient facts. Historians, often specialists in the period being discussed, did not shrink from administering such reproofs; in their turn they were often chastened when their own efforts at generalization were found to fall short of that minimal illumination meant to be produced by any causal explanation. The atmosphere was such that men came to know and respect not only one another, but their respective disciplines. Gradually to the professional superegos of each of them was added another. If a sociologist or a political scientist did not know what constitutes professional craftsmanship for the historian, he in time learned. Similarly, historians came to see that some sorts of theoretical explanations may make them better students of their subject. For their part they came to distinguish among sociologists and political scientists and to decide for themselves how valuable to their own work is one or another method or theory used in these subjects.

Through staff meetings, then, there emerged an enlightened set of judgments about the work of the course. From this common effort arose new answers, reformulations of problems, or dismissal of them as unanswerable in principle or because of the evidence available. The profound changes in Social Sciences 2 from one phase to another have been due as much to the criticisms made by the staff as to their encouragement in this attitude by Professor Beer. What Professor Beer has contributed are powerfully-stated alternative theories meant to explain the case in issue. Each of these statements are in turn presented with as much persuasiveness and energy as the lecturer can muster, and his audience is often hard put to determine which are his own preferences. Both students and staff are thus provoked into vigorous reactions. However, it has come to be understood that any critique of a theoretical position ought itself to transcend mere disagreement and proceed to another explanation. Suggestions of unexplored alternatives or restatements of those previously put forth characteristically receive a full and sympathetic hearing. Surprisingly often the staff has found the formal lectures, reading assignments, and examination questions modified or transformed in response to criticism accompanied by suggestions for improvement. The unique intellectual atmosphere of this course has been created by the combination of clear and vigorous hypothesis with receptivity and open-mindedness. Changes tend to be introduced piecemeal. Their nature and direction become more apparent over periods of five or more years than from year to year.

IV

About 1950 began the second phase of the course's development, that of a declining emphasis upon the Western heritage and liberal values, together with a new interest in the nature of comparison and explanation in the social sciences and the attempt to discern what was involved in the passage of a social system from a traditional to a modern condition. For the first time the purpose of the course was declared to be the application of theory to the analysis of history — to clarify historical cases by general hypotheses that might explain them and to test such hypotheses against evidence available in the record. Such an enterprise was in large part made possible by the translations of Max Weber into English by Hans Gerth and C. Wright Mills in 1946 and by Talcott Parsons and A. M. Henderson in 1947.[9] Weber combined an extraordinary mastery of detail in the history of many societies and periods with the even rarer capacity to formulate categories that made possible meaningful comparison among them, and thus the formulation of powerful general hypotheses. With his work as model and guide the way was opened to an approach at once more systematic and broader in scope than that used in the first years of the course. For Weber contrasted the development of Western societies with those of Asia, including patterns of authority and other political relationships, social structure, religious orientations, and economic development. Another related influence was that of the Harvard Social Relations Department, founded in 1946 by Talcott Parsons, Clyde Kluckhohn, and Henry Murray to bring together the teaching of sociology, social anthropology, and some aspects of psychology. The impulse that originated in this enterprise spread throughout the social sciences at Harvard.

Thus a number of influences converged to create a transition from the original concerns of the course to this next phase. The importance of ideas and values had been given a prominent place in its first version. Professor Beer had been a student of A. D. Lindsay (later Lord Lindsay of Birker), who attempted to preserve the essence of Oxford Idealism by giving up its metaphysics and epistemology, while insisting upon the importance of thought and will as social and political forces. This he did by tracing the ways in which human action is defined and directed by a society's "operative ideals." After Weber was translated, it began to be seen how he, perhaps the greatest of social scientists, had assigned a similar importance to ideas, ideologies, religions, and all other world views, which "define the situation" and thus make certain types of behavior significant to those taking decisions. Professor Parsons, then involved in formulating his own theory of action, was likewise influenced by Weber, whom he had studied so thoroughly and translated. It is not difficult to perceive how philosophical idealism in one or another form provided indirectly the starting points for all the authors mentioned above. Of course some others, such as Vilfredo Pareto, who play a part in the critiques of positivism synthesized by Professor Parsons in his *Structure of Social Action,* were not idealists.[10] But all converged in the attack upon Marx's version of positivism, which he had formulated in deliberate opposition to all forms of idealism known to him. Thus among the alternative explanations considered in this new version of Social Sciences 2, none was more prominent than Marx's theory that the objective situation, as determined by the mode of production, was to be regarded as decisive, and the rejoinder by Marx's critics that the orientations and emotional dispositions of the actors may in some cases be more significant.

Such a juxtaposition of divergent grand theories could easily have remained an exercise in abstract and ideological argument. But in the course these explanations were repeatedly applied to concrete historical situations. In this way, by trial and error, by making significant modifications and qualifications proved necessary by the recalcitrance of the data, the original act of faith in human will and reason that had been the basis of the course and the Harvard General Education Report was transformed into a complex and powerful theory of explanation. One of the steps along the way may be charted by reference to Norman Birnbaum's paper on Weber and Marx, which was a revision of lectures given by him when he taught in Social Sciences 2 during the early

1950's.[11] But the ultimate form assumed by this juxtaposition of Weber and Marx is best observed in Professor Beer's *British Politics in the Collectivist Age*. There in setting out five types of political behavior, he finds the essential element of each in the theory of representation contained in the political culture of its time. It is essential to his method that he begins by stressing operative ideals, but he then goes beyond idealist practice to specify how their effects may be observed, explained, and tested:

When I say "theory" of representation I am thinking of the work of political philosophers only insofar as these tell us something about our real object of concern: the images and sentiments that function as operative ideals in a community, or section of a community. Taken in this sense, each of the five theories of representation defines a more or less coherent system of roles for political formulations and their members. My procedure in each section of the historical discussion is first to set out this theory and then to examine the corresponding behavior.

Two further points need immediately to be made. I do not assert, nor have I found, that there is an exact and one-to-one correspondence between theory and practice. Political culture, its values, beliefs, and emotional symbols, while a major variable, is only one of the variables determining behavior. As interesting as the correspondence of practice with theory are its not infrequent deviations . . .

In any case, structures of political action, like other social structures, often have unanticipated consequences, and the question of whether these are functional or dysfunctional to the political system is a matter of inquiry by the political scientist.

Moreover, I do not say that for each period there is only one type of behavior dictated by a single, reigning theory of representation embraced in a clear, unclouded, and perfectly integrated political culture. On the contrary, a lack of integration in political culture may be a main source of conflict in the practical politics of the day.[12]

Another telling extension of the contrast between Weber and Marx has been made by Michael Walzer in *The Revolution of the Saints*, where he rejected the interpretation of Puritanism made by both.[13] However, his own theory that "Puritanism appears to be a response to disorder and fear, a way of organizing men to overcome the acute sense of chaos," is derived from a mode of analysis much closer to Weber than Marx.[14] In a paper setting forth his approach to the study of Puritanism as a revolutionary ideology, Professor Walzer has argued: "What must be studied, then, is a mind, or a group of minds, coping with problems and not passively reflecting them. For the mind mediates between the 'objective' situation and the human act and if the act is to be understood, the mind must first be known." [15]

Although these Weberian themes and techniques bulked large in the new directions taken in the second phase of Social Sciences 2, there were other innovations as well. Among them was the new role assigned the political theorists, who had in the course's earlier form been read as spokesmen for one or another set of values or formal philosophical positions. Now they came to be regarded as valuable for their general explanations of how and why men behave as they do under certain circumstances, as for example, Hobbes's treatment of human action in extreme situations where there is no authority to enforce order. This was one of the theories brought to bear upon the rise of the Nazis to power. Such a use of the political philosophers was a good deal closer to the way they understood themselves than to the interpretation now favored in some quarters that their theories are normative only and have no empirical component worth taking into account. Surely the historical truth is otherwise. Although much concerned with values, all political philosophers prior to Hume, and many after him, never segregated judgments of value from generalizations about how men in fact behave. Many of the hypotheses worth investigating about political and social behavior are stated with compelling force in political philosophy. In Social Sciences 2, Hobbes, Locke, Burke, Rousseau, and Nietzsche are presented as addressing themselves to the same range of problems as Marx, Weber, Elie Halévy, Freud, Erik Erikson, and Parsons. If nothing else, such a treatment provides unusual training in the imaginative formulation and application of general theory.

It was at this time that the topics were reduced to the six that have since remained constant: 1) the political structure of medieval England; 2) the religious structure of medieval England; 3) the Puritan Revolution; 4) the French Revolution; 5) Britain during the great age of reform; 6) the Nazi Revolution. Henceforth, not only the topics but the techniques of analysis would remain the same: each topic would be broached in terms of a theorist, whose views would first be illustrated and then tested by the historical materials. History, in short, was regarded as furnishing the data that would count as evidence for or against the hypothesis in question. As the course went along during the academic year, the range of theoretical concepts available was thus expanded. An increasingly broader set of hypotheses became familiar to the students. At the beginning, indeed in the first assignment, came Weber on the types of legitimate authority. Often the abstraction, not to mention the prose style, of this selection had an overpowering effect upon the freshmen and sophomores taking the course. At this point few complaints were heard about oversimplification or of repeating work done in high school. The trauma thus inflicted had on the whole salutary results. Many, if not all, of the students recovered and came in time not only to understand why Weber had chosen such terms of analysis, but to be able themselves to use his categories to some effect. In any case, what was being asked of them in the course clearly could not be identified either with narrative history or with dogmatic assertion of causal relationships. The two tasks of theorizing and testing hypotheses against evidence were emphasized in the papers that had to be written on every topic. But the subjects were devised by each section man for his charges. In many ways this work was the most valuable part of the course for both the section men and their students, for it brought home their own command or lack of it over the matter being discussed. Here again was a counterbalance to the impersonality of lectures delivered to large classes. And the graduate students teaching sections had to grapple with both the theory and the details of the historical situation.

How were term papers to be graded? On the whole, the staff took the position that completely professional standards were to be applied from the beginning, without any allowance made for the novelty of the enterprise to most students. Once again this resulted in a certain amount of damage inflicted upon students' self-esteem, particularly when great effort on their side was greeted by acid rejection on the other. But significant improvement could be noted after the first essay, which in turn bore almost no resemblance to the sixth and final one. With such importance given to essays, examinations did not bulk as large as they did in most other courses. Tests at the end of each term continued as before, to be taken from a list of questions made available early in the term. Sometimes study groups were formed by students; sometimes, section men or groups of section men met with them to discuss or to argue issues growing out of the questions. Such procedures made examinations at once more sporting and more serious, a combination that reflected the élan and good humor which characterized the course. One year the students requested and were granted time to put on a musical comedy taking off on the themes of the course. The occasion was a great success, recalling Montesquieu's words about the spirit of his own countrymen: ". . . For we do nothing better than what we do freely, following our natural genius. If the spirit of pedantry is imposed upon a nation that is by nature gay, the State gains nothing either at home or abroad. Let what is frivolous be done with seriousness, and what is serious with gaiety." [16]

V

A further transition has been under way since the late 1950's. This constitutes the third phase of the course's evolution. Analysis and justification of values has receded still further from the liberalism that once characterized the course. In its second phase, even after Weber had become the single most important focus of theory, there remained the objective of helping students to understand the premises of those arguments and ideologies upon which their society and form of government were said to rest. The study of Nazism was still that of the pathology of liberalism, with lessons that were potentially relevant to any industrial society subject to the strains and traumas that had brought an end to the Weimar Republic. Thus it was asked: What went wrong with German liberalism? Were the decisive causes for the advent of Nazism specifically German, or may they be said, *mutatis mutandis*, to apply to other liberal political systems undergoing similar pressures? Is it possible, on the basis of the Nazi experience, to avert such development in our own society?

Now the same topic tends to be treated as part of the dynamics of personal and group identity, as part of the turbulence accompanying a society highly modernized and rapidly becoming more so. Weber, with his interest in the growing rationalization and bureaucratization of modern Western society had already begun to create interest in the theme of "development" among some of those teaching in the course. This was reinforced by some of the principal trends in American social science during the 1950's: theorizing, combined with quantitative research, on the new states; the requisites of democracy; the political consequences of industrialization; and the new political forms, such as those of parties, characteristic of modern societies that have made the transition from their antecedent form. Michael Walzer treated Puritanism as a way of creating a group identity for a group reacting to change by hardening itself so that it could create a world shaped by its ideology. Charles Tilly made economic development, urbanization, and political centralization into prominent themes in his study of revolution and counterrevolution in the Vendée.[17] William Nisbet Chambers became concerned with the problem of how new states develop forms of association and organization adequate to supporting their political structures, and he studied this phenomenon in the early development of American political parties.[18] In a number of ways the approaches characteristic of Social Sciences 2 in its second phase prepared the way for joining in the formulation of a general theory of social and political modernization.

Another change has been the extension of the technique and scope of comparison. This had already been emphasized by the methods of Marx and Weber, with their comparison of whole societies and periods. But as used in the course, comparative analysis tended in fact to be limited to two societies of the same period. In the present phase of the course's movement there is a deliberate attempt to develop theory that is more general and less bound to a particular time or place. For example, in the final examination for January 1967 every question specifically asked students to utilize in their comparisons matter taken from two or more of the periods studied. And in addition to making more of comparison, Professor Beer has also redefined what he means by that procedure in a way that is tantamount to a drastic revision of the strategy of inquiry.

In some styles of comparison, for example, that which used to be practiced under the name of comparative government, the efforts of most investigators went primarily into the accumulation of data about the respective arrangements of different governments, their executive or legislature, or the working relationships between them. To the extent that method was deliberately considered as such, the stress fell upon description and induction rather than upon theory and deduction. Nor was there much attention given to categories and levels of analysis.

Now Professor Beer approaches comparison through theory, rather than theory through comparison. Beginning with a theory of a high level of generality, hypotheses are deduced from it. Then these are tested against the facts by reference to a number of comparable instances. If the role of radical intellectuals in the French Revolution is offered as an explanation of why such an upheaval occurred in France and took the pattern that it did, then it is appropriate to apply the same hypothesis to the English or Russian revolutions and to determine what part radical intellectuals played in each of them so as to test the generalization that began the inquiry. Needless to say, such a mode of comparison is not simple. It presupposes a procedure for specifying what is meant by radical intellectuals (for example, a typology like Michael Walzer's); it likewise makes it necessary to provide criteria for what sorts of phenomena are to be classified under the same rubric as the French Revolution, whether the degree of change or the degree of collective violence, or both combined, are to be regarded as constituting revolution. Nor can any one instance confirm or falsify a general theory. Thus the range of cases should be as great as possible. But throughout theory incites and guides comparison.

Perhaps the greatest single difference between the modes of comparative analysis used in the course's second phase and at present has to do with the purpose behind such extensive reference to theory. Gradually there has been a shift away from pedagogical to professional or scientific goals. Originally the device of stating two alternative theories of explanation was aimed at sharpening wits, developing a theoretical capacity, including that of critical evaluation, and demonstrating that the study of history need not be restricted to the careful accumulation of data with a view to describing discrete situations. Now when competing theories are considered, this is done to show what each of them explains and omits so that a more adequate general theory may be attained. Whereas before, any answer was treated purely on formal grounds, such as adequacy of evidence to theory and internal consistency, now what counts most is the positive contribution to a general theory of modernization. Comparison is regarded as the indispensable means of testing a causal theory by applying to different instances the questions: Why did this phenomenon occur at the time that it did and not before? Why did it occur where it did and not elsewhere? So conceived, the utility of comparison is not limited to breaking down simplistic thinking or parochial frames of reference.

This course has also made its own response to the behavioral trends so powerful in American social science. Although quantitative techniques, including use of a computer, have not as yet been introduced into the course, such a step is under active consideration, for a growing number of the staff already use such methods. This movement, which registers what has been going on in the separate disciplines, should serve as a reminder that no general education course such as this can be considered apart from its context.

The steadily rising level of undergraduate abilities has also had its effects. As their teachers see it, every year brings students with the capacity to master much more reading than had predecessors. And their analytical powers are greater as well. Such changes have led to an alteration of the examination system requested by the students. In their view, to take all questions from a previously prepared list is to encourage stereotyped "ideal answers" prepared by committees that stifle creative individual responses. Thus examinations now contain some questions not previously revealed.

Changes in the student body have reinforced trends toward greater specialization in the social and behavioral sciences. One staff member contrasted the course with that he had himself taken in general education as an undergraduate at the University of Chicago. What distinguished them, he found, was that at Chicago, he was being presented with a body of knowledge deemed essential to the well-educated man; in Social Sciences 2, he was on the growing edge of a professional discipline.

This impression has been strengthened on the part of student and staff alike by the fact that Social Sciences 2 has generated much scholarship on the topics it treats. Thus an increasing portion of the reading is drawn from the work of those who have taught in the course. It had always been the case that section men who believed that they had something to contribute were encouraged to deliver formal lectures. In addition, a number of the course's alumni appear every year to lecture on subjects about which they have written. Thus the course has come to appear as a continuing collective enterprise. Contributions continue to be made on topics that have been under intensive scrutiny for a decade. Thus students and staff come to feel that they are part of an intellectual community, that their insights and dissents, if sufficiently documented and properly argued, will find an interested audience and one not confined to their contemporaries. For those committed to interdisciplinary inquiry, such a sense of concerned audience is peculiarly important. The informal testimony of one former teacher catches what has been said by many more:

> In my case, I think, the course served to sustain and guide me in directions I was already moving in . . . so that I already thought of myself as a sociological historian . . . And of course the discovery of a new reference group was terribly important. The biggest problem of all, perhaps, for people who want to open up new lines of inquiry, is the feeling that no one is listening, that one is writing in an absolute vacuum. Learning about and meeting the Soc Sci 2 cadres helped a good deal in overcoming that feeling in my case.

VI

On two occasions conferences have been held of those who at various times have taught in Social Sciences 2. The first of these took place in the summer of 1961 and was relatively small. Designed as a working session for those who were finishing books, it also included a few other members of the course. Most of the three weeks in Cambridge were taken up by the discussion of manuscripts, which were circulated in advance. The participants came to appreciate how many pains they might have been spared had they from the beginning been able to address themselves to a group that understood what was involved in each of these efforts to state a complex argument resting upon evidence collected over years of research. Each of the writers had begun his enterprise with some faith in its originality. But not infrequently, as individuals moved from general education at Harvard to teaching in their respective departments elsewhere, they became aware of hostility to their interdisciplinary work, or what was worse, indifference. But in this gathering there was no need to defend the purpose of applying comparative and general theory to history. Service in the course had produced a spontaneous convergence of concepts, problems, and method. Criticism in the 1961 seminar was frequently sharp, but always impersonal, as had been the case in staff meetings. The focus of argument tended to be not on minute matters of fact, but rather upon the overall adequacy of the evidence to the hypothesis being presented. And this was what the authors regarded as most valuable to them.

Although there were a few meetings with such theorists as Louis Hartz, Talcott Parsons, and Herbert Marcuse, almost all the working sessions were devoted to discussing manuscripts. These included Samuel Beer's *British Politics in the Collectivist Age*, William Nisbet Chambers's *Political Parties in a New Nation*, Melvin Richter's *The Politics of Conscience: T. H. Green and His Age*, Charles Tilly's *The Vendée*, and Michael Walzer's *The Revolution of the Saints*.[19]

With some few exceptions, the group was made up largely of those who had been together on the course's staff during the early 1950's. The first meeting proved so useful that a second three-day meeting was organized in April 1967, made possible by a grant from the Carnegie Corporation. About fifty former members of the course and their guests attended. At it, formal papers were presented and discussed, but there was much time for informal talk as well. Former members came to Cambridge from as far away as England and California. A number of the papers given appear in this volume, which also includes some work first printed elsewhere or not presented at the meeting.

So prevalent was the sense of intellectual gain that it may be worth considering why these two meetings were so superior in quality to larger scholarly conferences. It may be that the conventional rationales for mammoth conventions and omnibus journals no longer hold. The scale of university faculties has so expanded that in most disciplines, annual meetings of professional associations have become unmanageable intellectually, if not administratively. At them a dozen or more panels meet simultaneously, thus dispelling any pretense that the subject has any unity as a whole. Nor is this difficulty overcome by the coming together of specialists in the panels of a particular section. Where there is no intellectual community, dialogue is unlikely. It may be that professional associations have become, in the terms of Troeltsch, churches, whereas they ought to be sects, where fellowship is more often found. Intellectual life ought to be decentralized and put on a human scale. The conferences held by former members of Social Sciences 2 are one model of what might be done.

VII

In the section that follows, the papers in this volume will be considered primarily in terms of those intellectual qualities, those shared assumptions about method which derive from their authors' experience in Social Sciences 2. Historians of ideas often isolate what is distinctive about a writer or school by pointing up the dominant interests or motifs of their thought, their preference for certain intellectual values that impose some modes of pursuing inquiry and interdict others. When viewed in this way, the writers in this volume can be seen to prefer complex to monistic theories of explanation; paradoxes and antinomies to simple, elegant laws formulated in disregard of the characteristic waverings and irresolutions of the working historian. These authors frequently resort to a dialectical strategy of argument which seeks to mediate among several alternative explanations rather than to discredit all theories other than their own. And throughout there is a commitment to rigorous self-criticism, to what might be called intellectual prophylaxis through the systematic consideration of potential objections, particularly in the use of historical sources, if one is not a professional historian, or in social and political theory, if one happens to teach in a history department. Such sensitivity to two sets of norms is one of the ways in which this group may be said to be interdisciplinary in practice; another is the insistence of those who comprise it to take it upon themselves to seek out those materials relevant to their enterprises rather than attempting to synthesize research or explanations performed from disparate points of view; a third is to be found in a disposition toward political sociology, the treatment of politics within a larger framework in a way that neither separates behavior, process, or institutional structures from their social context, nor reduces them to epiphenomena derived from economic or social organization. The same resistance to reductionism is no less marked in such uses as are made of the sociology of religion and the sociology of knowledge — the relating, that is, of belief systems to the social positions of those holding them. To acknowledge the standards both of theory and history is to make things difficult for oneself, and whatever merit may be attributed to the work of this group, rapid production in great quantity is not among its characteristics.

Something will be said about the substantive concerns of these papers, but for the most part their authors will be allowed to speak for themselves on their chosen subjects. Needless to say, nothing in this introduction should be construed as a claim that the work of this group is unique in form or matter, or that its members stand apart from their respective disciplines, from which they derive nothing, while owing everything to their service in Social Sciences 2. Rather these essays are united by a style of analysis, a cluster of qualities and intentions regarded by their authors as essential to their own work and which they seek to recommend. Although this approach to history evolved from general education, it has by now become autonomous and is no longer dominated by pedagogical purposes. On the one hand, history is considered as the indispensable means to developing a generalizing, analytical theory; on the other, these writers refuse to accept as their model that notion of general law derived from the natural sciences and erected into a central position in the philosophy of the social sciences. Rather they are committed to the notion that if social scientists are to make an explicit pursuit of theory, it ought to be of such a kind as may be shaped and adapted to history. Such a position is in no way incompatible with quantitative techniques and new forms of research and analysis. As will soon appear, those members of this group who are engaged in projects relying upon advanced techniques of processing data are among the most vehement champions of the view that sound theory requires taking history into account. Central to its conception of how this is to be done is the emphasis upon comparative analysis.

Comparison is regarded throughout as the indispensable means of testing theory. Generalizations about one society are compared and contrasted either to states of affairs found in other societies or in that same society at a different time. Similar operations are performed upon hypotheses said to apply to more than one society. Any arrangements alleged to be unique are put beside potential analogues in other societies or periods. It is assumed that patterns of behavior or of institutional organization cannot be fully understood without stipulating what alternatives to them exist. Thus much attention is given to typologies and systems of classification and the assessment of the phenomenon under study to one or more of the categories belonging to the taxonomy adopted. Although there is little explicit methodological discussion of real and ideal types, and of patterned variables as tools of comparative analysis, these writers seem to have made use of one or another of them after consideration of the rest. Sydney James applies Weberian ideal types to the transition from one pattern of authority to another in colonial Rhode Island. But he modifies Weber's type of traditional authority in the light of subsequent research on the nature of the Old Regime in the sixteenth and seventeenth centuries. Thus Mr. James is in a position to deal far more precisely with the phases of development than those theorists who contrast European "feudal" institutions with the fresh start made by Americans. What merits attention is that Mr. James, although working in colonial history, has chosen a problem in historical sociology, and rather than being dominated by Weber's formulation, has known how to adapt it to his materials.

It would be misleading to give the impression that the contributors all possess precisely the same notion of what is entailed by comparison. In fact the term is profoundly ambiguous, holding in suspension a number of quite different and even incompatible intentions and methods. As practiced in the nineteenth century, the comparative method was evolutionary in its thrust and thus envisioned comparison as a means for creating a general theory that would chart and explain genetic sequences. To trace complex developments back to a simple beginning by a scheme of stages was the common purpose of comparative anatomy and comparative philology — subjects which were created toward the end of the eighteenth century. This genetic aim established the now archaic use of the term "comparative" in these subjects (in linguistics, the present meaning of the term is typological, the comparing and contrasting of entire structures by systematic classification).[20] It was this older usage that E. A. Freeman had in mind when he gave currency to the term "comparative politics" in the lectures he published under that title in 1873.[21] Freeman declared the comparative method to have been the greatest intellectual achievement of his time, and he took as the model for politics comparative philology, because it was fully established as science. It might be remarked that the work of Max Müller, whose version of comparative philology was singled out for praise by Freeman, is now quite discredited. In any case, the comparative method sought to construct the stages of human development, social and political, by three means: by conjecture about the earliest stages of human history and the evidence taken from primitive peoples still extant, who were assumed to be in a state that all human societies once were; by distinguishing between simple chronological sequence and what J. F. McLennan called "human progress considered as development"; and finally, by classifying societies "by their structure, as higher or lower (in the manner of comparative anatomy) in the scale of development." [22]

Another purpose of comparison may be the almost exclusive concern with establishing similarities. Investigators with this temperament tend to ignore differences; their interest extends only to qualities shared by all men and groups. Much late eighteenth-century comparative work, particularly in "philosophical history" was of this sort, a disposition fully described in A. O. Lovejoy's essay on deism and classicism.[23] A later variety of this intention, and one often combined with the comparative method, was work done with the purpose of classifying all human societies under one or another rubric, conceived as a real type induced from the data, such as Herbert Spencer's "military" and "industrial" societies, or Durkheim's "mechanical" and "organic" forms of solidarity. Sometimes comparison in this style has been undertaken in order to establish the laws governing all human associations. Such theorists as Comte — and J. S. Mill, to the extent that he was influenced by Comte — seem to have cherished comparison because of its promise of one day making it unnecessary to compare, a state that will be attained when laws of society similar to those of Newton are discovered.

In other hands comparison may be intended to prove quite the opposite point, namely, the radical and irreducible diversity among societies, epochs, or civilizations considered as individual organisms. Hence, it is argued, the impossibility of grouping them or finding traits common to them. The notion of national character, the *topos* of attributing to every society its own distinctive mode of politics, or social relations, or music, or lovemaking is one that has found adherents for a very long time. Thus the notion of distinctive character may be used as a comparative concept designed to exhibit singularity. This is its characteristic deployment by certain forms of romanticism, nationalism, and historicism. Sometimes, however, the emphasis upon national or societal differences has been combined with the theory of a natural law common to all men. But there exists a version of comparative analysis that seeks to destroy the periodization or theory of general laws or categorical apparatus of those comparatists obsessed with similarity. This attack may take the form of insisting that all phenomena and arrangements are embedded within a unique context. It may, on the level of evidence, center its attention upon the dangers of generalization extracted from reports that have proved unreliable in even the most carefully studied societies.[24] Finally, it may dismiss similarities on the ground that they are outweighed by differences.

To round out the inventory of intentions that may prompt comparative analysis, two more must be mentioned. The first, which will be illustrated by reference to Max Weber, cares equally about the use of comparison to develop generalizations, although not universal laws, and its use to explain particular cases, although not limiting itself to them. The second, which will be illustrated by reference to Montesquieu, seeks by comparison the universal laws governing society and politics and yet at different moments, however inconsistently, uses the same technique to establish the permanent differences individuating human societies. Weber, for better or worse, did not believe in universal laws or in theories of stages common to all societies; nor did he carry *Historismus* to the length of denying that comparison was in principle impossible among phenomena drawn from quite different settings.

In his introduction to the new complete translation of Weber's *Economy and Society*, Guenther Roth has made a penetrating analysis of Weber's method of comparative sociological study. Reference to this way of proceeding both will clarify Weber's purpose in comparative analysis and will later enable us to understand better the extent to which Montesquieu and Tocqueville may be said to have used a variety of ideal-type analysis, a point critical to any analysis of their practices and purposes. Professor Roth points out that Weber, in his use of comparison, did not conceive of his purpose as the creation of a transhistorical, functionalist theory. Rather, he wished to create the tools of explaining major historical phenomena, such as the origin and nature of capitalism in antiquity, the Middle Ages, and modern times, together with the forms of political rule and social stratification peculiar to them. Comparison was meant to establish the differences between older and modern conditions and to explain the causes of the differences. Weber's comparative strategy was directed against theories simply assuming historical identity (of ancient and modern capitalism, for example) and evolutionary theories such as the "Comparative Method," which established stages or phases applicable to the development of all societies.[25] As Weber wrote in his treatment of Roman agrarian law: "A genuinely critical *comparison* of the developmental stages of the ancient polis and the medieval city . . . would be rewarding and fruitful — but only if such a comparison does *not* chase after 'analogies' and 'parallels' in the manner of the presently fashionable general schemes of development; in other words, it should be concerned with the *distinctiveness* of each of the two developments that were finally so different, and the purpose of the comparison must be the causal *explanation* of the difference." [26]

In order to realize this program Weber made use of a number of comparative devices: the ideal type, the identification of similarities as a first step in causal explanation, the negative comparison meant to elicit differences and prompt generalization, the illustrative analogy, and the metaphor.[27] All of these devices appeared in the operational practice of Montesquieu and Tocqueville, as will be seen later in my article. But the function of each such method is determined by the analyst's purpose in undertaking comparative work. Every purpose is involved in a distinctive set of presuppositions, although this is not necessarily true of the devices used to realize this purpose.

The essays in this volume abound with comparative work executed with one or another of the intentions described above. Yet most of their authors count similarities and regularities as having more significance for them than differences. Increasingly, not unlike the development followed by the course itself, they have tended to regard comparison primarily as a means of testing theory. The only exception is the late Klaus Epstein's treatment of conservatism. In setting out the phenomenon he was investigating, he dismissed both its functional definition (as any defense of the status quo) and its substantive definition (in terms of an unchanging ideology expressing absolute and unchanging values). Instead, his conception of his task was to seek the specific reactions of German conservatives to those issues explicitly raised by the "party of movement" within the conditions found in Germany as it was in the last third of the eighteenth century. Thus conservatism, in his view, because of its reactive and defensive nature, must be studied in relation to its specific context within each society. Thus viewed, if an adequate history of European conservatism is to be written one day, its author "will be required to immerse himself in the specific conditions of every European country in order to secure a realistic understanding of what different conditions conservatives wished to conserve." Thus such a comparative study of European conservatism would principally serve to exhibit uniqueness, although some similarities might appear as well.

The part played by comparison in these papers is in large part determined by their authors' understanding of what is meant by history. Professor Beer's paper is directed to a clarification of three ways in which history can serve the social and political theorist: 1) history as past behavior; 2) history as duration; 3) history as development. By the first of these is meant that use of history which prevents generalizations from being rooted upon too narrow a basis of fact and range of experience. History is to be consulted for the sake of difference from our contemporary experience. But the difference is not understood as deriving from its pastness in time. The second notion, that of history as duration, however, does emphasize the dimension of time. It is essential that the social scientist realize that certain things may be studied only through consideration of long-term change. Among the great problems of inquiry in the social sciences is the identification of those structures and processes worth study. The sense of history as duration teaches us to ask whether a short-lived fact is to be understood as constituting a part of some more general structure or function. To identify the phenomenon is to raise the question of how to explain it, and indeed sometimes itself suffices to explain it. In any case, such identification of phenomena makes possible the comparison and contrast of similar facts. If the social scientist extends his range of concerns backward in time, he may find not only continuities, but also discontinuities that he would otherwise never have suspected. For example, Messrs. Burnham and Chambers, in extending the study of American political parties back to their beginnings, have found differences sufficiently significant to lead to their distinction of five different types of party systems.[28] Thus the concept of history as duration serves two purposes: on the one hand, it brings to light structures persisting through time and performing characteristic functions; on the other, it is relevant as well to another type of concern, that with changes in structures and functions through processes which we attempt to classify in typologies and account for by explanatory theory, as in the study of revolutions and counterrevolutions, themes that have figured prominently in the work of this school, both in this volume and elsewhere.

The third and final sense of history distinguished by Professor Beer exhibits his growing interest in the theory of modernization and calls attention to history as development. By this is meant that social and political forces occur in series of successive stages; that each stage is in some sense produced by the previous one; and that throughout this process, there is a direction or trend toward greater modernity, rationality, productivity. But it is not to be assumed that the purpose of inquiry is to establish laws of the sort identified and discredited by such methodologists as Karl Popper. An awareness of the pitfalls awaiting the social scientist who comes to history without knowledge of historiography is everywhere evident in this volume. Historical materials cannot be used to the greatest advantage without knowledge of the criticism and controversies that historians for good reason have carried on among themselves as well as with philosophers.

Historiography, although never a rival to social and political theory, has always played a part in Social Sciences 2. The journal *History and Theory* was founded by George Nadel, who exerted considerable influence upon the course when he taught in it, has participated in meetings of its former staff, and continues to draw heavily upon them as contributors. In the essays found in this volume, the effects of historiographical discussion may be seen at work whenever there is some danger of the analyst falling into what Popper has called "moral futurism," or Butterfield, the "Whig philosophy of history" — the emphasis upon those causes, parties, groups, and individuals victorious in their own time, or who have contributed to trends predominant in our own. Although vitally interested in the connections between collective violence and development, economic and political, Charles Tilly takes particular pains with those groups that have been losers, and whose resort to certain types of violence represents their last cries of protest against their fate. To them he accords at least as much sympathy and understanding as those classes and groups on the ascendancy. Stephan Thernstrom in his work on social mobility is no less concerned with those at the bottom, or those who fall back, than with those who make it to the top, or some part of the way. He calls attention to the extraordinary geographical mobility of the workers who passed through Boston, and he notes that probably this rate of turnover in the working force was an index of failure on the part of those who departed. In any case, such mobility has political and social significance. As a group, they did not "remain long enough to make their weight felt, and were tossed about from city to city, alienated, but invisible and impotent." The mere existence of an electoral law that required voters to live for a year in Boston was enough to disenfranchise 25 percent of the population. The same resistance to moral futurism is to be found in Dean Burnham's denial that present voting alignments permanently obliterate older alignments and configurations of voting behavior. Under certain circumstances the past, or some part of it, may be reinstated. Critical realignments do not render history insignificant to the student of voting behavior.

Another example of sensitivity to questions of historical method, and indeed to those of objectivity in the social sciences, is to be found in the contribution by Klaus Epstein. During the time that he taught in the course and served as its head section man, no issue received more attention than that of ideology, both in the form given to it by Marx and Engels, and in the more eclectic version of Karl Mannheim. Max Weber's well-known lectures on science and politics as vocation served as touchstones in the discussion that raged about the scholar's obligation to be objective. Although most of those involved willingly conceded that it was impossible for a scholar to divest himself of all prejudice and interest, there was general agreement that to the greatest extent possible, political preferences should be excluded from one's professional work, although not from one's life as a citizen. This conviction was shared by Klaus Epstein. What turned out to be his last book is animated by its author's aspiration to objectivity.

After a distinguished first book on Matthias Erzberger and a virtual torrent of extended essay-reviews published in the United States and West Germany, Mr. Epstein embarked upon a grand project combining his chosen field of modern German history with his longstanding interest in the history of conservative thought.[29] The first volume of his study appeared just before his death in an automobile accident in Bonn.[30] In his introduction, here reprinted, Mr. Epstein, with great integrity, succeeded in making impossible any ideological use by others of his book. For in it he achieved a remarkable balance. Without equivocation he stated what in his view have been the principal deficiencies of conservatism: the incapacity to analyze and understand the long-run needs of society, complacency about dismaying conditions, its nostalgia for the past, and its callousness about the sufferings of the many considered by conservatives as naturally inferior to the well-born. This is not to say that he became any less severe toward eighteenth-century rationalism, that "party of movement" he regarded as responsible for so many of the evils of the modern world. But what he wrote had to transcend partisanship if it was to satisfy his own demanding standards.

It was remarked above that prominent among the intellectual values of the writers in this book is the taste for complexity, paradox, irony. In his treatment of revolutionary repression Mr. Walzer ends on an irreducible antinomy. Revolutionaries, to the extent that they are authentic and radical, call for the end of state repression, which in their view is cold, external, and immoral because it depends upon brute force. For it they would substitute the self-repression of a pledged group whose members acknowledge that their common purposes require such discipline. But such governance is at least as repressive as that practiced by the state it destroyed. And either the revolutionaries maintain this phase of self-coercion at a high cost of individual liberties and private life (which is incompatible with spending all one's evenings at meetings), or else they transform terror into routine anxiety manifested in economic competition. What cannot be dispensed with is repression of some kind, some one of the three moments set out by Mr. Walzer. Thus summarized, the conclusion does less than justice to the subtle procedure of this essay, for among its principal virtues is the way it puts the reader's mind in motion, dispelling comforting morals and convenient rationalizations on whatever side and bringing him back to the phenomenon of repression, a problem that cannot be dismissed either by those who believe in the creative and liberating effects of revolution, or those who would prefer to forget the repression practiced by their own state.

Nor is this concern with the quality of argument absent from those papers that begin with statements of the discrepant theories that have been offered as general explanations of the problem in question. This dialectical strategy of argument owes much to the procedure that dominated the second phase of Social Sciences 2 and is still prominent at the present time. In his paper Charles Tilly defines his central problem as the effects produced by modernization upon a society's political stability, protest movements, and forms of collective violence. During his initial survey of the alternative theories that hold the field, Mr. Tilly emphasizes two such hypotheses. The first takes as its focus the disruptive consequences produced by modernization: *anomie,* the uprooting of a population, and the consequent dissolution of its former norms, controls, and social attachments. The second such explanation centers upon the discrepancy between actual improvements and those expectations aroused by improved communications, by the slogans used to mobilize an unprecedented national effort, and by the extension of participation in political activity to groups formerly parochial in their concerns. One part of Mr. Tilly's paper may be read as an attempt to mediate between these two views. In the course of this dialectical process Mr. Tilly suggests that each theory catches some part of the total process of collective violence. Yet both, even when taken together, omit something, and this, he argues, may be caught by a further hypothesis linking collective violence more directly to the political process. This phenomenon is most likely to occur when and where new groups are struggling to acquire membership within the political community, or when long-established groups are seeking to avoid the loss of the role they once played. And thus Mr. Tilly adds a third theory, emphasizing the political process, to the two sociological hypotheses with which he began his paper. This additional explanation has been necessitated by the data collected by the author and his analysis of it. And it is an excellent example of a historical political sociology.

A similar mode of proceeding is to be found in the contribution by Sydney James. His general problem is how a rational-legal form of authority arose in colonial America; his particular case is that of Rhode Island. Beginning with the theories of Louis Hartz and R. R. Palmer, Mr. James suggests that although ostensibly incompatible with each other, these theories are in fact complementary, each of them serving to explain different phenomena or classes of phenomena. Thus Hartz's theory was right in describing the repudiation of monarchy in the American Revolution as easy, wrong in explaining it by a total exemption from a local feudal order in the past. "Palmer was right in looking for the overthrow of an Old Regime, but looked at the wrong time period, and so unduly magnified a small change while missing a great one." Mr. James thus makes use of an intellectual strategy not unlike that of Mr. Tilly. A third theory is introduced, in this case not a causal hypothesis, but a taxonomy that enables the analyst to distinguish an Old Regime or corporative social order from one that might legitimately be described as feudal. Without exaggerating the significance of the fact that Messrs. Tilly and James are both engaged in explaining aspects of a modernizing process, it may be said that the structure and strategy of their papers are similar. The same dialectical pattern is applied by a historian to the early history of Rhode Island and by a sociologist to collective violence in nineteenth-century France.

It is striking to observe how the emphasis upon the importance of history for political and social theory is so stressed by precisely those writers in this volume who use the quantitative method and are most concerned with the type of questions now receiving the greatest attention from American researchers — Dean Burnham, Stephan Thernstrom, and Charles Tilly. The last of these in the conclusion to his book on the Vendée remarked to his colleagues: "Sociologists have cut themselves off from a rich inheritance by forgetting the obvious: that all history is past social behavior, that all archives are brimming with news on how men used to act, and how they are acting still." [31] Although their purpose in using history is to develop general theory, these three writers have found it necessary in their respective dialogues with their colleagues to emphasize both the importance of the historical perspective and of the full and careful investigation of context when historical materials are employed.

Dean Burnham, in addressing himself to political scientists of the behavioral school, has asserted that the absence of historical perspective has produced significant distortion in the study of American political behavior. A general model which has been implicitly and widely assumed to characterize American politics is probably of maximum validity only during very recent times. What is more, its utility as a description of the real world of electoral politics can undergo major erosion even in the present, granted the existence of certain conditions. In his paper Burnham seeks to demonstrate that patterns of voting which have been assumed to be archaic can prove to be of startling relevance to contemporary electoral politics, that the existence of this relevance constitutes a major anomaly within the received conventions of the field, and that theories of American voting behavior must be revised accordingly. Without disputing that critical realignments of party allegiance periodically occur in American politics, Burnham argues that earlier patterns of behavior may lie dormant for a very long time and yet be elicited by issues and conflicts among groups and sections analogous to those that produced the original reaction. Indeed, explicit recognition of this phenomenon should help students of the field come to a clearer understanding of the properties of these realignments and of the dynamics of American electoral politics generally. Although based in part upon the Survey Research Center's careful analysis of the 1964 election, Burnham's paper should be understood as part of his earlier proposal that American politics be studied historically in such a way as "to reorganize the conceptual map which we have of American politics in such a way as to relativize all those things which we have taken to be absolutes; to make way for a recognition of discontinuities, jumps, and anomalies where before we saw only uniformities." [32]

Much the same position in the relevance of the past to the study of social mobility in the present appears in the work of Stephan Thernstrom. His book on Newburyport demonstrates how Lloyd Warner's Yankee City series was deformed by erroneous and uninvestigated assumptions about the sort of place Newburyport in fact had been.[33] In what still remains the most intensive community study yet made, Warner simply assumed that Newburyport at the time he came to it was problematical and required careful investigation, whereas its character in the past could easily be ascertained and in any case was irrelevant to his inquiry. In a paper on recent work on social mobility Mr. Thernstrom found that it suffers from a parochialism, not national as Burnham has argued about American political science, but rather a parochialism of time.[34] It is Mr. Thernstrom's position that many of the most interesting questions that ought to be asked about the nature of a class structure today cannot be answered without detailed knowledge about class and mobility over the long term preceding it. Yet, as he remarked, "Despite the recent avalanche of empirical research on social mobility, appallingly little is known about the process of social mobility in the past and about long-term mobility trends in any society — certainly not in our own." [35] Again like Burnham, Thernstrom has not been content to rest his case on the basis of admonitions to future researchers. Even when most overtly programmatic, he has translated his advice into operational terms. That is, he has proposed two general principles for the comparative historical study of social mobility: first, the need for investigators to construct finely calibrated instruments of analysis applicable to societies very differently constructed from our own; second, the need to pay close attention to the entire social context of the phenomenon under consideration. What this would mean in the study of changes in the relative openness of American social structure since 1900, he has indicated:

> . . . I think we would proceed in a manner somewhat different from that in which many contemporary sociologists would proceed. Rather than taking the currently fashionable index of social mobility, the rate of inter-generational movement between manual and non-manual occupations, computing occupational mobility rates at selected intervals, and constructing a simple time series, the historian would insist that a scrupulous examination of the class structure at several strategic points in time and an assessment of social mobility in terms of categories appropriate to each point in time would be required and that to arrive at a simple conclusion about trends might be impossible because of the lack of comparability of the historically specific categories used. Did the Polish peasants in the mills of Gary in 1910 hold the same relative position in the class system as the indentured servants of Salem in 1710? . . .[36]

Mr. Thernstrom's purpose is not to argue the uniqueness of every historical moment, but rather that "historical data be employed to edit and refine social theory . . ."[37]

His contribution to the present volume uses some of his findings in the study he has been making by computer of 8,000 families living in Boston between 1880 and 1963. His aim is to deal systematically with occupational, social, and geographical mobility in terms of the categories and principles he has himself formulated. It is his stated conviction that such matters as he treats must be based on quantitative evidence or be doomed to mere impressionism. And yet his awareness of historical context makes him careful and self-critical. He consistently specifies what it is that he is leaving out of his analysis, or the grounds on which either his evidence or his conclusions are open to objections. Although many of his findings about Boston are both unanticipated and striking, in this paper he constantly alerts his audience to those places where caution is in point. For example, he finds that Boston had no stable lower-class population, no permanent proletariat, and he surmises that the great volatility of workers has retarded the development and expression of distinctive class loyalties. But the reader has already been warned that the data used in this study cannot throw any direct light on political and cultural history. By this Mr. Thernstrom means that his is not at all a study of attitudes or expectations. Thus he plays down the significance of his extraordinary finding that 40 percent of working-class sons in Boston went on to hold middle-class jobs, a figure for the rate of circulation among occupations that Mr. Thernstrom found to remain constant throughout sweeping changes in the economy, political structure, and ethnic composition of Boston. With integrity, he refuses to overexploit his data. Instead he warns that we may conclude that "variations in objective mobility opportunities, between nations, or over time within a nation, do not in themselves explain very much, that mobility data are meaningless except within a context of well-defined attitudes and expectations about the class system, and that these attitudes and expectations may be most unstable and susceptible to change." Professor Beer's emphasis upon the method of *Verstehen*, of the difference between objective data and what men make of them, is here rephrased in the assertion that "the austerely objective facts uncovered by empirical social research influence the course of history only as they are mediated through the consciousness of obstinately subjective human beings."

More could be said about the larger projects of which these papers constitute some part. In a good many cases the posing of a theoretical question has led to the imaginative use of what the Germans call heuristic, the technique of research with the purpose of discovering evidence that could confirm or falsify the investigator's hypothesis. Sydney James has dredged up materials by a sort of microanalysis of documents and texts found not only in public archives, but in legal collections. Charles Tilly in his study of the Vendée made use of the provincial archives to provide data relevant to issues hitherto unstudied about the relative urbanization and development of a market economy in contiguous areas. In his present work he has put together widely scattered data bearing on collective violence in France, including statistics on strikes, police records, government reports, including those of prefects and the Ministry of the Interior. Stephan Thernstrom has availed himself of little used census schedules and city directories in order to study social and geographical mobility.

The use of political theorists as a source of empirical theories in the course was among the forces impelling me to undertake my study of a French school of comparative political sociology that begins with Montesquieu and Tocqueville. And again the operational techniques of Social Sciences 2 have led me to begin explorations of the methods used by great practitioners of social and political analysis in the past.[38] As yet no analogue to the history of science exists for the social sciences, although a positivist philosophy of science is the accepted orthodoxy used to indoctrinate students. Long after strict logical positivism has been discredited among philosophers, it lives on among social scientists. Virtually no careful studies have been made of empirical inquiry in the past; we know next to nothing about the most obvious questions, such as the history of the logic of the social sciences, the conceptual schemes used for comparison and analysis, or the reasons for the replacement of one general scheme by another.

This course has also prompted an unusual number of studies in the effects upon action of such definitions of the situation as are provided by religions, ideologies, and philosophies. Sydney James's book on the Quakers' varying seriousness about their social obligations to their fellows, my work on the relationship between Evangelicalism and the strange victory of philosophical idealism in Victorian England, Norman Birnbaum's studies in the economic origins of the Reformation in different settings in Germany and Switzerland, Michael Walzer's view of Puritanism as a modernizing radical ideology are all examples of sustained inquiry combining theory and history in an area that otherwise has not received much attention from American social scientists.[39]

This book has its origin in its authors' concern with a number of questions: Is it possible to have intellectual communities in the age of the multiversity? Can settings be created in which teachers and students may without subservience explore questions worthy of inquiry even though they cut across the heavily fortified boundaries of departmental interests? Can graduate students be trained both as professionals and as individuals who put their own unmistakable stamp on everything they take up? The corporate experience of Social Sciences 2 may be found to be of some interest to those concerned with such questions; at the very least, the publication of this volume will serve to identify its collective style.

Melvin Richter

December 1969

THEORY

1. POLITICAL SCIENCE AND HISTORY

Samuel H. Beer

The subject of this paper is how history can be used by political science. My concern is not to encourage the study of history for its own sake, but rather to show the benefits that political science can get from various uses of history. More specifically, I am interested in the use of history to develop analytic political theory. If I speak for history, it is because of my ultimate concern for theory — for bold, generalizing, political theory. Moreover, although I focus my attention largely on political science and political theory, most of what I have to say would, I believe, apply generally to the social sciences.

THE LIMITED GENERALIZATION

If political scientists are going to make an explicit pursuit of theory — as I wholeheartedly think we should — we need to be wary of misleading notions of what it is that we pursue. One of the more oppressive of such notions is the belief that if the study of politics (or any subject matter) is to be a science it must seek and discover laws that are universal in their application, regardless of time or place. This view is a commonplace in discussion of method. Karl Popper writes: "To give a causal explanation of a certain *specific event* means deducing a statement describing this event from two kinds of premises: from some *universal laws*, and from some singular or specific statements which we may call the *specific initial conditions*." [1] Similarly, Carl Hempel in a well-known article argues that a "genuine" or "scientific" explanation is based on "general laws" and defines a general law as "a statement of universal conditional form which is capable of being confirmed or disconfirmed by suitable empirical findings." [2]

In this view the task of political science, or indeed of any science, is not simply to capture uniformities in generalizations widely corroborated by empirical evidence. Such an empirical generalization will be limited to some region, or regions, of space and time. Causal explanation on the other hand requires universality. The explanatory generalization is a statement cast in universal form stating the causes or conditions which are always followed by the kind of event in question. If, therefore, political scientists wish to be truly scientific, that is, to find causal explanations, they should proceed by framing hypotheses in such universal form and testing them against the evidence. Moreover, if there is hope for a true political science, there is some reasonable chance of achieving such universal laws.

In the abstract, the idea that universality is the clue to what we mean by causal explanation and scientific law is plausible. If one accepts Hume's notion that causation merely means regularity in sequence, then it is sensible to conclude that a law is a statement describing an invariable sequence. In other words, if we think of causation merely in terms of association or sequence, then how do we distinguish causation from accidental association or sequence? What is the characteristic of those statements we call "laws"? Given the initial assumption, there is not much choice except to say that causal sequences are sequences that invariably occur and that laws are statements describing these invariable sequences. Trouble arises, however, when one tries to act on this notion. If the political scientist takes the doctrine of universality seriously, that is, tries to shape his research to accord with it, he will be confused and misled.

In one sense the criterion of universality is only too easy to satisfy. For it is no great problem to take a statement which refers to specific objects and by certain verbal changes give it a logically universal form.[3] For instance, the statement "These apples are red," a singular proposition, can readily be converted into some such statement as "All apples in basket b at time t are red," a proposition which is universal in its logical form. If, therefore, the political scientist takes such logical universality as sufficient to make a statement lawlike, or nomological, he will have no trouble finding "laws" among even his most limited and unambitious achievements. In this sense the doctrine of universality acts not to spur, but to relax the effort toward bolder theory building.

The advocates of the doctrine, of course, deny that logical universality is sufficient to establish nomological universality. In the case of the proposition just mentioned, the continuing reference to specific objects in a limited space-time region is quite clear. It is further stipulated, therefore, that to be a law, a statement must not only be universal in logical form, but also free of such local reference. Or to put the matter more positively, all predicates, it is said, must be "purely qualitative." [4] There is still a problem, however, for it is far from easy to say precisely when a predicate is purely qualitative. Hempel concludes a searching examination of the question with these words: "The characterization of a purely qualitative predicate as one whose meaning can be made explicit without reference to any one particular object points to the intended meaning, but does not explicate it precisely, and the problem of an adequate definition of purely qualitative predicates remains open." [5]

The difficulty of knowing when predicates are "purely qualitative" can become quite real to the person engaged in political analysis. It caused me some troubling doubts and confusion on one occasion, which incidentally was the beginning of my own dissatisfaction with the universalist view of scientific explanation. When writing the methodological section of an introduction to a textbook on comparative politics,[6] I accepted and set forth Popper's view of what is required to establish causal explanation. At the same time I was confident that my coauthors had made some quite significant progress in explaining the various events and institutions that came under their attention. Did their achievement, however, fit the Popperian definition? Explicitly or implicitly, the premises of their explanations usually seemed to be confined to a time-space context, for example, a particular country, or Western Europe, or the West of the twentieth century. The terms of crucial explanatory propositions — such as "industrialism," "feudalism," "democracy," and their adjectival forms[7] — looked like universal concepts, yet also were so embedded in European history that one could hardly hope to make explicit their meanings without reference to the specifics of that history. The lesson of this experience for me was that causal explanation does not necessarily entail universalist pretensions.

I say "necessarily" because my purpose here is to open doors, not close them. It is not my intention to lay a ban on social scientists who attempt to frame theories with nomological universality. Such an effort might very well have pragmatic success, yielding explanations that could be corroborated in a very wide variety of time-space contexts. Indeed, the universalist doctrine can be very useful if taken in the right spirit. That is, if we think of it as a kind of utopia which urges us continually to try to develop and expand the generality of our hypotheses, but which should not be taken as a paradigm of what must be achieved. Like utopias in other contexts it can be a useful guide to conduct. Similarly, the danger is that it will lead us to disdain and downgrade what is practically within our reach. The universalist doctrine is misleading if it turns the social scientist away from an important kind of general knowledge which his disciplines are quite capable of achieving, that is, knowledge which is causally explanatory but which is explicitly or implicitly restricted to certain contexts. This kind of social science consists of generalizations, but they are limited generalizations.

Consider, for example, the achievement of *The American Voter*. It is an understatement to say that this study has vastly extended our understanding of American voting behavior. Nor is this a matter of mere description. The authors have been continually concerned with tracing "the intricate pattern of causality leading to behavior at the polls." [8] Yet it would be an obvious absurdity to try to judge the value of the study by submitting its findings to the test of nomological universality. The study draws on general psychological theory and there are, to be sure, suggested hypotheses for testing in other contexts. Overwhelmingly, however, its achievement lies in its system of explanations of voting behavior in mid-twentieth-century America. The authors, moreover, are explicitly aware of the limitations put upon their work by what they call "the historical context." They write: "It is evident that variables of great importance in human affairs may exhibit little or no change in a given historical period. As a result, the investigator whose work falls in this period may not see the significance of these variables and may fail to incorporate them in his theoretical statements. And even if he does perceive their importance, the absence of variation will prevent a proper test of hypotheses that state the relation of these factors to other variables of his theory." [9]

In looking for and restricting himself to such limited generalizations, the political scientist shares a practical rule of method with many historians. Discussing the question of "generalization in the writing of history," William Aydelotte repudiates the notion that a generalization must be "a statement about an unrestricted class of cases which comprises an 'inductive leap' and which implies a prediction for all

44

undescribed cases of the type that may ever exist, past, present, or future." Historians, he goes on, do generalize, but most of them do not traffic in universals but restrict themselves to particular contexts.[10]

Once we rid our minds of the doctrine of universality we are not only less embarrassed to call ourselves political scientists, but also better able to appreciate the scientific achievement of historians and historically minded political scientists with a taste for analysis and generalization. Marc Bloch's *Feudal Society* is a superb example of the work of the analytic and generalizing historian. In its last chapter his summary of "the fundamental characteristics of European feudalism" is the capstone of a complex system of generalizations, descriptive and explanatory, referring to Europe during a thousand-year period of its history — for example, his brilliant analysis of the relation between disorder and the fragmentation of authority. Moreover, as one would expect from a founder of the *Annales* school of French social history, Bloch was anything but unaware of the comparative implications of his study and devotes one of the final sections of the book to the suggestion that the "feudal model as abstracted from European history should be tested in other contexts." "Feudalism," he wrote, "was not an event which happened only once in the world." [11] In spite of its broad scope and its potential for further development, however, his analysis is confined to the limited generalization and makes no claim to universal validity.

I do not mean to imply, of course, that the work of historians is a sufficient paradigm for the political scientist. As compared even with the analytic and generalizing historian, the political scientist will no doubt seek to make his conceptualization more explicit, his use of theory more deliberate, his effort to derive hypotheses for further testing bolder and more systematic. Yet the tendency of my argument is to erode the absolute barrier between history and the social sciences which has sometimes been set up in discussions of method. It is sometimes said, for instance, that the historian's main focus of concern is with the concrete and the particular, while the social scientist's is with the general and the theoretical. The limited generalization, however, even when broad and abstract, always retains some reference to the concrete and particular — for example, the twentieth-century American voter. Likewise, even when the historian is trying to characterize a limited period, he will in some degree generalize. Indeed, the biographer himself will not write a minute-by-minute account of his subject's career.

Once we give up the doctrine of universality, social science becomes far more feasible and also more like history.

If we are to pursue theory for theory's sake, I repeat, it is helpful to have some notion of our quarry. The doctrine of universality offers a familiar definition of what we seek — of the essential nature of law, science, and causal explanation. To try to accept it, however, leads one into serious methodological difficulties. More important for this paper, to try to act on it leads the social scientist into serious practical difficulties. For both reasons we should give it up as a definition of explanatory theory.

In the abstract this rejection has troublesome implications. It may well seem in some sense self-evident that when we say a proposition is a "law," we mean that if its prescribed "initial conditions" are present, the consequence must follow. In other words we believe that a true law will hold in any time-space context — precisely as the doctrine of universality asserts. To reject this doctrine means, therefore, that we will be ready to accept as lawlike and explanatory propositions which do not hold in all contexts. Naturally, when any such case arises in research, we shall wish to seek more penetrating analyses which explain these differences. We shall try to find the more comprehensive laws from which these more limited generalizations are derivative and which tell us why the "initial conditions" have a certain consequence in one context and not in another.

Yet what "law" means is best determined not by our *a priori*, but by fact. It is bootless for us to insist that empirical reality "must" be such and such — for example, that there must be ultimate natural laws or that nothing can happen by chance. We should rather accommodate our notion of law and causation to such characteristics as social and political reality display. The definition of what we seek as political science must take its character from what actually happens. In this basic sense theory must make its peace with history, not vice versa.

THE METHOD OF VERSTEHEN

The case for the limited generalization shows that the actual practice of historians and social scientists is much closer than methodological discussions usually suggest. If we accept this argument, we can also better appreciate the need to reject another distinction that has often been drawn between the two sorts of inquiry. This distinction relates to procedure and approach. Social scientists, it is said, use the method of empirical generalization, building their theories by carefully observing fact and testing hypotheses in the manner of the natural sciences. Historians, on the other hand, it is claimed, use the method of *Verstehen*, or subjective understanding.

This distinction was first made by certain philosophers in the latter part of the nineteenth century. Violently reacting to positivism, they put their case in extreme terms, asserting that the method of empirical generalization, although suitable to natural science, could not be used in the study of history, that *Verstehen* was the method of study exclusive to history, and that history was concerned only with understanding the concrete, unique occurrence in itself and in series. This point of view involves a sharp distinction between the product of the two methods — on the one hand universal truth, on the other particularistic truth. The case for the limited generalization enables us to criticize this rigid distinction and so prepares us to consider the further point that not only in product, but also in procedure, the two sorts of inquiry are not sharply set apart.

My purpose, in a sense, is to save the method of *Verstehen* from its originators. For though I disagree with much of what they say — I think they are wrong on all three points mentioned above — the method itself seems to me to be a fruitful one which in actual fact is constantly used not only by historians but by social scientists as well. Nor does this imply a rejection of empirical generalization. On the contrary, the two methods are most usefully employed in conjunction with one another. They are, however, distinct and independent and neither can be reduced to the other. Yet both, I will argue, lead to knowledge that is general and to explanations that are causal; in this sense both are "scientific."

These contentions I think reflect the actual practice and achievement of social science. They will no doubt meet with objection from students of methodology. Yet we must recognize that philosophers disagree on what is the right method or methods for studying human behavior. While not clearly vetoing the method of subjective understanding, Nagel, for instance, obviously much prefers what he calls "the causal-functional approach of natural science." [12] Wittgenstein, on the other hand, argued that as an agent who acts on reasons, man must be distinguished from all other objects, since his activities, unlike theirs, cannot be explained in a causal way.[13] Following this line, some of his followers are deeply critical of the whole idea of social science.[14] Given this disagreement among philosophers, the social scientist, it seems to me, will do well to look to his own practice, sorting out whatever methods and approaches have proved useful, regardless of whether they may or may not accord with the prescriptions of methodologists.

The best guide, it seems to me, is Max Weber, and in what I have to say I accept the general lines of what I take to be his methodological argument. Rather than add one more commentary on Weber, however, I will try to explain the meaning and defend the use of *Verstehen* by referring mainly to examples from some of my own work. I am thinking of the typology which I developed for the analysis of British politics and which distinguished among five types of political behavior — Old Tory, Old Whig, Liberal, Radical and Collectivist.[15] In analyzing each of these types of politics I used in the first instance what I call an "intentional" model of political behavior, the adjective being chosen to bring out the contrast with "situational" models which I will discuss at a later point.

An intentional model is a product and an illustration of the method of subjective understanding. Consider, for instance, the model of Liberal politics which I used to analyze the behavior of a large section of the political community in the early Victorian period, in particular to characterize and explain the forms and modes of action of the various political formations of the time. In terms of this model a principal source of Liberal behavior consisted in certain premises of value and belief which I call the Liberal theory of representation. This is not the place for a complete description. One essential element, however, was political individualism, the notion that what ought to be represented is not estates or corporate groups, but rather the rational, independent man. This whole mentality, moreover, was penetrated by an exceptionally high commitment to instrumental rationalism.

This model is explanatory in the sense that it does not simply summarize and describe certain uniformities of behavior, but also tells why the uniformities occurred, that is, exhibits the Liberal theory of representation as a cause of the action constituting these uniformities. The new form of pressure group which arose in this time, for example, was sustained, if it was not initially produced, by the rugged political individualism of the Liberal perspective. Thus an essential feature of these formations was that they were voluntary associations based upon agreement among a number of like-minded individuals who set themselves to pursue certain explicitly stated objectives. The model gives a causal explanation in that it shows why a particular kind of behavior was chosen — that is, as a means to the end or value of political individualism.

Moreover, and contrary to what most defenders of *Verstehen* themselves have argued, the knowledge provided by such an analytic model is general. In the first place it is not confined to explaining a single concrete occurrence. That might be the case when the method of subjective understanding is used, let us say, by a biographer to explain some particular decision in a statesman's career. But in this analysis of Liberal politics, the model applies to a great many events over a substantial period of time, for example, to the founding of a number of different pressure groups and to the multitude of decisions constituting the process in which their structures were sustained. In the second place the model yields knowledge which is general not only in this temporal sense but also, so to speak, spatially. It applies not only to one kind of uniformity but to a large number, helping to explain not only pressure groups but also the behavior of M.P.'s, the organization and action of political parties, and methods of propaganda.

Finally I should say that the knowledge derived by means of this model of intentional behavior is general in the sense that the time-space reference can be still further broadened in order to get hypotheses for testing in other contexts. It was developed from a study of ideas and behavior in one political system in a particular period of time. The reference to Great Britain, however, is not intrinsic and the general propositions constituting the model can be used as hypotheses for studying politics elsewhere. It is, I strongly suspect, culture-bound to Western countries. Nevertheless, its level of generality is quite broad.

In short, the knowledge derived by the use of the method of subjective understanding in this instance is explanatory, causal, and general. I see no reason why we should deny it the final accolade of "scientific."

The nature and strength of the method can be made clearer if we take up some of the usual criticisms.

One would be the basic thesis of the behaviorist — the really rugged behaviorist — that ideas, feelings, attitudes, and such "subjective" elements are not to be considered as causes of behavior. If this thesis were accepted, it hardly needs to be said, the case for *Verstehen* would be destroyed. Since true behaviorists are very rare today, I will not pause to take up this argument. As behavioralists, nearly all of us in the world of social science agree that ideas can be causes. Where the critics part company from the defenders of *Verstehen* is in asserting that one can know that an idea, feeling, or attitude is a cause of some behavioral effect only by means of an empirical generalization validating the connection. When a social scientist seems to achieve knowledge of a causal relation by *Verstehen*, they contend, it is only because he makes some implicit reference to such an empirical generalization supporting the inference with which he is concerned.

Let us consider how this objection might be deployed with regard to my intentional model of Liberal politics. The model consists of the following elements: 1) the norms of political individualism and instrumental rationalism; 2) a certain situation perceived in a certain way; and 3) a need or desire — which we need not further analyze here — for some mode of concerting action for political purposes. We observe the rise of the new type of pressure group and say that the premises of individualism were an important cause. We are, however, able to say this — so runs the objection — only because of a further element: 4) an empirical generalization based on previous observation and asserting that people with the value of instrumental rationalism will, very probably, follow the logical implications of their substantive values in making particular decisions. In other words, we have seen this kind of rationality work in the past and so conclude that probably it will again.

This further element must be added, the critic emphasizes, because otherwise we would simply have a description of the antecedent conditions, individualism and rationalism (i, r,) the situation (s) and the need (n), but no proposition linking these conditions $(i + r + s + n)$ with the particular kind of action, voluntary association, (v) which we wish to explain. Since this additional and empirical generalization $(i + r + s + n = v)$ is necessary for the validity of the explanation, the independence of subjective understanding as a method falls to the ground. The dynamic causal phase of our analysis will be reducible to the method of empirical generalization.

This criticism, it seems to me, does not strike home. The analysis of political and social behavior is, and can validly be, conducted by means of the method of subjective understanding and without reference to such additional empirical generalizations, implicit or explicit. The crux of the reply is that the actors themselves, when making this decision, certainly did not need to refer to such an empirical generalization; therefore, neither does the student of their behavior. It may be that the group being studied were the first people ever to behave in the specified way. A fortiori they could not have acted on a generalization derived from previous instances of the specified behavior. But even when there have been such previous instances, groups and individuals, it is needless to say, often act without knowledge of them, making their way by thought and feeling from the initial elements to a determination. In either case, since it was possible for the members of the group to make their decisions without reference to such a generalization, it is also possible for the social scientist to reconstruct in imagination their process of decision making without such help.

To return to the model of Liberal politics: the analyst gets a grasp of the political culture of these early Liberals — men like Cobden and Bright with their hatred of hierarchy, deference, and aristocracy and their fierce commitment to the free, rational individual. He reconstructs the situation as they perceived it in economy and polity. He then follows through their processes of reaction and decision and sees how it was natural and logical, if not exactly inevitable, that they should invent and sustain these new tools and modes of individualistic political warfare.

The crucial phase of the analysis is not the reconstruction of the initial elements from which the process of reaction and decision followed. I do not mean that to do this is easy. The analyst will use whatever data and whatever general knowledge are relevant to make as sure as possible that his conception of the initial elements is correct. He certainly does not make an "intuitive leap" into their subjective consciousness. Where imagination and empathy are involved, however, is in the dynamic causal phase of the analysis when, having grasped the initial elements, the analyst follows their inherent behavioral tendencies. This phase of imaginative enactment is not something mysterious — not at any rate in the sense of being unfamiliar. It utilizes the same capacities that enable us in everyday relations to anticipate the reactions and appreciate the feelings of people around us. This ability to "put oneself in the position of another person," that is, this capacity for vicarious experience, may be a little puzzling, but it is certainly a commonplace of social existence.

To describe the process by saying that the analyst puts himself in the position of the people he is studying may be helpful if it is made clear that it means that he puts himself in their position with *their* values and confronting the forces of the time and place as *they* saw them.

51

It does not mean that he puts himself in their position as he is with his values and beliefs and understands what they did because it is the same thing he would have done in the same situation. Moreover, and this is much the same point, the method of subjective understanding does not mean that he personally must identify with the people he is studying. The student of Soviet Russia does not need to identify with Stalin in order to reconstruct his deliberations. Similarly, the analyst need not himself go through the emotional experiences — the hate, anger, jealousy — of the people he is studying. Subjective understanding is an intellectual process and insofar as emotion enters in, it is, so to speak, emotion reconstructed in tranquility. Nevertheless, as Weber observes, the analyst must share with his subjects some common substratum of human experience, thought, and emotion. The ultimate values of some groups or cultures, for instance, may differ so greatly from those of the social scientist that he will find it impossible to reconstruct their character and tendencies in imagination.[16]

The method of subjective understanding is plagued by the criticism that it depends on some kind of mysterious intuition. The simplest way to clear up this point is to observe that one of its most successful uses has been in the study of rational action. In his discussion of explanation as practiced by historians, William Dray describes one mode which he calls "rational explanation." The essential technique is a "reconstruction of the agent's calculation of means to be adopted toward his chosen end in the light of the circumstances in which he found himself."[17] The inquiry begins when the historian finds himself puzzled by some action of an individual or group. As an example Dray cites a question raised by G. M. Trevelyan in his history of the Glorious Revolution, when he pointed out the curious behavior of Louis XVI in removing military pressure on Holland at the very moment Willian of Orange was about to invade the England of Louis's ally, James II. Trevelyan's explanation is that Louis "calculated that, even if William landed in England, there would be civil war and long troubles as always on that factious island. Meanwhile, he could conquer Europe at leisure."[18] In fact this calculation proved wrong when a virtually unanimous England drove out James and welcomed Willian. Yet Trevelyan's reconstruction of Louis's motivation shows it to have been an "appropriate" means to his ends at the time the decision was made. In thus explaining its "rationale," he shows why the action was taken.

In his discussion of "rational explanation," Dray is concerned only with the action of individuals in the past. The method he illustrates, however, can be applied *not only to individuals but also to groups and not only to action in the past, but also to action in the present and in the future*: to the probable behavior of a politician trying to advance his fortunes, a pressure group seeking some advantage from a government, a nation acting to expand its power. Game theory in some of its phases utilizes this mode of analysis, focusing, as Richard Snyder points out, "on the reasonable policy maker who weights values (or utilities) with probabilities and maximizes the weighted sum of the two." Echoing language often used in describing *Verstehen*, he continues: "The theory of games is also directed to the question: What would I reasonably do if I were in the other fellow's shoes?" [19]

Although economics also uses the method of empirical generalization, in its deductive phase it employs similar techniques of rational explanation. The laws of economics, as Weber writes, "state what course a given type of human action would take if it were strictly rational," not subject to error or emotional influences and directed to one end, maximizing economic advantage.[20] By itself, such a system of projections has no predictive value. Insofar, however, as people are identified who possess the purposes presumed by economic analysis, the actions indicated by its rational calculations have more or less probable predictive force.

It may be objected that we can never be sure that people will act rationally upon their purposes or values. Even if the inquirer is sufficiently acquainted with the conscious thought and feeling of his subjects, it is always possible that nonconscious forces are compelling them to act. The observation is obviously correct and this possibility is why depth psychology is an important instrument of social science. Unless, however, we are going to deny all causal force to conscious processes and intentions, we must allow for the fact that an understanding of how these conscious processes operate — how, in cases of rational action, for instance, they lead to decisions embodying and expressing goals and norms — has real predictive (or retrodictive) power.

Rational action provides ready and intelligible illustration of the method of subjective understanding and helps dispel any shadows of obscurantism that may still cling to it. But the method itself applies as well to nonrational action and, of course, to that much more common case of mixed rational and nonrational action. Weber recognizes this application to the nonrational when he writes of the "sympathetic participation" which enables the inquirer adequately to grasp the emotional context in which an action takes place. We imaginatively participate, he writes, in such emotional reactions as anger, anxiety, pride, and so forth, "and thereby understand the irrational conduct which grows out of them." [21] The observer, for instance, understands how "pride" prevented a person from taking some action which was clearly to his advantage or was perhaps required by his ideals or affection for others. He understands in the sense that he imaginatively reconstructs the situation and himself enacts the process of "decision" of the actor or actors.

It is in this connection that one can see most clearly the link between the social sciences and the humanities. Novelists and dramatists have often remarked how sometimes in the process of composition their characters take on life and begin to act on their own. Recently, for instance, Edward Albee remarked that when writing a play he first creates his characters and then tests them by putting them in various situations — such as aboard the *Titanic* — in order to see how they behave. In this way he finds out whether they are fully developed and credible.

The novelist or dramatist conceives of a certain sequence of behavior by his characters. This process of artistic conception is enormously complicated and there is surely no single "method" by which it is carried on. Many writers make great use of social theories — compare the impact of Freud on the novel — as well as those loose, but not wholly unreliable, generalizations of common sense. In the present context, however, we are concerned with a different approach, as suggested by Albee's comment. When the writer takes this approach, the sequence of behavior conceived by him derives not from his knowledge of laws of social or individual behavior, but directly from his imaginative enactment of his characters' experience.

We are dealing here with art in which the actors are fictitious, the creatures of the artist. This does not make the process of creation irrelevant to the social scientist. For although the characters are fictitious, there are standards of credibility to which they and their behavior must conform. In analyzing a work of art we can often detect this dual concern of the artist. On the one hand are his distinctive aesthetic and dramatic purposes. On the other, however, is his need to make his characters and their action behaviorally convincing. If, for instance, he needs a certain action for dramatic or aesthetic effect, he must create characters for whom such action is credible. For once a certain character has been placed in a certain situation, it is no longer the mere creature of the writer, but acquires a behavioral tendency of its own.[22]

A social scientist using the method of subjective understanding will similarly deal with the causal interconnection of character, situation, and action. He works with reference to values, beliefs, and attitudes of a group; the situation confronting it; and the action which has been or will be taken. His task is by imaginative participation to grasp the behavioral tendency of the group. Yet like the novelist or dramatist whose character and plot are contrived and mechanical, the connections he suggests may be unbelievable and subject to criticism and correction by another inquirer with more sensitivity to the human qualities involved.

Both approaches, subjective understanding and empirical generalization, are legitimate paths to new knowledge. Though distinct, they can nevertheless be fruitfully combined. To illustrate this latter point I should like to conclude this section of the paper by showing how the two types of analytic model, the intentional and the situational, can be used in a single piece of analysis.

The illustration comes from my discussion of British politics in the collectivist period.[23] Initally the analysis is based upon an intentional model which finds in the collectivist theory of representation the major premises for a great deal of behavior which otherwise would not appear to be related. This intentional model is explanatory in that it enables one to see the causal relation between these very general norms and a mass of institutionalized political behavior. Particularly important is the fact that in contrast with the norms of nineteenth-century liberalism, these norms centering on party government and functional representation in effect legitimize and even require a massive concentration of power in political parties and pressure groups.

Observation of this behavior, however, shows that it is not fully described by these norms and that such unanticipated consequences are not merely random, but constitute uniformities which can be described in empirical generalizations: in short, that the structure described by the intentional model has latent functions as well as the manifest functions of party government and functional representation. One is greatly helped in identifying these latent functions and seeing how they are interrelated by another analytic device, a situational model.

The outline of this model was taken from economics in which the study of concentration has shown how this growing feature of the economy tends to supplant the typical behavior of the free market with managerialism, bureaucracy, bargaining, and manipulation of consumer demand. Political concentration has similar effects. According to the norms of collectivist politics, for example, trade associations and trade unions ought to be brought into close and continuous contact with government in order to give it the benefit of their advice and expertise. In fact, however, because of certain features of the situation — namely, the high level of organization of these producer groups and the government's need for their cooperation in carrying out its policy of welfarism and economic management — this process of ostensible advising becomes a process of bargaining.

This process of bargaining is not intended by the norms of collectivist politics. Yet neither is it the result of some kind of conspiracy; indeed, at least in the initial stages of development, it is not recognized for what it really is — bargaining rather than advising — even by people participating in it.[24] An unintended uniformity resulting from certain features of the situation, above all concentration, it is one of several latent functions of the structure of collectivist politics which the situational model enables one to identify. The model is explanatory in that it sheds light on the causes of these unintended uniformities, the causes being in particular a high degree of political concentration joined with a high degree of government intervention.

The model is general in that it unifies the explanation of a number of different kinds of uniformities, for example, bargaining, bidding, bureaucracy, and manipulation. It is also general in that it applies to British political behavior over a substantial period of time. Moreover, the time-space reference can be broadened and the propositions constituting the model — that is, asserting the connection between concentration and these consequences — can be used as hypotheses in the study of other political systems.

No more than the intentional models, however, does it pretend to universality. Further comparative research may well show it to be limited to certain time-space contexts. It is dependent for its validity upon such contexts, that is, upon various as yet undetected conditions, positive and negative, which must be present if the causal connections it asserts are to obtain. The political scentist will try to reduce this unanalyzed context and to discover those conditions, positive and negative, which have a causal bearing on the sequences asserted by these empirical generalizations. At the same time it would be self-defeating not to recognize that the model, insofar as it is true, has explanatory power and can claim to be a piece of scientific knowledge.

This example illustrates only one way in which the two types of analytic model can be combined. The nature of the problem being investigated may, for instance, make it more productive to begin with a situational analysis. Discussion of this and other related points will be more appropriate, however, at a later point. In this context my object is to explain and illustrate how the two methods — subjective understanding and empirical generalization — far from being incompatible, are natural allies in the work of political science and indeed the social sciences generally.

For our concern with the pursuit and development of analytic political theory this discussion of *Verstehen* has the principal value of helping us further define what we pursue. My argument has been that this sort of intentional analysis can produce knowledge which is general, causal, and therefore scientific. Hence, explanatory theory, as it develops, can be expected to include such knowledge. My emphasis in these concluding pages, however, has been to suggest there are not two sorts of knowledge, derived respectively from intentional and from situational analysis, but rather that the two methods can be so joined as to integrate harmoniously both sorts of scientific achievement.

The products of *Verstehen* do, to be sure, have a specific reference and a localistic taint. This reference, I strenuously insist, need not be to a single individual human being. It can be to a group which extends widely in time and space so long as there is a pattern of behavior which the imagination can credibly link with a pattern of motivation. Subject to this requirement, the group could be a family, a political party, a nation, or perhaps even one of Toynbee's civilizations. Even in such extreme cases the specific reference remains. But as I have suggested in the first part of this paper, such specific reference seems to taint all general knowledge in some degree. Neither the method of empirical generalization nor the method of subjective understanding gives us knowledge that is purely theoretical or purely historical, purely universal or purely particular. In each case the knowledge produced has both aspects. This is one condition of their compatibility in models of analysis.

Samuel H. Beer

In the previous pages we have been concerned with the usefulness of history to political science, in particular analytic political theory. Among other things it has been argued that theory must shape and adapt itself to history. This raises the question of what one means by "history." It seems to me that there are three meanings which bear on our general question and which for the sake of identification I shall term 1) history as past behavior; 2) history as duration; and 3) history as development.

One must admit that the rejection of history by the social sciences can provide itself with a plausible rationale. It can be argued that confining one's attention to present events, precisely because it shows unconcern for the particulars of this or that time, thereby reflects the truly scientific thrust for the universal. In defense of this antihistorical position one might point to the success of the natural sciences and what it seems to teach the sciences of society.

Physical nature, for instance, also has a historical dimension which, in the case of the earth, is studied in geology. But consider how much the progress of geology in the nineteenth century owed to the belief that, as Lyell wrote, "all phenomena of the earth's crust were caused by causes like those studiable today." This great pioneer of geology constantly urged and acted on his "uniformitarian" presupposition, fiercely attacking the "doctrine of the discordance of the ancient and modern causes of change" and confidently asserting that "amid all the revolutions of nature, the order of nature has been uniform." [25]

Similarly, the social scientist might argue that the laws governing human behavior are the same regardless of time or place, and that therefore he can derive them from a study of contemporary behavior alone. Judged from this point of view, history has a modest function. It may suggest problems which then turn the social scientist to renewed investigation of present-day behavior. Also, as he makes progress in developing the general laws of human behavior, he can go back to history to identify and clear up problems of causal explanation. In this view, however, the data of history are not needed for the essential progress of social science.

In the premises of this reasoning we have one source of that dogma of universality which has done so much damage to the progress of social science. It was precisely this way of interpreting the success of natural science that led to the abortive striving for universal social laws in the nineteenth century.[26] As Bloch remarks, the advances of natural science in the nineteenth century so impressed people that they thought the only kind of knowledge worth having was in the form of "imperiously universal laws." Today, however, as he points out, we are free of this old and restrictive model and are much more flexible in our notion of what can be called scientific.[27] The metaphysic of "the uniformity of nature" is no longer generally accepted by philosophers as a picture of the human or the natural cosmos.

Whether or not the metaphysics of social scientists is up to date is not in itself of much importance. An old-fashioned addiction to uniformitarian doctrine, however, can have bad results for practice. It can, for instance, provide a rationale for what is in fact simply American parochialism. That we are parochial has been and still is a familiar criticism of American political science. Its basis is not merely our concentration on American affairs, but also our lack of historical perspective. It is still common for the introductory course in political science to be in fact a course in American government and politics which, after a brief initial bow to the Federalist papers and the making of the Constitution, leaps into a detailed discussion of American voting behavior, pressure groups, parties, and the like during the past ten or twenty years. Can anyone doubt that such parochialism cries out for a deepening of historical perspective and a new stress on comparative political history?

Some find the source of this parochialism in certain peculiarities of American political culture. Walter Dean Burnham notes that a hostility to history has persisted through the older "institutional" phase on into the present "behavioral" phase of the discipline.[28] This has meant, he says, that although both the "old" and the "new" political science have been marked by a high level of intellectual competence, it has been a competence at home especially with "the solution of technical problems within tacitly accepted boundaries of 'giveness' which ultimately reflect the kind of political culture Hartz described in *The Liberal Tradition*." Whatever the cause, Burnham goes on to argue that the lack of historical perspective has had unfortunate effects on our understanding of political behavior. In his view it has, for instance, led some political scientists to elevate such features as incrementalism, bargaining, and low ideological profile into a general model of American political behavior, although inquiry with historical depth shows this emphatically not to be the case. On the contrary, such historical inquiry, he continues, will oblige us "to reorganize the conceptual map which we have of American politics in such a way as to *relativize* all those things which we have taken to be absolutes; to make way for a recognition of discontinuities, jumps and anomalies where before we saw only uniformities; and to require, e.g., a much more complex and multi-level theory of the American voter — one much more likely to make room for his 'rationality' — than those theories which now dominate the field."

When one asks whether political scientists should be concerned with history, the answer is clear. Their subject is political behavior wherever and whenever it takes place. Just as the discipline will not confine itself to Western countries, so also it will broaden its concern to seek out and welcome evidence of political behavior in times past. As Charles Tilly remarks when concluding his sociological study of the Vendée rebellion: "Sociologists have cut themselves off from a rich inheritance by forgetting the obvious: that all history is past social behavior, that all archives are brimming with news on how men used to act, and how they are acting still." [29]

Stated in these terms the case for the study of history is strong. Yet it is a case for the study of history in only one meaning of the term. To study history as past behavior will broaden the basis of fact on which to build the discipline. Like the extension of our studies to non-Western countries, it increases the varieties of political behavior coming under inquiry and so widens the scope of our knowledge. To argue for history in this vein, however, implies that though past behavior will often differ in many vital respects from present behavior, this difference does not consist in or come from the fact of its pastness. History is to be consulted and used for the sake of difference, but not for that special kind of difference which resides in its pastness. In short, this case for studying the past presumes that the time-dimension is irrelevant. But when we say that political science can benefit from the use of history, we also mean that in some sense the time-dimension is of the essence.

HISTORY AS DURATION

The first point that we mean to make when we stress the time-dimension is the contrast between short-range and long-range change. In urging the importance of historical study for social science we are saying that certain things can be discovered from the study of long-range change that cannot be discovered from the study of short-range change. An entity is its history, displaying its characteristics and its effects through process. If the time-dimension of our inquiry is too narrow, we may miss the significance of the entity or even fail to perceive it at all. As we have already had occasion to observe, variables of great importance may change very little during a given period.[30] If we are to assess their significance and their relationship to other variables, we must therefore extend the historical dimension of our study.[31]

Structural persistence

One of the great problems of inquiry is to identify the important structures and processes to be studied — those with major causal influence. They do not automatically leap to the eye from the manifold of experience, but must be selected. One of the marks of the professional is that he will quickly perceive important variables in what seems to the amateur a mass of confused fact. A principal aid in this task is theory, which enables us to see structures and functions that would otherwise go unnoticed. It is by theory, so to speak, that we educate our perception to a professional level.

Similarly, a sense of history as duration is a spur to this broader and more sophisticated perception. It teaches us to ask: Is this present and short-lived fact a part of some more general structure or function? Is this seemingly unique arrangement or event actually one more embodiment of some persisting and deep-rooted feature of the political system? Is this particular party system, for instance, to be seen as simply the present form of a mechanism of interest aggregation produced and supported by long-run forces of the political system? There is no guarantee that the answer will be "yes." But if it is, we will have found something common and invariant in what appeared to be diverse and particular.

To find such a common element has the advantage, first, of raising the level of generality of our knowledge and so facilitating comparison. One of the barriers to the development of social science is the uniqueness of social events. This is not just a trumped-up objection, but a hard fact that any social scientist continually runs into. How, for instance, can he quantify certain phenomena without first being able to make the qualitative judgment that they are similar? Like theory, history can help us break through the particularity of things and locate comparable and quantifiable identities.

To identify these common structures of processes will also further our pursuit of causal connection. Let us say we began with a concern for the causes of some contemporary event and at first found them in a high correlation with certain other recent events. A broader historical perspective, however, shows this correlation to be the recurrence in a particular form of a persisting relationship in the political system. As a result our study of causation now shifts to the long-run factors. This is vitally important. For if we were content simply with our short-run correlation, it is quite possible that the events we were trying to explain would continue even when the correlation no longer held.

A quick illustration of these points. We began, let us say, by trying to explain McCarthyism in terms of a high correlation with Catholicism. A longer look at American history, however, shows that outbreaks of rightist radicalism have been recurrent, their roots extending into long-run processes, such as urbanization. This does not invalidate the initial correlation but we interpret it differently, making a different qualitative judgment as the basis for our quantification. The important characteristic is now not something peculiar to Catholicism, but rather some common feature shared with similarly situated and affected groups in other times. A sense of history as duration thus may enable us to move farther from a merely narrative account of such a phenomenon and look at it in a much more scientific way. We may see it, for instance, as an instance of "fundamentalist reaction" which not only has its roots in long-run processes in American history, but can also now be compared with similar occurrences in other countries.

In description and explanation in social science we use the present tense rather freely, creating for purposes of analysis a kind of "extended present." We say that a party system "has" such and such functions, that the power structure of some organization "is" oligarchic, democratic, or the like. This should not conceal from us the fact that we are including a good deal of history within this extended present. Our subject matter exhibits itself only through process and so over time. If, for instance, we are going to talk about the functions of our party system — or indeed if we are going to say what we mean by the American party system — we will be right not to focus narrowly on the contemporary, but look at these structures and functions over a long period of time. This kind of historical perspective will help us not only to identify the structures we wish to describe, but also to locate the causal explanations of them.

The concept of history as duration, however, does not mean that the long-run perspective will always identify the more important entity or the more important causal influence. It by no means implies that if, in the study of the American party system, we will extend our historical perspective we are sure to find a single party pattern which remains identical through periods of change. On the contrary, a great virtue of a longer perspective may well be to show us discontinuities we never suspected. Thus, a recent study which powerfully exploits the historical approach finds five party systems.[32]

The novel, the unprecedented does happen from time to time, making fruitless the search for similarities in the past. Fascism, for instance, was something radically new and the early efforts to assimilate it to models of military and authoritarian dictatorship in the past were misleading. In this sense the concept of history as duration is heuristic only. It is a way of saying: Do not fail to consider the possibility that your immediate subject of investigation may actually be part of a more inclusive long-run entity. This will often prove to be the case and, when it is, the rule will have helped us develop our knowledge of causes. This rule, however, is not a theoretical finding that the causally most important will also always be identical with that which has endured the longest. It is tempting to imagine that longevity is an index of what is causally fundamental. Some historians seem to make the assumption that the most powerful causes in a society or polity are those which have been in existence for the longest time. It would be an aid to much research if this were always true. But whether or not it is, we can tell only by checking out the facts in each case.

Structural Change

In this discussion of history as duration I have been concerned with structures persisting through time and continually performing certain characteristic functions which we describe and analyze in the extended present of social science discourse. But the concept is also relevant to our concern with changes in structures, that is, to our concern with processes themselves as subjects which we try to classify in typologies and account for in explanatory theory.

An obvious example is our concern with revolutions, particularly those we call the great social revolutions. Some are longer, some shorter in terms of physical time, and the question of when each begins and ends is a problem for inquiry. In any case, however, the event has a time-dimension that is substantial. The revolutionary process is a unit with parts that we understand by relating them to one another in the whole. We can describe the event only by referring to a complex of action which stretches over years. Of the French Revolution we say, for instance, that "the ancien régime was overthrown and a liberal order established." To perceive this fact, however, we must look at the revolutionary process as constituting a unit. That is, we would never arrive at this descriptive statement, let alone an explanation of it, if we considered in isolation the subordinate events of each year or month during the revolutionary period. As a result, therefore, these great social revolutions with their substantial periods of duration have become units of analysis and comparison for political scientists concerned with the study of "internal war."

Structural Interdependence

Lipset has observed that the revival of historical interest in sociology has gone along with a shift of interest from microscopic (small unit) to macroscopic (total society) problems.[33] Is there any intrinsic connection between the two sorts of concern? Certainly work with small units does not necessarily bar an interest in general theory. To be sure, as Robert Dahl has pointed out, much work in the behavioral mood in political science in recent years has at once concentrated on small units and neglected both theory and history.[34] Yet small-unit inquiry can have a powerful thrust toward the general. The investigation of small-group behavior, for instance, has led to advances in general theory[35] and the work of psychologists dealing intensively with a few individuals has shed light on the nature and sources of aggression.

On the other hand, a long historical perspective and a concern for broad theory were intertwined in the work of many of the founders of sociology and political science. There is an intrinsic connection in the sense that a concern with history as duration will tend to lead to the discovery of more important causal influences and to the development of more general theory. Indeed, it would seem that the importance of duration in the identification of structures and processes for study is related to the fact that we are dealing with social, that is, highly interdependent, elements. Political events as we find them are embedded in complex systems. Each element we select for study, whether an individual, or group, or institution, is causally related to others. This complex interdependence in space involves a complex interdependence in time, so that acts or responses of the system as a whole will have substantial duration.

If not a necessary connection, certainly this is a familiar fact: that political systems in comparison with their subunits exhibit their characteristic features only in relatively longer periods of time. In consequence, political systems as a whole cannot be studied without being viewed in an appropriate historical perspective. In this sense the traditional influence of history on political science has helped sustain our concern with macroscopic problems. Similarly, the rising interest in the study of political systems in recent years is related to the renewed interest in the historical dimension of the discipline.

HISTORY AS DEVELOPMENT

To be aware of history as duration — of the extended present of an event and of the interdependence of its parts — is important for political and social analysis. But the notion of a dimension in time which is called up when we speak of history also has another important aspect. We say that a structure or institution or system has "grown out of" or "developed" or "evolved" from its history. We feel that there is something important to be learned about that entity by studying its past. Such notions take us beyond the concept of duration. That idea calls attention to the fact that the entities that are analyzed in social and political inquiry have a temporal dimension which may be of substantial magnitude. Still, in this perspective, the entity, even if it is some massive event such as a great social revolution, is treated as if it could be isolated from its past and so compared with other similar units. Although admitting that it may thus be necessary and legitimate to isolate units of social and political process for purposes of comparative study, we cannot avoid the further question of whether we can understand the unit without study of its particular past. This sense of history I call the notion of history as development.

I have left the notion only vaguely defined because it is in this form that it is often found pervading the work of social scientists and especially historians. It can, of course, be formalized. One could try to derive a meaning from the use of the concept of development in sciences, such as embryology or psychology. No single meaning of the word can be excogitated from the nature of things or of thought. There are, however, three elements often connected with the term in common usage and in social science which make it useful. The first is the notion that social and political process occurs in a series of successive stages. The second is that each stage is produced by the previous one, that is, the line of causation is endogenous. At any transition, causes from outside the system may affect what happens. The source of causation, however, to which the concept of development directs our attention here, is the preceding stage. The third element is the idea of directionality, or trend, in the whole process, for example, toward greater modernity, rationality, productivity, freedom, or the like. Moreover, the concept assumes, of course, that we have identified something which continues through these changes — "the system," "the country," "the group" — and within which the endogenous line of causation takes place. Only if we can identify such an underlying subject of change can we know that we are dealing with stages of the same entity rather than with two different entities and determine which causes are endogenous and which exogenous to the process.

Several successive stages of an entity, each caused by the preceding stage, with the whole process showing a trend — this is the distinctive pattern of change to which the concept of history as development calls our attention as a possibility for research and theorizing.

Needless to say, this concept in one form or another has been very important in social and political thought. Sometimes it has taken an evolutionary form in which gradual change makes the succession of stages hardly discernible. It has also provided the framework for revolutionary theories, which sharply mark the transition from stage to stage in catastrophic outbreaks. It can be focused on entire social or political systems; it can be used to organize the history of particular institutions or structures. It has been exhibited not only in some of the grander philosophies of history, but also in the work of hardheaded and empirical social scientists such as Weber, Durkheim, and MacIver. To discover such a pattern in some area of events would be an important advance. To be able to think of this concept as a possible way of organizing historical data would be a help to social and political theory. Whether such a pattern can be found, needless to say, is to be determined solely by empirical research. If, however, history sometimes does take this form, then our analytic political theory will not be adequate to the facts unless it is sensitive to this possibility.

If we are to make the concept useful, however, two things need to be done. First, we must confront the suspicion that its use will involve us in the fallacies of historicism.[36] Second, we need to make the meaning of the concept clearer by showing the kind of process to which it directs our attention. As I have just suggested, it has been put in the service of a wide variety of social and political interpretations. We cannot begin to cover them all, but the discussion of historicism itself will naturally lead to an illustration which bears particularly upon the work of the social scientist as social critic.

The concept surely can be used in objectionable ways. If, for instance, it is taken to mean that there has been a single line of development constituting all human history — as in many of the great philosophies of history — then it is improper to speak of the description of this process as a "law" of social science. Such a description, as Popper points out, is "not a law, but only a singular historical statement."[37] It may, of course, be a correct description. The point here is simply that it may not be treated as a hypothesis or law because, in the nature of the case, the proposition cannot be tested by other instances.

This criticism no doubt applies to some of the older applications of the concept. It does not apply, however, where the social scientist finds several instances of a pattern of development, as is the case with most modern developmental or evolutionary theories. Even Alfred Weber, whose rhetoric resounds with the old-fashioned thunder when he declares that "social evolution . . . runs through a predetermined number of stages and reaches a predetermined result," holds that this pattern recurs in "the various great historical organisms."[38] This criticism reminds us, however, that even though we may have discovered a series of stages, we still confront the task of finding the general laws that explain the transition from stage to stage and, if there is a trend, the further task of identifying the persisting conditions which promote it throughout the whole process.

We get closer to a central criticism of historicism with the objection that it fails to state its predictions in conditional form. Popper strongly defends a scientific study of society which involves predictions that certain changes will take place "under certain conditions."[39] The historicist's vice — his misuse of the concept of development — is to make the prediction unconditionally, that is, to fail to specify those "initial conditions" which observation and testing have shown are followed by the predicted consequence. The rhetoric of the historicist is: "The revolution will come." That of the social scientist is: "If conditions A, B, C are present, and if possible offsetting conditions X, Y, Z are not present, then the revolution will come." [40] The historicist makes prophecies; the social scientist predictions.

This good advice applies to the natural scientist as well as to the social scientist. If either wishes to predict that a certain consequence "will" occur, he must specify the presence of all the conditions which promote it and the absence of all those conditions that could offset it. Discussing this question with his usual lucidity, J. S. Mill was led to define cause as follows: "The cause, then, philosophically speaking, is the sum total of the conditions, positive and negative, taken together; the whole of the contingencies of every description, which being realized, the consequent invariably allows." [41] As John Dewey remarked, "there is always the *theoretical* possibility that *some* conditions which affect the observed phenomenon have not been brought under control. The postulate of a closed existential system is thus a limiting ideal for experimental inquiry. It is a logical ideal which points the direction in which inquiry must move but which cannot be completely attained." [42] Rigorously pursued, this ideal could take one a long way. Normally of course, the experimenter can assume the continuation of a massive unanalyzed context of conditions — from the presence of oxygen in the air to the absence of colleagues who will suddenly smash his equipment.

Social Self-Knowledge

In the social sciences there is a special form in which this problem of "offsetting causes" presents itself. This arises when the generalization describing or explaining certain behavior becomes known to the persons with whose behavior it is concerned. As a result, as Nagel observes, well-established generalizations and predictions of social science will be rendered invalid, if and when they are made public and people alter their behavior in the light of this new knowledge. [43] To recognize this problem of "social self-knowledge" — the phrase is Dankwart Rustow's — is not a reason for despair, but rather for inquiry. [44] To begin with, it means that social science is doing what it should, that is, giving men greater control over their history. Being made aware by social science of what in their own behavior is causing the results they dislike, they are enabled to modify that behavior and so to eliminate those undesirable results — or to create and maintain desirable conditions.

Moreover, the laws and theories that give them this power are not necessarily invalidated by being so used. Keynesian economics explains what causes economic equilibrium at less than full employment and shows how government loan-financed expenditure can change the situation. The Keynesian propositions, however, are valid whether society chooses the line of action that leads to deflation or the line that leads to full employment. In general, explanatory social theory has this capacity to explain both "health" and "sickness" in a society, as medicine explains both the course of a disease that is untreated and the treatment that will cure it, or as depth psychology applies to both the neurotic and the normal.

Admittedly, it is hard to deny that if men choose, they can invalidate even the best established of our social laws and theories. *Once they understand how a series of acts leads to certain consequences, the possibility arises that they may choose not to perform these acts.* Of course, they may not alter their conduct because they are content with what is going on, because they are emotionally incapable of a different choice, and so on. In short, how men will react to social self-knowledge is one of the more interesting subjects of social science. Nor is such knowledge exclusively an incidence of the growth of formal social science. It arises all the time on the plane of practical everyday group behavior. A family realizes how some routine is the source of disorder or discomfort and makes adjustments in its behavior. A university continually sets up committees to try to find out the effects of a certain curriculum or grading system and, if necessary, to recommend corrections. *Common sense and everyday behavior continually take advantage of the fact that if we can discover the "laws" controlling social behavior we can, if we so desire, modify them.*

For the individual or group or nation, on the plane of common sense and of social science, this process of social self-knowledge leading to self-criticism is a common feature of societies and one of the principal motors of their development. At first sight it would seem to undermine the utility of the concept of development. That concept supposes that we have discerned a pattern of stages and of the causes leading to them. Such knowledge, becoming widely disseminated, raises the question of whether the subjects of inquiry — a whole society, or participants in some structure — may not now choose a different line of conduct. We cannot exclude that possibility. It confronts not only historicism, but any generalization of social science, whether macroscopic or microscopic. It is the hopeful converse of Santayana's melancholy words that those who will not learn from history will be obliged to repeat it. It illustrates a kind of freedom that is present only in human behavior. Yet it is a special source of instability affecting social processes and continually threatening social science with obsolescence. It means that in the social sciences laws themselves develop and that, in Daniel Bell's phrase, the social sciences are "emergent."

Social Self-Knowledge and Rationalization

At the same time it is obvious that this view of the effects of social self-knowledge itself suggests one general way in which social and political development may take place. To admit this possibility is not to commit the fallacy of historicism by saying that such change is bound to happen. Yet we have a clue here to an important kind of historical change, which moreover, is related to one of the more persistent hunches of social science, namely, that the development of social and political systems tends to show a trend toward rationalization.

This model of rationalizing development was implicit in the earlier discussion of the methods of subjective understanding and empirical generalization and it may help clarify it by a brief reference to the terms and illustration of that discussion.[45] In analyzing collectivist politics, it will be recalled, an intentional model was used in order to elicit the manifest functions of institutionalized political behavior and alongside it a situational model in order to identify and explain the latent functions. The latter were shown to be in some degree dysfunctional to the normative system, for example, by "distorting" advising into bargaining.

Initially unanticipated and unrecognized, these latent functions are in time perceived, described, and explained. Depending on whether or not people feel them to be desirable, this new social self-knowledge may lead to acceptance or to reform. In the case of bargaining in British politics the effect has, on the whole, been acceptance, and, accordingly, new norms have emerged to match the realities of behavior.[46] Even in this case of acceptance, however, development has taken place, in the sense that recognition and control have been extended to a new area of the political process.

Let me repeat that I am not trying to set forth a formula covering all sorts of development. I am not here concerned, for instance, with the situational forces which might make a class or group the spearhead of historical change. Moreover, while I am speaking of a process of rationalization, I am not concerned with that kind of change which begins with criticism of the basic norms and beliefs of a system — for example, the kind of function which we normally attribute to the political philosopher. I am rather describing a function akin to that of the social scientist, that is, his function of discovering and explaining by empirical generalization the latent functions of a system or structure. This work is shared in by the social scientist, but it is not exclusively his province. Many other intellectuals take part in it. According to Lionel Trilling, for example, the "field of research" of the "classical novel" has also been to penetrate beneath social appearance to social reality — "to record the illusion that snobbery generates and to try to penetrate to the truth which, as the novel assumes, lies hidden beneath all the false appearances." [47]

As I have suggested, the newly recognized sequence of social behavior may be accepted and provided with appropriate justification in the normative system of the political culture. In this case, what was at one point of development an empirical generalization with an ambiguous ethical standing becomes a normative standard. Thus, for instance, the relationships of cabinet government arose in eighteenth-century Britain as latent functions of the "balanced constitution" of that time. Gradually these were recognized — for example, the dawning awareness that His Majesty had a "first" minister; ultimately they were embraced as rules of the British constitution, the classic formulation not being achieved until Bagehot. More interesting no doubt is the emergence of social self-knowledge leading to efforts, whether reformist or revolutionary, to change the newly recognized uniformity. This effort may involve the abolition of old institutions which have been proved responsible for the undesirable consequence, or the creation of new institutions in order to establish a different relationship.

A third possibility is, of course, that the latent functions of a system may not be discovered, but continue in existence, not merely repeating themselves, but producing further social or political change — a process of "objective" development unmediated by criticism. In relation to the totality of social and political process, this third possibility is perhaps the most common. Our social science, achieved by whatever method, never comprehends the whole of society; our explanations remain incomplete and relative. There always remains an unanalyzed context which the effectiveness of our social and political knowledge presupposes. In one sense, then, rationalization means that more and more sectors of social and political process are being subjected to human control. On the other hand, that which is to be controlled may not stay the same, but may develop new stages out of sight of our scientific binoculars. We may say that rationality has advanced, but we cannot be sure that human power has also increased.

Social self-knowledge remains a real problem. Its tendency is to render social science theory, whether of the commonsense or professional variety, obsolete or invalid. The growth of such social knowledge is one instance of the growth of knowledge in general which, as Popper has argued, makes it impossible to have "a historical social science that would correspond to *theoretical physics*." [48] Quite apart from other reasons, the prospect of such new causes entering history is alone enough to undermine the dogma of universality. The unpredictable effects of our own advancing theory are one reason why that theory will remain limited.

Verstehen and Novelty

We admit the ultimate limitation, but constantly struggle to push it back. The study of patterns of development can be an important instrument in this effort. By widening our comparison and extending the generality of our theory, we may be able to detect the invariant pattern in what initially appear to be diverse and incomparable processes. Thus the method of empirical generalization can help the political scientist cope with what seems to be novel and unique. Yet sometimes radical and irreducible novelty does occur. Although there is no method or approach that can assure us of comprehension and control in such cases, we may conclude with a word on the possibilities of *Verstehen*.

The method of subjective understanding, while originally identified as peculiar to the study of history, is in a real sense profoundly nonhistorical. In our earlier discussion it by no means figured solely as a means of understanding the past.[49] On the contrary, it was shown to be a method of prediction, as well as retrodiction, an approach opening up possibilities of not only imaginative enactment, but also what one might call imaginative preenactment. Thus, the game theorist can make well-founded, if not apodictic, projections of what the Russians will do in response to various possible moves by the United States. Thus also a Churchill could grasp the behavioral tendencies of Hitler and his gang when our generalized knowledge of such movements was in its infancy. So, too, as a sociologist has recently remarked, Kafka could write *The Castle* a number of years before the commissars built it.[50]

The method of subjective understanding is nonhistorical in the sense that it does not depend upon empirical generalization founded upon observation of past behavior. We may think it fortunate that there is this kind of social science, since it gives men a chance of coping with radical novelty in events. Even though unprecedented in history, and therefore beyond the reach of our empirical generalizations, a new turn of affairs need not find us totally without resources for understanding and so perhaps influencing its future tendencies. The method of subjective understanding, once thought to be peculiarly historical, actually offers us a chance to escape from some of the compulsions of history.

2. THE USES OF THEORY: TOCQUEVILLE'S ADAPTATION OF MONTESQUIEU

Melvin Richter

This paper is an effort to investigate in detail how Tocqueville made use of Montesquieu's theory in that crucial chapter of *Democracy in America* entitled "The Principal Causes that Tend to Maintain a Democratic Republic in the United States." [1] There Tocqueville stated his conclusions in terms of theoretical categories derived for the most part from Montesquieu. This link, although often asserted, has never been established. At the height of the success attained by the first part of the *Democracy*, in which this chapter is found, Royer-Collard had hailed Tocqueville as Montesquieu's successor, a judgment repeated shortly thereafter by John Stuart Mill. [2] Since then this connection has become a commonplace repeated by nearly every commentator without further analysis. This view remained unchallenged until the appearance of Professor Pierson's magisterial *Tocqueville and Beaumont in America*. [3] His assessment of Tocqueville, which concludes what remains perhaps the most valuable book yet written about him, begins with these words: "Royer-Collard was mistaken when he proclaimed his young follower as a second Montesquieu. For the resemblance was superficial. Tocqueville did not owe his greatness to any Olympian disinterestedness, still less to an adroit inspiration and a beguiling humour." [4] In the discussion that follows, its author concedes only one authentic similarity between the two writers, and that in the style of their chapter titles.

This paper is in one sense a defense of the older thesis against Professor Pierson's attack. But the relationship between these two authors is not treated here as one of "influence," that astrological concept which has too long bemused intellectual historians. Rather Tocqueville's use of Montesquieu is considered as a means of understanding how one indubitably great theorist of politics and society made use of a predecessor's conceptual scheme both to frame questions that directed his own research and to order the data thus found into generalizations distinguished by their abstraction, theoretical elegance, and applicability to situations far removed in space and time from those studied by their author. Tocqueville's debt to Montesquieu was nowhere greater than in such general categories of analysis and explanation. For few of Tocqueville's substantive conclusions about the United States bore any literal resemblance to Montesquieu's observations about democracy.

From the correspondence of the later writer, we know that while writing the *Democracy*, he read three authors every day: Montesquieu, Rousseau, and Pascal.[5] Of the three, Tocqueville owed most to Montesquieu, but this was not due to mere repetition of his model. This was true in part because of differences separating those democracies known to Montesquieu and that one observed by Tocqueville in the age of Jackson; in part because Tocqueville as a thinker was careless, unsystematic, forgetful, but for all that, extraordinarily subtle and imaginative. Often he preferred to formulate distinctions anew or to invent hypotheses rather than to check his source in Montesquieu where he could have found much of his work already done. This mode of proceeding merits attention, if for no other reason than for the light it casts upon one type of creative achievement in the social sciences that has gone largely ignored by those concerned with its philosophy and method. Much the same type of neglect may be attributed to historiography, both in its earlier technical form in manuals and in its present manifestation as analytical variations on a theme by Carl Hempel.

Montesquieu and Tocqueville were aristocrats trained as magistrates, not university professors with advanced degrees in the social sciences or history. Both were great theorists despite defects that might have reduced to insignificance authors of lesser stature. It may even be that their achievements in some curious way depended upon their defects. Whitehead once remarked that the great advance of the German universities in the nineteenth century (and all other modern universities have emulated their organization) consisted of making it possible for third-rate minds to make contributions to their subject. But precisely those canons of method and organization of knowledge within the university may make it more difficult for certain types of first-rate minds to function at their best.

75

As yet, little is known about the conditions of creativity for grand theory, or about what promotes acceptance or rejection of conceptual schemes in the social sciences. Although the history of the natural sciences has been studied in this way, almost no equivalent work is to be found in the study of man. It may be, as has been argued, that the history of science is irrelevant to the philosophy of science. Such a generalization is defensible at a very high theoretical level. Yet what is carried away by students from many books and courses on the scope and method of political science, or for that matter, from courses in historiography, is the impression that the best work can be achieved only under conditions of strict antisepsis applied to analytical tools, of constant self-consciousness about methodological canons, about the nature and limitations of certain materials and types of evidence. It may be that the minor virtues apt to be possessed by most professors are the precondition of those creative capacities demonstrated by very few, but little evidence yet exists for such a comforting conclusion, indeed for any conclusions whatever.

The truth of the matter is that almost none of the great theorists of the social sciences have been studied in action, in terms of their operating procedures and investigators, and their reflections, hesitations, and ultimate decisions in theorizing. This study attempts to do so. In the case of Tocqueville, it may provide some basis for considering the views of his method held by a philosopher of science, J. S. Mill, on the one side, and by a historian, Professor Pierson, on the other. Mill, who for the most part took his model and method from the natural sciences of his day, praised Tocqueville's mode of inquiry: "The importance of M. de Tocqueville's speculations is not to be estimated by the opinions which he has adopted, be those true or false. The value of his work is less in the conclusions, than in the mode of arriving at them. He has applied to the greatest question in the art and science of government those principles and methods of philosophizing to which mankind are indebted for all the advances made in modern times in the other branches of the study of nature." [6]

It is symptomatic of the gap that has existed between the philosopher and the historian that what Mill regarded as the "true Baconian and Newtonian method applied to society and government" has been systematically deprecated by Professor Pierson in the closing chapters of his book. Yet this work, it must be said, has created that genre of Tocqueville studies most relevant to many of the questions treated here. In addition to Professor Pierson's own close analysis of Tocqueville's mode of proceeding as investigator and theorist in the United States, there now exist further works on him in England, Ireland, and Algeria.[7] And in the Tocqueville holdings at Yale, carefully built up by Professor Pierson from the collection left by Paul Lambert White, there are manuscript materials that cast much light on the processes of Tocqueville's mind and method. Whatever criticism may be made of Professor Pierson's evaluation, it must be remembered that it is he more than anyone else who has made it possible for others to disagree with his own findings. To the resources provided by such scholarship and such materials for this enterprise may be added the techniques of intellectual history: textual analysis, comparison of key terms and organizing concepts, the assessment of what has been borrowed, confused, or creatively transformed of Montesquieu's work. All these materials and methods have something to tell us about Tocqueville's use of Montesquieu and the conclusions that may be drawn from it. In order to make detailed analysis possible, this paper will be confined to that single summary chapter in the *Democracy*.

Tocqueville, Professor Pierson tells us, followed the same sequence in all his investigations. First, by documentary research, interviews, and personal observation according to an established protocol, he attempted to determine the pertinent facts in the case under study. The second step was inductive and interpretative. Caring little for his facts, Tocqueville sought to discover the basic idea (*idée mère*) of which they were an expression. Having thus obtained his key, he would then deduce by logic what were the consequences of the principle he had discovered. Thus in turn he relied on observation, induction, and deduction. Of this procedure Professor Pierson takes a dim view. In his opinion Tocqueville overreached himself in his second and third steps. Too logical and insufficiently inquisitive, he tended to gather only those facts that suited his theory, once the "true explanation" had occurred to him. And particularly in the second part of the *Democracy*, he slipped into an a priori method by which he spun his ideas out of theory alone and thus ended up in the purest nonsense. For whatever consolation it may offer, Professor Pierson adds that if Tocqueville was no true historian, if his techniques of observation and generalization were both faulty, he nevertheless was a great sociologist.[8] Professor Pierson takes Tocqueville's goal to be the achievement of "the basic laws of human association, in order to find out — as one might study the gravitational movements of the stars — what makes societies act the way they do." [9] Mill attributed to Tocqueville a more psychological aim — the formulation of laws of human nature.* It would be instructive to ask which version is more nearly exact, or, if both are to be rejected. But this would involve a rather more detailed discussion of method than is here possible. Among other issues that would have to be posed are uses of "ideal types" by Montesquieu and Tocqueville respectively and the compatibility of this method with a theory of deductive laws. Such considerations will be undertaken in another place.

There is still another dimension to this paper. No question appeared more crucial to Montesquieu and Tocqueville than that of the nature and principle of governments. It is well known that Montesquieu conceived of democracy as one form of the republican state and believed its spring to be civic virtue. Thus seen, a democracy could not function without consistent self-abnegation on the part of its citizens, who place its interest above their individual interests. Among Tocqueville's major dilemmas in the application of Montesquieu's theories to Jacksonian America was the fact that Americans followed their self-interest, and yet were able to make their democracy function. This flagrant incompatibility between Montesquieu's category and facts about the United States, as Tocqueville found them, might have led him to abandon his predecessor's mode of analysis. But this Tocqueville did not do. Instead he rephrased Montesquieu in a way that made him applicable to American reality. In the process Tocqueville created a new moment in the development of a theme first articulated in the ancient world and then revived with significant consequences for Europe, England, and America by that movement Hans Baron has called "civic humanism." [10] Both Montesquieu and Tocqueville played considerable roles in the subsequent development of that current of thought, roles that emerge with some clarity from this relevant chapter in the *Democracy*.

---

* Mill wrote of Tocqueville: "His method is, as that of a philosopher on such a subject must be — a combination of deduction with induction: his evidences are laws of human nature, on the one hand; the example of America and France, and other modern nations, so far as applicable, on the other. His conclusions never rest on either species of evidence alone; whatever he classes as an effect of Democracy, he has both ascertained to exist in those countries in which the state of society is democratic, and has also succeeded in connecting with Democracy by deductions *a priori*, showing that such would naturally be its influences upon beings constituted as mankind are, and placed in such a world as we know ours to be." (*Essays on Politics and Culture*, p. 233)

II

Montesquieu's knowledge of democratic republics was limited to the city-states of classical antiquity. These were small and intimate polities, which, forced to distribute a quite finite quantity of wealth, often destroyed themselves by bitter class warfare. The United States in the 1830's was at once far larger and wealthier than Montesquieu's models. An acquisitive society, its members were animated rather more by the passion to improve their material condition than by civic virtue or class hatred. Nor was the political structure of the United States what Madison had called pejoratively, "pure democracy." The Constitution of the United States had been devised by men who had studied classical history. To avoid both tyranny and faction, those characteristically fatal diseases of ancient democracy, was high among the aims of those who drew up the Constitution. They succeeded so well in their projects that they rendered most of Montesquieu inapplicable. Nevertheless they themselves regarded Montesquieu as among the political theorists most worthy of being taken into account, and they defended their own innovations by glossing his texts.

There were other reasons that turned Tocqueville away from the literal application of Montesquieu. Principal among them were the most recent French revolution, that of 1830, and the two eighteenth-century revolutions which had created the United States and destroyed the Old Regime. Montesquieu, of course, had taken France as the model of monarchy, and monarchy as that type of government best fitted to governments of moderate size, just as democracy could exist only in small states and despotism was the form natural to far-flung empires. Both the power exerted by contemporary political arrangements over Montesquieu's mind and his own affiliations and preferences, that of the *parlementaires*, were anchored in a now-vanished society.[11] Taken literally, his analysis of politics and society was inapplicable to France after two revolutions, and to the United States at any time.

Yet there were other ways of using Montesquieu. His political values could be applied to those institutions and practices he had neither known nor could have anticipated; his analytical tools, consciously devised to make possible classification and comparison of "the laws, customs, and various usages of all peoples" could be adapted to serve Tocqueville's purposes as investigator and theorist.[12] Montesquieu's preferred values in

79

politics were the maintenance of political liberty by preventing the concentration of power in the same set of hands; the minimization of centralized bureaucracy; the primacy of pluralism and of diversity; the need to multiply centers of power with a view to creating institutionalized conflict of a sort that would make the central power bargain and compromise with groups and interests outside the state structure. As for his method, it was comparative, historical, sociological, and based on the analogy between the aspects of a society and the qualities of a system.[13] In his most extensive treatise on method, an essay continually revised before, during, and after the completion of the *Spirit of the Laws*, Montesquieu declared that comparison is the single most valuable capacity of the human mind for the analysis of human collectivities.[14] In order to explain why a given society has certain characteristics and not others, we must apply hypotheses to general effects discovered by the use of the comparative method, rather than from particular effects inferred from a unique case. In making comparisons it must be remembered that "nothing in nature is perfectly uniform (with other members of the same class) but is more or less so.[15] This point was to figure prominently in Montesquieu's typology of regimes, the first conscious effort to apply to comparative analysis that technique later called by Max Weber "ideal types." Montesquieu also understood the theory of a social system, which he applied to such phenomena as laws. These he treated as forming part of a system, within which they function together with its other parts. In comparing French and English laws punishing false evidence, Montesquieu remarked: "The three French laws form a system whose parts are closely interrelated and mutually dependent; the same is no less true of English laws on the same question." [16] No less essential to the understanding of a system is the historical dimension of development in time. To explain why laws exist, it is necessary to follow the process by which they have taken on meaning within the context of a given system, which may no longer function as such. It is this genetic method that Tocqueville called *"le point de départ."* It may be used to compare not two different societies, but the same society at different periods.

What, then, constitutes an adequate explanation of why a society has a given set of laws, political organization, and social structure? Montesquieu stipulated that such an explanation must take into account two major types of causes, physical and moral.[17] Principal among physical causes, in his view, is that of climate, which produces a number of physiological and mental consequences. Also to be taken into account are the quality of terrain, the density of population, and the territorial scale of a society. Montesquieu, who made much of such physical causes, nevertheless rejected the notion that they alone directly and irresistibly determine a society's mode of life. His position was that moral causes may predominate over physical ones, that by political and religious means even the effects of climate may be minimized and overcome.[18]

Together physical and moral causes form a society's *esprit général.* This general character of a society is to be found in the style of education it gives to its members. For every society passes on to those who live in it three types of training: that gained from the family; that from the schools; and that of life.[19] A society's general spirit is affected by a number of moral causes: religion, laws, maxims, precedents, mores (*moeurs*), customs (*manières*), its economy and trade, and its style of thought, usually created in capital or court.[20] Montesquieu believed that every society is dominated by an ordering of principle, or general spirit. As he formulated his theory, there is nothing mysterious or metaphysical about it. He directed attention to a number of moral causes whose respective effects can be rationally assessed after empirical investigation. To the extent that any one of the secondary causes predominates, the rest to that extent recede in importance. Montesquieu put much stress upon the notion of functional equivalence — the notion that certain prerequisites of a system may be fulfilled by a variety of means, including unplanned interactions. Political order may be secured either by sanctions or by self-restraint on the part of individuals or groups.

The title of Montesquieu's major book, the product of twenty years' work, called attention to the ways in which laws affect human behavior. As has been remarked, Montesquieu's treatment of law left much to be desired: he confused uniformities of behavior with moral rules, customs, and civil laws; he treated descriptive and prescriptive laws as though they belonged to the same type.[21] Montesquieu meant by "law" any rule of conduct supported by sanctions of the political authority against those who disobey such a rule. He also used the term to refer to rights and obligations protected or enforced by courts, and to basic rules of a constitution restricting those who hold power under it.

In the most significant parts of his book Montesquieu treated law as but one way of affecting human conduct. It is the method peculiar to government. The society uses other distinctive means: religion, mores (*moeurs*), and customs (*manières*).[22] Montesquieu did not underrate the power of laws backed by the coercive power of the state. But he wished to emphasize that almost everything resulting from the operation of such sanctions could also be done by social forces. In short, that restraint of human passions, wills, and imagination requisite to the maintenance of order in society could be achieved by means other than the state. Here again was the theory of functional equivalence. Montesquieu opposed the theory that the state must be omnipotent. He was not committed to the thesis, however, that society should do everything and government nothing. As a theorist, he cared most about establishing the numerous and complex ways in which the political and social systems interact. He did not attempt to reduce government to a derivative function of society. Yet there can be no question but that his political sympathies and interests led him to seek theoretical justifications for the semiautonomous existence of *"corps intermédiaires,"* groups and institutions set between the Crown and the people.

Among the forces outside government punishments and rewards that may affect political behavior, Montesquieu emphasized religion. Going beyond the Machiavellian theory of elites manipulating credulous masses, Montesquieu's position was that if religion is an effective force in a state, there is, to that extent, less need for the exercise of repression by the state. But the effects of religion vary with the type of state. Disastrous consequences may be produced by the most sacred dogmas, if they are incongruent with the general spirit of a society. In a republic it is dangerous to allow the clergy to gain strength; in a monarchy, a strong clergy helps maintain liberty. Other aspects of society are affected as well by religion, which may also determine a population's orientations toward politics, economic activity, liberty, and reproduction.

Two other secondary causes contributing to the general spirit and closely resembling religion in their operation are mores (*moeurs*) and customs (*manières*). Both may serve as surrogates for the sanctions of the state. "When a people has good mores, its laws need not be complex." [23] Montesquieu compares and contrasts *moeurs* and *manières* with much greater precision than does Tocqueville. *Moeurs* and *manières* are alike in that they put limits on men's action and aspiration qua members of their society; laws, on the contrary, limit them qua members of a government unit. There is this difference separating *moeurs* from *manières*: the first apply internalized restraints to conduct and aspiration not specifically prohibited by law; the second, external restraints upon such conduct, but the sanctions applied are social rather than legal. Although Montesquieu conceded that the distinctions among laws, *moeurs,* and *manières* are analytical, he maintained that one and only one of them can set the tone of a society's general spirit. In Sparta, it was *moeurs;* in China, *manières.* The Chinese made all aspects of human conduct subject to ritual. When the rites were observed exactly, China was in order and functioned well in all regards; both society and government were dominated by the same secondary cause. But whenever rulers sought to make extensive use of sanctions, the state fell into anarchy and everything went wrong. The contradiction between state and society produced revolution.[24]

Montesquieu thus emphasized social determinants of behavior as much as legal sanctions. But he did not contend that there exists a hierarchy of causes, of which the most significant are nongovernmental. The general spirit may be established by the operation of any one of the seven secondary causes he had identified. Thus in Tocqueville's summation of his argument, he was operating in Montesquieu's style of analysis when he concluded that the success of the democratic republic in the United States had been due more to the Constitution than to the climate, terrain, and position relative to the world's major powers, but that most important of all had been the *moeurs* of its inhabitants.

III

The term "democratic republic" used by Tocqueville to classify the United States was itself a derivation from Montesquieu. For Montesquieu had divided all governments into three types, each of which is characterized by a nature and principle. By nature, he meant the person or group holding sovereign power; by principle, that passion which must animate those involved in a form of government if it is to work at its strongest and best. If that passion is absent, the government will be corrupted and decline or be overturned from inside or without.[25]

When classified by their nature, governments fall into three categories: a republic is that form in which the people as a whole, or else certain families, hold sovereign power; a monarchy is that in which a prince rules, but according to established procedures designating those channels through which the royal power legitimately flows (an aristocracy administering local justice, parlements with political functions, a clergy with recognized rights, cities with historical privileges); and despotism, the unrestricted rule of a single person who takes into account only his own wishes and interests.[26]

The principles of these three types differ: civic virtue is that of republics; honor, that of monarchies; fear, that of despotism. Montesquieu subdivided republics into democracies and aristocracies. His image of the first was taken from classical Greece and republican Rome. When he defined "virtue" as their distinctive principle, he meant that it was that quality requisite to their maintenance: self-subordination of personal or group interest to the common good. Its distinctive forms were love of country, belief in equality, and principled frugality and asceticism. It was with this conception of civic virtue that Tocqueville was to wrestle with when he attempted to fit the facts of American democracy into Montesquieu's theory as he understood it.

Whatever were Montesquieu's virtues as a theorist, internal consistency was not among them. Few thinkers with such claims to greatness have had so low a resistance to new ideas or to variants of old ones that called into question his own original position. And it was altogether exceptional for him to return to his earlier statements and amend them. After having set forth with the full power of his mind the notion that the spring of democracy is civic virtue, Montesquieu blithely made a series of admissions about democracies that virtually undermined the validity of his earlier and highly influential formulation.

It is true that when democracy is based on commerce, it can very well happen that individuals may possess great riches without corrupting the mores (*moeurs*). For the spirit of commerce brings with it frugality, economy, moderation, work, wisdom, tranquility, order, and measure. Thus, so long as this spirit is operative, the riches it produces have no bad effect. This occurs when excessive wealth destroys this spirit of commerce. Suddenly this creates all the disorders of inequality, which up to now had not made itself felt . . . In Greece there were two types of democracy: the first was military, like Sparta; the other, commercial, like Athens. In the first, it was desired that the citizens be idle; in the other, an attempt was made to create the love of work . . .[27]

Yet, in another sense, Montesquieu was attempting to adapt his previous analysis to the facts. For if Athens was not a democracy in the Age of Pericles, what polity had a title to that name? Yet Athens was commercial, and great fortunes were accumulated. How could this be explained? Montesquieu chose to maintain that under certain circumstances the spirit of commerce may perform functions equivalent to that of civic virtue. It is worth remarking that Montesquieu was familiar with early versions of the notion of the invisible hand, in which each by seeking his own private interest unwittingly contributes to the general good. Montesquieu was deterred from taking this way out of his dilemma with democracy by the fact that he had chosen to make it the distinctive mechanism of monarchy, which he declared to have honor as its principle. In his discussions of England this issue is further blurred. For in Book V, Chapter 19 of the *Spirit of the Laws*, Montesquieu described England as "a republic disguised under the form of a monarchy." But if England was a republic, it surely was not a democracy, nor did it fit into the category of an aristocracy, as defined by Montesquieu. In his second extended discussion of England (Book XIX, Chapter 27), Montesquieu's profile of England emphasizes the connections between its free government, the commercial nature of its society, the individualism of its citizens, and the existence of political parties. Though full of penetrating and suggestive insights, this analysis further endangers Montesquieu's vital distinction between civic virtue and honor. If only one type of human character provides the spring of each distinctive type of regime, how can Montesquieu contend that a democracy is based on principled self-abnegation? For he admits that in some democracies citizens devote most of their time and energy to enriching themselves. And the same is true of England, however it is classified. How important, then, is virtue as a principle?

Perhaps enough has been said here to indicate both Montesquieu's characteristic strengths and weaknesses as observer and analyst. In these traits Tocqueville bears a strong family resemblance. And yet for all the similarities between Montesquieu's treatment of commercial democracies and Tocqueville's analysis of Jacksonian America, there is no evidence in Tocqueville's notes to indicate that in his reading of Montesquieu he had noticed these emendations by his predecessor on the theme of civic virtue. Tocqueville had to perform similar modifications on his own. This he was able to do because he had mastered so well Montesquieu's functionalism. But what cannot be ignored is the carelessness on the part of both authors: Montesquieu in matters of logic, Tocqueville in matters of careful reading and checking of his predecessor's texts.

Montesquieu's model for aristocracy he found in contemporary Italian republics such as Venice. Although such aristocratic republics required virtue on the part of its governing class, the form it took in them was moderation of aspiration and conduct, for their characteristic weakness was immoderate internal rivalry. As for monarchy, its principle, honor, the esprit de corps, the sense of belonging to an exclusive and superior social group, which demands and receives preference on the basis of birth. When such privileges are granted, the aristocracy of a monarchy becomes a semi-autonomous, intermediate group that resists any attempt by the Crown to exceed its constitutional prerogatives. Montesquieu summed up his conviction that such an aristocracy is essential to a monarchy (as opposed to despotism) in the phrase "Without a monarchy, no nobility; without a nobility, no monarchy. For then there is only a despotism." [28] And despotism, in his view, has no virtues whatever. Based upon the fear generally felt by its subjects, it tolerates no intermediary powers and is moderated, if at all, only by religion.

Throughout this discussion Montesquieu clearly understood himself to be introducing a new method. His explanation of it did not protect him from critics who failed to understand his meaning. In this regard Montesquieu suffered the same fate as would Tocqueville and Max Weber, who anticipated in theory and practice the objections of the literal-minded. Montesquieu wrote:

> I have had new ideas; I have had to find new terms, or else to give new meanings to old ones . . . It should be noted that there is a great difference between saying that a certain quality . . . or virtue is not the spring that moves a government, and saying that it is nowhere to be found in that government. If I say that this wheel, this cog are not the spring that makes this watch go, does it follow that they are not in this watch? . . . In a word, honor exists in a republic, although political virtue is its mainspring; political virtue, in a monarchy, although honor is its principle.[29]

In a free government, powers must be separated, and each of them given the capacity to resist any other, in the event that it goes beyond its assigned sphere. This is the burden of perhaps the best-known sections of the *Spirit of the Laws*, those describing or idealizing the government of England.[30] Montesquieu had distinguished among the executive power, which included foreign affairs, the legislative, and the judicial. Taken purely as constitutional doctrine, this theory seems to have had not much more to recommend it at the time that Montesquieu wrote it than it does today. But it had another dimension, which made it distinctly more interesting. Obviously there can be no guarantee of political liberty unless each of the three powers is in the hands of a different group or class. When that is the case, liberty will be the outcome of a struggle among groups. Such politically useful conflict is of a particular and limited kind that varies with the type of government. Montesquieu had adopted this argument, which he had found in Machiavelli's *Discourses*, to explain the positive effects of class warfare in the Roman republic.[31] It fitted into his definition of monarchy, which is differentiated from despotism by the fact that semi-autonomous intermediary groups, such as the aristocracy, have the constitutional power to enter into negotiation with the Crown whenever they feel their rights or interests menaced. Only in despotism is there no conflict among groups.[32] Thus the existence of intermediary groups set between the Crown and its other subjects, the recognition of the right to negotiate, and the obligation on both sides to compromise — this theory of institutionalized conflict as the condition of political liberty was at the heart of Montesquieu's doctrine of the separation of powers. Among the glosses of Montesquieu made by Madison, this presupposition of the original is made explicit. Tocqueville was to make much the same interpretation of Montesquieu. If even the separation of powers depended upon the assumptions about the nature of a society that could support free institutions, then clearly Montesquieu could not be said to stress the absolute worth of political arrangements. Indeed his method precluded any such position: law is but one of the potential determinants of the general spirit of a society.*

IV

Chapter XVII, Volume I, organizes Tocqueville's observations and conclusions into a coherent scheme. The Conclusion is rather more of an exercise in projecting the trends Tocqueville saw at work into the future.

From the notebooks preserved in the Yale Collection, it is evident that Tocqueville had collected his data and directed his inquiries in terms of categories heavily influenced by Montesquieu. The national character, religion, *moeurs*, centralization, associations, slavery, equality were among the topics Tocqueville thought would most illuminate his subject.[33] All of these played a large part in Montesquieu. From him Tocqueville had also learned to make use at every turn of the comparative method. In his earlier chapters Tocqueville had both contrasted what was novel about United States society and government with that of Europe, and espe-

* This point is not perhaps so self-evident as might appear. Professor Pierson, for example, speaks of Tocqueville's "discovery — which only America had been able to suggest to him — that there was no absolute value in political institutions. The usefulness of a given constitution depended upon the physical environment, and on the inherited characteristics of the society to which it was applied . . . (G. W. Pierson, *Tocqueville and Beaumont in America*, p. 722).

cially France, and he attempted to extricate those elements that were comparable between the egalitarian society before his eyes and the developments in the same direction of that at home. Now the time had come to summarize both the contrasts and the comparisons, to explain why American society and government had their distinguishing characteristics, to draw out those lessons that might be practically applicable to France, after allowance had been made for the difference in conditions. Later he described his use of the comparative method:

Should you explain the resemblances and the differences between the two countries, or write so as to enable the reader to find them out? . . . In my work on America, I have almost always adopted the latter plan. Although I seldom mentioned France, I did not write a page without thinking of her, and placing her before me, as it were. And what I especially tried to draw out and explain in the United States, was not the whole condition of that foreign society, but the points in which it differs from our own, or resembles us . . . I believe that this perpetual silent reference to France was a principal cause of the book's success.[34]

At a number of crucial places in this chapter Tocqueville made adroit uses of comparison. While conceding the significance of the frontier to American developments, he has no difficulty in demonstrating that opportunities afforded by nature are less important than the character of peoples. This point he established by comparing the behavior of Canadians of French origin to Americans. And he concluded that while under European conditions American laws would have to be modified considerably, nevertheless these laws were relevant to France and other European nations. Democracy need not take in these countries precisely the same form it had assumed in the United States. Because of the contiguity of powerful neighbors, greater centralization was wanted in Europe. But there was no reason why there should not be a type of democracy in which the citizens would govern less directly than in the United States, and yet each, with certain rights reserved to him, would take part in government.

For a number of reasons, theoretical and practical, the comparability of the United States to Europe was critical. If it could be established that the success of democratic institutions in the United States was due to its unique geographical conditions, then Tocqueville's work could have no relevance to his own country. Among the most striking aspects of this chapter was Tocqueville's use of Montesquieu's most characteristic arguments to establish that sustained comparison and contrast were in point.

What were the elements that had to be taken into account? How was their relative weight to be assessed? Tocqueville subsumed them into three categories of causes: accidental, these were largely although not exclusively physical; legal; and habits and mores. As for the special conditions of the American case: climate, the absence of powerful neighbors, the open frontier, great natural resources, the lack of a great capital, the ease of attaining a high level of material well-being, the fortunate political *"point de départ,"* or historical inheritance — all these Tocqueville considered important, but not determining. This point he again argued comparatively: the same advantages when found elsewhere in the New World had not produced the same beneficent effects as had those of the United States. It followed that some other type of cause was responsible for the differences. Tocqueville here followed Montesquieu's lead: the use of inverse deductive method to prove that physical causes were not necessarily decisive.

What about legal and constitutional arrangements? These Tocqueville placed above physical and accidental causes. The framers of the American Constitution had done their task well. As a result, three features of the legal system contributed significantly to the maintenance of the democratic republic: its federalism, which enabled the union to enjoy the power of a very large republic but with the internal security of a small one; its local institutions, which mitigate the tyranny of the majority and simultaneously impart to citizens both the taste for liberty and the practical means for remaining in that condition; its judicial institutions, which likewise correct the deficiencies of democracy without directly obstructing its operation. Throughout this part of his analysis Toqueville remained close to Montesquieu. The principal objective of the *Democracy*, Tocqueville declared, had been to make known *les lois* of the United States. It was no coincidence that he here echoed Montesquieu's ostensible focus upon laws, since both had been trained legally, coupled with equal attention to other, mainly social determinants of the political system. And Tocqueville's eulogy of American federalism followed closely Montesquieu's praise of the confederative republic, a notion frequently referred to in the *Federalist Papers*. Tocqueville's words of praise for American self-government, the *commune*, may be seen as a revival in another form of Montesquieu's notion of civic virtue as the principle of democracy, as well as a reworking of his contention that liberty is to be found in the relations of semi-autonomous political entities to the central power. Finally, Tocqueville's analysis of the constitutional role of the American judiciary does not fail to refer to the position taken by the greatest of the *parlementaires;* Tocqueville, although referring to the claims of the Parlements under the Old Regime, shows how superior to them as a brake upon the central power is the role given to the judiciary by the American Constitution.

Despite his praise for the Americans' *lois,* Tocqueville attributed greater significance to their *l'Esprit.* It was the mores (*moeurs*) of the Americans which, in his view, were the principal reason for the success of their democracy. This emphasis upon mores, he wrote, is a truth which is the inevitable conclusion of all his research in books and practical experience; it is the central point of his reasoning, the basis of all his ideas.[35] Nevertheless, this had to be proved to others; it was not simply based on faith. Once again comparison was called into play. The Mexicans had adopted a federal system similar to the Americans; it had not produced the same successful results, for their *moeurs* were not the same as the Americans'. Even more convincing: compare the workings of democracy in the East and West in the United States itself. To Tocqueville it appeared manifest that in the East, American political institutions functioned better than in the newer parts of the Union. The older states had arrived at habits and ideas more favorable to the maintenance of democracy: internal checks were more efficacious; political passions, more restrained; civic education, at once universal and effective; religion, most thoroughly intertwined with political liberty. Taken together, these habits, opinions, beliefs, usages comprise the nation's *moeurs:* the most powerful forces supporting democracy.

It must be said that Tocqueville's argument was not without its difficulties. On its face it appeared to be an assertion that a political system derives its essential characteristics from the mores of the society in which it is placed. Yet actually this was not Tocqueville's position. His uses of the term democracy were slippery in just those places where precision was most critical. He slid from the narrower political meaning of the term to that of an egalitarian social system. As a result it is notoriously difficult to sort out his arguments. The same irritating failure to define his terms and maintain a consistent usage of them is manifest in his many discussions of revolution.[36] It is worth noting how Tocqueville at once derived the concept of *moeurs* from Montesquieu and by carelessness managed to make that term much less precise than its original. In this chapter Tocqueville gave his single most detailed definition of *moeurs:*

By the term *"moeurs"* I mean what the ancients conveyed by *"mores"*: and I apply it, not only to *moeurs*, properly so-called, what might be called the habits of the heart, but also to the different concepts men use, to the different opinions that divide them, and to the totality (*ensemble*) of their ideas that comprise their mental habits.

I include in this term everything connected with the moral and intellectual condition of a people. My objective is not to describe every aspect of American mores, but is restricted to an investigation of those only that support the political institutions of that country.

Montesquieu, it will be recalled, coined the term general spirit to characterize the organizing principle which, in his view, is to be found in every society. The general spirit is the outcome of both physical and moral causes. Principal among the latter category are religion, laws, maxims, precedents, mores, customs, its economy and trade, and its style of thought. It is obvious that although Tocqueville attended most closely to the range of considerations emphasized by Montesquieu, the disciple blurred useful distinctions present in his master. Tocqueville extended *moeurs* to cover all of what Montesquieu had meant by "general spirit," except for "laws," which now became an independent category in a three-fold set of distinctions among accidental, usually physical, causes; laws, including constitutional arrangements; and *moeurs*, Montesquieu had restricted *moeurs* to social restraints not covered by law and internalized by the members of the society; *manières*, also social restraints upon conduct not covered by law, were external in nature and backed by sanctions of the society rather than the government. Montesquieu also made religion and general style of thought into separate secondary causes affecting the society's general spirit. Tocqueville simply blended all the secondary causes into one category. No doubt this was due to the forgetfulness and imprecision of his method in general and his way with words in particular.

But these remarks do not exhaust all that there is to say about Tocqueville's use of Montesquieu. Although Tocqueville was careless about the letter of Montesquieu's theory, he made a brilliant application of its animating spirit to the quite new situation he was analyzing in the United States. Ultimately Tocqueville shared Montesquieu's assumptions about man's nature and passions; he therefore postulated that even in the freest of political regimes there must be a certain amount of repression, an effective limitation of human will and expectation. To the extent that this sort of repression may be carried out by individual or social rather than political means, political liberty is more likely to ensue. Indeed if political ties are loosened, there must be a substitution of some other type of restraint. This is especially true under democracy, where without some effective means of limiting the will and aspiration of the majority, a particularly onerous type of tyranny may arise. Despite this danger, Tocqueville remarked, he had never encountered anyone in the United States who asserted that everything is permitted that serves the interest of the majority, "that impious maxim, which seems to have been invented in a century of liberty to legitimize all the tyrants who were to come." [38] And what was that force that had so effectively countered the worst potentialities of democracy? Tocqueville found this in religion: at the same time that the law gives the American people great power, religion prevents them from conceiving the worst alternatives and thus keeps them from daring to do everything that they might otherwise attempt.

Like Montesquieu, Tocqueville treated religion from a sociological, or as he himself called it, a purely human point of view. Both cared most about the indirect and unintended consequences of religion, its latent rather than its manifest functions. Tocqueville, discussing the particular dangers of democracy, saw religion as a counterweight to the instability and agitation characteristic of the new form. Somehow men must have a guiding principle to orient themselves amidst rapid change.[39] If everything in a society is in flux, then its members become drastically disorganized, or *déreglés*. In the *Old Regime*, Tocqueville later argued in detail that the worst consequences of total revolutions stem precisely from their simultaneous destruction of all orienting principles. Tocqueville thus argued that much of the success of American democracy had to be attributed to the practical wisdom of Americans in recognizing that religion performed indispensable functions requisite to political freedom. This finding he recommended to his own countrymen, split since the Enlightenment on the question of the compatibility between liberty and religion. The revolution had further embittered this division to the point where men of good will felt they had to choose between liberty and equality on the one side and religious belief on the other. Tocqueville sought to end this division. Characteristically, he chose the strategy, intellectually pleasing, but politically ineffectual, of taking a position equally unpalatable to both camps. To those who argued that religion was incompatible with freedom and equality, he retorted that they placed their anticlerical prejudices above a careful study of that society that had most successfully realized freedom and equality. To those who condemned these values as anarchical and contrary to their faith, Tocqueville answered that they confused their image of a past now irretrievably lost with what was possible and desirable under modern conditions. Religion was compatible with democracy, he argued, but only on the condition that there be the strictest of separation between the state and the church. Under the Old Regime the church had been hated because of its privileges as a landowner and because of its support of the monarchy. The Americans, including all Roman Catholics, knew better than this.[40] And although Tocqueville did not here invoke Montesquieu, his predecessor had asserted that in a republic the church should not play any political role directly.

Throughout his discussion of religion Tocqueville waived the question of whether Americans honored religion because they genuinely believed in it or because they understood its social utility. From his point of view, as from Montesquieu's, this distinction was irrelevant to his analysis. Above all he was concerned to understand the nonpolitical conditions of this polity's success. Despite his praise for the American tendency to consider religion as an indispensable support of democracy, Tocqueville did not regard the citizens of the United States as having achieved a higher level of individual moral excellence than elsewhere. Indeed Tocqueville found Americans to be overwhelmingly concerned with material gain, calculating and economically rational, individualistic in the sense that they seldom acted in the spirit of that devotion to the general good that had characterized classical democracies. This finding could not but raise grave theoretical problems for a careful student of Montesquieu, who had of course made civic virtue into the principle of the democratic republic.

V

The position taken by Tocqueville can only be understood as a phase in the adaptation of civic humanism to a form of society and economy apparently incompatible with it. Both past and future versions of the relation between citizenship and democracy form the frame for Tocqueville's new version of Montesquieu's theory.

In a series of brilliant papers, Professor J. G. A. Pocock has traced the history and significance of civic humanism as a political theory up to the time that Tocqueville wrote this new chapter in its development.[41] In the city-states of Renaissance Italy, particularly Florence, it had been argued that individuals can fulfill themselves only when as citizens they participate in the decisions of an autonomous republic, and this with the purpose of attaining the general good. Thus seen, economic concerns on the part of the individual are incompatible with the claims of citizenship; the necessary condition of civic virtue is the rejection of private satisfactions, and a luxurious society may be identified with one in which corruption has set in. As Professor Pocock has written, "the concept of the citizen or patriot was antithetical to that of economic man, multiplying his satisfactions and transforming his culture in a temporal process; it encouraged the idea that change and process were entropic and that only a Spartan rigidity of institutions could enable men to master the politics of time." [42]

This civic humanism, or classical republicanism, put much stress upon citizens possessing a high degree of personal self-control and economic self-sufficiency. Professor Pocock has demonstrated how in the hands of Harrington and his followers there was created first an English and then an Anglo-American version of this doctrine. It was taken up in England by the country against the court, and the arguments forged in this context turned out to be highly useful to the American colonists in formulating their grievances. What this theory did was to identify the autonomous citizen with the freeholder of land, who may pass it on by inheritance. The function of property is to make the citizen independent of any of the agents of government and thus to prevent the process originally attributed by Machiavelli to Roman history — that by which certain citizens became dependent on others, until they identified their interests with those of the leaders rather than with the public good. The name given to this development was "corruption," by which was meant three things: "First, the degenerative tendency to which all particular forms of governments are prone; second, the specific cause of that degeneration which is the dependence of some men upon others when they should be depending upon all and upon themselves; and third, the moral degeneration of the individual, who, in these circumstances, is prevented from developing his virtue by identifying his particular good with the good of all." [43] Politically what was entailed in the minds of those using this second moment of civic humanism was the notion that the court by the use of government, bureaucracy, and public credit was attempting to replace an independent parliament by placeholders and the freeman in arms by the professional soldier. In England such views produced country gentlemen with leanings toward democracy, eighteenth-century commonwealth men; in America, agrarian radicals.[44] Both variants of the type assumed that there was one and only one proper relationship between individuals and government and that corruption became inevitable if that relationship were supplanted by any other. Hence the crisis created by change — whether political, social, or economic.

How could a republic subsist if its citizens no longer were independent and actuated by the public good? In America it was commonly accepted that Europe was hopelessly corrupt, that England was becoming infected by the same contagion. Separation was necessary if America was to escape this dread disease.

Social and economic change, then, were envisaged as menacing the only proper relationship of the citizen to the republic. In Montesquieu and in the Scottish moral philosophers rather more ambivalence is to be found on this point. Montesquieu remains faithful to civic humanism in his best-known statement of the theory of democracy: this, however, he qualifies when he distinguishes commercial from military democracies. Montesquieu thus does not confine liberty to republicanism or rural freeholders. But in monarchy the general good can be attained indirectly by the natural harmony of interests. Perhaps he believed that republics were *dépassés*, that monarchy was the form of modern European states. Democracies must by their nature be small; again an unequivocal assertion later diluted by the notion of a confederate republic.

Tocqueville came to the United States with the assumption of civic humanism about the preconditions of a healthy democratic polity. Citizens must be disinterested and active participants in political life; they must be actuated by common ends, the general interest, rather than by petty self- or party interest, a doctrine, which we shall see, he attributed to Montesquieu. In Book XI, and even more in Book XIX of the *Spirit of the Laws*, much was said about England that suggested how the self-seeking individualism of a commercial society could be made compatible with the general good and how membership in factions, interest groups, and even political parties likewise could be so treated. Of this aspect of Montesquieu's thought, there is little acknowledgment in Tocqueville. Although the style and thrust of Montesquieu's later books were clearly assimilated by Tocqueville, his own operative memory of Montesquieu's theory of democracy remained limited to the initial, relatively simple and unqualified statement. It is this formulation that is closest to Machiavelli and the first moment of civic humanism. Tocqueville's recollection may have been influenced by the fact that he was simultaneously dealing with Rousseau, whose version of citizenship was a heightened and far more intense restatement of the earlier doctrine.

Tocqueville was to suggest the notion of interest rightly understood as the solution to the problem of citizenship in a state characterized by a high degree of self-seeking activity in commerce and industry. Men, by participating in political life, particularly local government, come to see that their own private interests are better served by sacrificing short-term individual interests to those that are long-term and collective. From one point of view this theory must be understood as an attempt to salvage from the original theory of civic humanism some elements that could be integrated into the new set of economic and social arrangements characteristic of a society in the midst of rapid change. Participation was still regarded as crucial to the political health of democracy, now conceived as large in scale, using representative institutions and capable of devolving important political functions on units of local government. Tocqueville feared that potentiality of democracy which could lead its individual members to consenting to a despot ruling in their name and, as was usually claimed, in their interest. But in the *Democracy* he accepted the ideal of general participation, subject to certain checks, social and political. Principled abnegation of individual interests to the general good, however, was no longer regarded by him as crucial. And he thought that he had found a functional equivalent in the principle of interest rightly understood. By adopting it he followed Montesquieu's lead in seeking to reconcile civic humanism with quite another style of thought, that known to Montesquieu's generation from Mandeville's theory of private vices leading to public goods, and to Tocqueville's from the theory of the invisible hand celebrated by the economists, some of whom were essentially members of the Scottish school, others more explicitly Benthamite utilitarians. Like Montesquieu before him and Elie Halévy after, Tocqueville called attention to the resemblances among the asceticism of the classical republican citizen, the practicing Protestant Christian, and the commercial and economic man. In large part the analysis depended upon internalized repressions of spontaneous impulse, passion, or expectation; upon deferred pleasures and subordination of immediate gratification to goals regarded as ultimately more satisfying. Such discipline was requisite if a man were to govern himself, and, as part of a republic, a sect, or a commercial society, participate in self-government on the political level. Of course, such an attenuation of the ideal qualities of the citizen was purchased at a price: the outcome of a common good was emphasized rather than the good will of the individual citizen. Throughout this process, on his own part, Tocqueville was sustained in his faith that participation could educate citizens to their long-term stake in the common good by both the political theory and the social condition of the Americans. For the second moment of civic humanism, that of belief in the political virtue of freeholders in land, still exerted a powerful hold over part of the American mind and social experience. It was not urban America that inspired Tocqueville's confidence, not immigrants, not the commerce of city dwellers apart from the rural base of freeholders.*

There is good reason to believe that Tocqueville's qualified optimism about the possibility of a democracy based upon the principle of interest rightly understood did not long survive his return to France and his entry into political life. Both the principle of self-interest and that of voluntary association seemed less attractive in France under the July Monarchy. After the Revolution of 1848 and the coup d'état of Louis Napoleon, which drove Tocqueville out of politics, he began to search for the distinctively French roots of corruption in the sense of civic humanism; his answers are to be found in the *Old Regime and the Revolution*. These need not be rehearsed here, but it is worth noting that among Tocqueville's most weighty hypotheses is that emphasizing the transformation of his own class from an aristocracy to a caste, from a group performing indispensable functions on its lands in the country to one that continued only to claim privileges at court.

Tocqueville's analysis of societies in terms of elites was not a negligible

---

* "America does not yet have a large capital, but already has very large cities. In 1830, Philadelphia's population came to 161,000; New York's, 202,000. The common people (*le bas peuple*) who inhabit these great cities comprise a rabble more dangerous even than that of Europe. First of all, it is made up of freed negroes, condemned by law and opinion to a condition of degradation and hereditary misery. Also there is a multitude of Europeans daily pushed on to the shores of the New World by misfortune and criminal behavior. Such men bring to the United States our greatest vices without any of the interests that might combat their influence. Inhabitants of the country without being citizens, they are ready to profit from all the passions agitating it. Thus for some time serious riots have broken out in Philadelphia and New York. Such disorders are unknown elsewhere in the country, which is almost unconcerned by them since the population of the cities has hitherto exercised neither any power nor influence on that of the country.

Nevertheless I regard the size of certain American cities, and, above all, the nature of their inhabitants, as a real danger menacing the future of the democratic republics of the New World. I have no fears about predicting that this is the way they will perish, unless their government succeeds in creating an armed force, which, although subordinate to the will of the majority, nevertheless is not subject to that of the cities' common people, whose excesses it can put down." (Tocqueville, *Oeuvres* [M] I, i, 290n.–91n.)

spur to the thought of Mosca and Pareto. In their hands and those of Ostrogorski and Michels, to mention only the more scientific forms of a theory that revived aristocratic modes of thought in a democratic age, there grew up a critique of the one remaining strand of civic humanism that Tocqueville sought to preserve and maintain.[45] This was of course the notion of general participation in political activity by all members of a democratic polity. Elitist theorists in the twentieth century argued that not only was such participation unknown in any functioning democratic state, but that it was a priori impossible for it to occur. The logic of large-scale organizations, whether private, voluntary, or public simply precludes such participation. In time the argument came to be accepted, and one more reformulation of democratic theory took place because of the incompatibility of civic humanist postulates with the facts of political practice. Schumpeter, Sartori, and Dahl are only a few of a great many who have argued that a modern democratic theory is possible if we abandon the notion of direct participation by citizens seeking to attain the common good.[46] Instead democracy is to be viewed as the free competition of elites for responsibility granted by the citizens, now envisaged as possessing only the capacity to choose among alternative programs, a capacity in its turn increasingly called into doubt by psychologists and specialists in public opinion. They question even the means citizens possess to understand the choices offered them. Of late signs have begun to appear of challenges to the present orthodoxy in democratic theory. Interestingly enough, such challenges seem to rest more upon the original postulate of civic humanism than upon any evidence that the world has not changed in the unpleasant ways that have undermined successively the social and economic assumptions of that mode of thought. Indeed the very newest attacks upon elite theories of democracy more or less unwittingly return to a further outcome of civic humanism, once again charted by Professor Pocock.

Under the impetus of still another aspect of Montesquieu's thought there emerged in Scotland such thinkers as Adam Ferguson, Adam Smith, and John Millar. Instead of freezing the relationship between freeholders of land and republicanism as had Harrington and his latter-day followers, the Scots set up a "historical scheme of modes of production — hunter, shepherd, farmer, trader, manufacturer — through which mankind moved according to a law of increasing specialization and division of labor . . . A historical science of culture now seemed possible: 'President Montesquieu is the Bacon of this branch of philosophy,' wrote Millar, 'Dr. Smith is the Newton.' " [47] Yet these Scottish social theorists viewed as "corruption" that point in human development when man's capacity for citizenship, for concerning himself with the common good, became reduced by the division of labor and consequent specialization. It is perhaps here that the origin of the conception of alienation is to be found: "The undistracted, unspecialized man — hunter in the morning and critic in the afternoon — whom Marx and Lenin hoped to restore to his universality is in long view an Aristotelian citizen, participant in all the value-oriented activities of society, and his history is in part the history of civic humanism." [48]

It might be added that Tocqueville was not unaware of some of the implications of the division of labor. He regarded the intelligence of the American voter as higher on the average (although the greatest Americans were not to be compared to the greatest Europeans) than among any other people he knew about.* This he attributed to their system of education and to the fact that division of labor was little developed.

Great differences of wealth among the citizens were also viewed as incompatible with republicanism by the theorists of civic humanism. As has been noticed, Montesquieu took this position with respect to democracies, except for the passage where he distinguished between their commercial and military forms. Tocqueville, dealing with the United States, had to deal with economic inequality. In part he followed Montesquieu's lead when he emphasized the necessity for the laws to combat excessive economic concentration; in part he raised the level of abstraction and emphasized the nature of the function requisite to democracy: "What is most crucial to Democracy is not the total absence of great fortunes, but that they do not remain in the same hands. In this way, there are rich men, but they do not form a class." [49] Elsewhere he specified that downward mobility was as necessary as upward mobility for the functioning of equality.

In any case Tocqueville could not imagine how in the modern world

* "It has been remarked in Europe that the division of labor makes a man infinitely better fitted to deal with the details to which he applies himself, but diminishes his *general capacity*. Such a workingman becomes a master of his specialty, but a brute in everything else. Example of England. Dismaying conditions of the working classes there. What makes the American so intelligent is that the division of labor does not exist, so to speak, in America. Everyone does a little of everything. This he does less well than the European who does nothing else, but his general capacity is a hundred times greater. Hence the principal cause of superiority in all the everyday matters of life, and of the government of society." (Alexis de Tocqueville, "Sur la Démocratic en Amérique," [Fragments inédits], introduction de J. P. Mayer, *La Nouvelle Revue Francaise* [1959], 1–2).

the character structure needed for a society that combined democracy and liberty could be attained without commerce: "This is what I should like explained to me: how is it possible for a genuine taste for a high degree of political liberty, for independence in common action, how is it possible that such traits be developed by a man who has learned to obey another's arbitrary will in almost every aspect of his life, and particularly in those most intimately connected to the human heart." [50]

Tocqueville's answer is that such a taste for liberty is developed by commerce and by participation in the affairs of local government:[51] "Commercial institutions produce not only skill in making use of liberty, but also a real taste for it. Without commerce, such a taste for political liberty would amount to no more than childish desires or youthful fears . . ." [52] And once the taste for liberty is created, then it must be reconciled with the general interest of the society. This is best done by entrusting to the citizens the administration of minor affairs, by involving them in jury duty and local government, where they see how their own welfare is connected in the long run to the general welfare.

Despite the importance of these suggestions, we have not yet arrived at the heart of Tocqueville's reconciliation of the data he had collected in the United States with Montesquieu's theory of civic virtue. In a passage of his notes for the *Democracy* there can be caught a fascinating glimpse of Tocqueville's theoretical mind in action. His attention is riveted on the complex relationship between a political system and the principal concerns, the moral causes of its society's general spirit. The indirect and unintended consequences, the psychological and social restraints upon potential political excesses are what concern the analyst here once again in finding a principle, which performs the function equivalent to what Montesquieu had declared essential to the democratic republic:

The Americans are not a virtuous people, and nevertheless they are free. This does not constitute a decisive refutation of Montesquieu's belief that virtue is essential to the existence of republics. Montesquieu's idea must not be understood in a narrow sense. What that great man wished to assert was that republics may be sustained only through the operation of society upon itself. What he meant by "virtue" is that moral power which each individual exercises over himself, and which keeps him from violating the right of others. In the eyes of the moralist, there is nothing virtuous about such a triumph of a man over temptation if it should be the case either that the temptation is slight, or that the decision is made as the result of calculating the agent's personal interest. But

Montesquieu was concerned more with the result than with the cause, and so any such triumph over temptation is relevant to his theory.

In America, it is not that virtue is great, but that temptation is small, which comes down to the same point. It is not disinterestedness that is great, but it is interest, properly understood [in the long run] which again comes to almost the same thing. Montesquieu, then, was right, although he discussed virtue in the ancient world, and what he said in connection with the Greeks and Romans still applies to the Americans.[52]

Montesquieu's theory had provided the categories by which Tocqueville sought to explain what he had discovered by his empirical research in America. Tocqueville's own intellectual style determined in part the use he made of Montesquieu. But there can be no question but that theory guided heuristically Tocqueville's explorations in person and later in his sources, just as it contributed to the ultimate shape it took in his final version. Comparison was his most powerful weapon, and what he extracted from its use were conclusions applicable to the complex but crucial interrelations between the political and social systems. Ultimately Tocqueville believed that there were valid means for applying his conclusions about the United States to France. If the Americans were qualitatively different by the nature of their habits and opinions from Europeans, or if they were essentially the same in these respects, and it was their fortunate physical circumstances that produced results so discrepant with those of Europe, then American experience would indeed be irrelevant. But neither supposition is plausible. The passions of the Americans were fully analogous to those of the Europeans. Some of these passions derive from human nature itself; some, from the democratic organization of society. What Americans have been wise to do is to oppose the idea of right to that disease of democracies, envy; to use religion as a counterweight to the instability endemic to their form of government; to avail themselves of the political education provided by participation in free institutions against their absence of sound theoretical knowledge; to limit the impetuousness of their desires by a cool and rational calculation of long-term advantage natural to those whose passions are concentrated upon commerce rather than politics. Some of these considerations had occurred to Montesquieu in his treatment of England, for he had written that the English best knew how to combine religion, commerce, and liberty. But what was an insight on Montesquieu's part became in Tocqueville's hands a fully developed theory. Despite Tocqueville's liberties with his predecessor, he more than repaid his debt by restoring Montesquieu's mode of thought to the importance it warranted in a world so thoroughly different from that of the mid-eighteenth century.

It would be at once condescending and inaccurate to say that Tocqueville's analysis is notable not because of his way of proceeding, but in spite of it. For the thinker possessed of imagination, operating in terms of grand theory is not to be judged by terms appropriate to neat pieces of microscopic research unconnected to any major questions. Rather the capacity to deal with major variables and to formulate hypotheses about their relationships and significance is perhaps more often found in thinkers who are careless, as Montesquieu and Tocqueville were careless, in their handling of detail and even some elementary intellectual procedures. In dealing with the achievements of first-rate theoretical minds we often feel a sense of mystery as we attempt to understand how much that is extraordinary in their achievement could be combined with so much easily detected as inadequate by students and teachers of infinitely less worth. Tocqueville was the heir to a style of political and social theory that he transformed creatively in his encounter with a society and government unknown and unimagined by his predecessors. What he was able to do was not just a personal achievement, but a demonstration that such theorizing was and is worth continuing.

3. THREE TYPES OF CONSERVATISM

Klaus Epstein

Conservative individuals, in the broad sense of opponents to religious, socioeconomic, and political change, have existed since the beginning of recorded history; yet it is a truism of modern scholarship that a conservative movement appeared in Europe only toward the end of the eighteenth century. What explains the emergence of such a movement at that particular time? The answer must be sought in the dynamism introduced into Europe by the intellectual movement known as the Enlightenment, the cumulative impact of commercial capitalism, and the rise of a bourgeois class dissatisfied with traditional patterns of government. These three broad tendencies — whose interconnection is apparent today and was widely suspected by contemporaries — made for an acceleration of change, and a broad awareness of change, which was bound to provoke a strong conservative reaction.

A brief delineation of the new dynamic forces will serve to define the problem confronting conservatives at the end of the eighteenth century. The *Weltanschauung* of the Enlightenment constituted in its essence the triumph of this-worldly, materialist, and hedonist values over the other-worldliness, spiritualism, and asceticism of traditional Christianity. The principles and practices of the Enlightenment — however transcended in spirit and repudiated in detail by subsequent intellectual and political currents — drastically and irreversibly transformed man's picture of himself and the world. To live for the next world rather than this became an eccentric aberration from the generally recognized norm; to repudiate

Note: This paper is reprinted with minor changes from Klaus Epstein, *The Genesis of German Conservatism* (Princeton University Press, 1966) by permission of the publisher.

material values, the outlook of the saint and the crank; now happiness became the universally recognized desideratum of a "good society." Happiness was, moreover, not only desirable but attainable if only economic and political affairs were arranged by "enlightened" rulers with intelligence and good will.

The development of capitalism heralded the end of the predominantly rural stage of European history. Earlier society had been structured with a legally privileged landowning nobility standing at the apex. The forward thrust of capitalism was accompanied by the development of a dynamic, wealthy, and increasingly self-conscious bourgeoisie, resentful of aristocratic privilege; it demanded social mobility and "equality before the law," two goals incompatible with any hierarchic society. Economic advances made under capitalism — first in the form of the "domestic system," later in the early stages of the Industrial Revolution — led to the emergence of the vision, and to a lesser extent the reality, of a society in which all men could be liberated, for the first time in history, from the scourges of poverty and social degradation. The full achievement of these goals required the destruction of legal privileges and the active encouragement of capitalist enterprise by sympathetic governments.

This work was begun toward the middle of the eighteenth century by several "enlightened monarchs" in the name of reason of state; for the intelligent pursuit of power — the main preoccupation of eighteenth-century statecraft — required a prosperous and contented population. It became clear, however, that a complete orientation of government policy toward the general welfare, and more specifically the full achievement of legal equality, could not ultimately be left to monarchs who were, after all, by their nature part and parcel of the world of inequality; nor could they be expected — laudable examples to the contrary notwithstanding — to identify completely their dynastic interest with the general welfare. These considerations suggested the necessity of replacing the traditional monarchical-authoritarian state (what Germans call the *Obrigkeitsstaat*) by self-government (preferably of a popular character). The participation of the people in the work of government was bound, incidentally, to give a tremendous impetus to the sentiment of nationality, since the nation appeared as the "natural unit" of political self-consciousness at the end of the eighteenth century. Nationalism, though not immune to conservative appropriation, was originally progressive in inspiration; and it proved an additional dynamic element in the history of Europe as it discredited both supranational units (such as the Holy Roman Empire) and parochial territorial states (embracing but part of a nation, as was the case with that empire's component states).

The challenge confronting conservatives was not confined to these impersonal forces working to create a secular, egalitarian, and self-governing society; it was compounded by the emergence of a group of men who devoted themselves, with zeal and determination, to the repudiation of the status quo and the reconstruction of society in accordance with the principles of the Enlightenment. Many labels can be attached to these men: "radicals," because they wanted to strike at the roots of the existing society; "progressives," because they worked for a better society in accordance with their conception of progress; or "party of movement," because they believed that they were cooperating with the forward march of history. The terms radical, progressive, and party of movement will be used interchangeably in this volume for men who aimed systematically at repudiating the status quo in the name of a new pattern of society; it must be clearly understood that they name a genus which includes numerous species differing widely from one another. Among these species are liberals, concerned primarily with civil liberty, legal equality, and laissez faire; democrats, concerned primarily with popular sovereignty; and socialists, concerned with social equality and economic planning. In our context these species may be considered successive radicalizations of a single party of movement appearing in rough chronological sequence. Strong liberal demands began to be voiced in Germany after about 1770; a significant democratic movement arose only around 1790 without, however, crowding liberalism off the stage; while socialism, championed by isolated voices before the end of the eighteenth century, did not become an important movement until 1848.

The raison d'être of conservatism as an articulate movement is conscious opposition to the deliberate efforts of the party of movement to transform society in a secular, egalitarian, and self-governing direction. . . . the history of German conservatism [begins at] the moment — around 1770 — when the challenge of German radicalism had become sufficiently strong to provoke a significant conservative response. It may be noted that the conservatism here described and analyzed is a specific historical phenomenon during the specific historical period starting about 1770; its essence is resistance — or, in some cases, accommodation — to the specific challenge of German radicalism.

The definition of conservatism given here differs from other definitions employed by various authors which are either too broad or too unhistorical to serve our purposes. The definition of conservatism as any defense of the status quo, irrespective of the substantive nature of the status quo, is too broad to be useful; under it, all ruling groups which seek to preserve their power — and what ruling group does not? — would be conservative, including successful revolutionaries (for example, Robespierre and Stalin).[1] At the opposite extreme from this functional definition of conservatism stand various substantive definitions of conservatism in terms of an unchanging ideology expressing certain absolute values, valid (though, of course, not attained) everywhere and at all times. A recent critic of conservatism has described the key values of this ideology to be harmony and tranquillity, two qualities possible only where friction is avoided by the curbing of individual desire and the absence of conflicting interests. By this exalted standard it is clear that a conservative society has never existed and never can exist, and that all conservatives always fall short of their own professed principles (Q.E.D.).[2]

Many self-styled modern conservatives — especially in the ranks of America's so-called "new conservatives" — are highly arbitrary in identifying one specific historical form of conservatism with conservatism per se.[3] They tend to canonize the admittedly great figure of Edmund Burke and attach an absolute value to the principles of eighteenth-century England (or the pre-1789 regime generally) which he defended against the Jacobin challenge. These conservatives make themselves ridiculous when they try to apply the principles of Burkean conservatism to a contemporary America where its foundations (a landowning aristocracy, an established clergy, and an ancient monarchy) do not exist now, have existed only in a vestigial manner in earlier times, and are quite irrelevant to the solution of contemporary problems. Suffice it to say that the conservatism described [here] does not claim any universal significance; it only describes — let it be repeated — the specific response of conservatives to the specific challenge of the party of movement under the specific historical circumstances of Germany during the last third of the eighteenth century.

It is important to stress this specificity of German — or any other type of — conservatism, for in this quality lies the major obstacle to the writing of any general history of European conservatism. Ruggiero, the brilliant historian of European liberalism, confronted a manageable task in writing his general history; for liberalism was a general movement which aimed at creating a liberal society, with relatively homogeneous characteristics, in every European country.[4] It possessed common intellectual roots (such as the Renaissance, certain aspects of the Reformation,

Cartesianism, and the Enlightenment) and a common program.[5] Conservatism usually appears, on the contrary, as a specific defense of a concrete and ever-changing status quo, and is therefore as variegated as the conditions which it defends. Its thinkers — excepting the special case of Burke — rarely exercise much influence outside their own countries and times, whether one thinks of Coleridge in England, Maistre and Bonald in France, or Möser, Müller, and Haller in Germany. The future historian of European conservatism will be required to immerse himself in the specific conditions of every European country in order to secure a realistic understanding of what diverse conditions different conservatives wanted to *conserve*. In the light of these considerations it appeared overambitious and premature to deal with European conservatism on a comparative scale at this time. The author has instead selected the more limited topic of German conservatism during its formative stage; he hopes that it will prove significant not only in itself but also will serve as one of many preliminary studies for the general history of modern European conservatism to be written in the future.

THE THREE TYPES OF CONSERVATIVES

Three major types of conservatives can be identified in the period following the emergence of self-conscious conservatism around 1770. They are all confronted by the advance of modern forces outlined above: they all deplore that the institutions, conditions, and principles of the ancien régime are placed on the defensive. The three types, which will be labeled defenders of the status quo, reform conservatives, and reactionaries, constitute three different responses to this common challenge. Each is characterized by a distinct outlook and a special set of problems. The three will be initially characterized as "ideal types"; the reader must remember, however, that the real conservatives . . . are frequently mixed breeds that do not conform to these stereotypes. Nevertheless, an analysis of these types has value in pointing up the difficulties and dilemmas encountered by conservatism in its various forms.

The first type is the defender of the status quo. He is fundamentally contented with the world, whereas the reform conservative is restless and the reactionary, embittered. The status quo conservative is satisfied with enjoying what he *has* rather than pursuing something he *wants*. He is usually ahistorical in his outlook — a tendency connected with his essentially static view of the world. He has no reason to quarrel with past historical development, since it has led to a society satisfactory to himself; but any future development is considered a departure from the eternal principles of "natural society" embodied in the status quo. The defender of the status quo is generally a member of the upper classes, enjoys the external and internal advantages of high social status, and sees positions of authority occupied by men like himself.[6] He tends to deify the existing social framework and to identify it with the dictates of justice itself, and he naturally places a high value upon order, authority, law, and established institutions. He refuses to see that all these have an ephemeral element and must be adapted to changing conditions in order to retain their vitality; and that they benefit primarily the upper classes and cannot be expected to retain the loyalty of the lower classes permanently.

The main difficulty confronting the status quo conservative is the fundamental hopelessness of his overall goal — hopeless because of the ever-changing nature of the status quo he seeks to defend. It is clear that the preservation of the status quo is, in the long run, impossible; the dynamic flow of modern history is no more tolerant of the present than of the past. It relentlessly changes society and daily alters the task of society's defenders. Conservatives are doomed to fight what is essentially a rear-guard action in which victories are at best successful holding operations. As the status quo changes, its defenders find themselves in the ridiculous position of justifying today what they had assailed only yesterday, because it has meanwhile prevailed despite their best efforts to the contrary. Frequently the only way to escape this position is to become a reactionary, and this is one reason why the dividing line between the two tends in practice to be fluid. The status quo conservative's theoretical position in the political spectrum is, however, easy to define: unlike the reformer, he does not want to adjust to modern needs; unlike the reactionary, he recognizes the impossibility of moving backward; wishing things to remain as they are, he is dragged along by history instead of voluntarily cooperating with it.

Voluntary cooperation with history is the main characteristic of the second type of conservative, here called the reform conservative. He has an understanding of the course of historical development and sees the inevitability of certain changes, although he does not pretend any enthusiasm for them. He is, however, impressed by their inevitability (in the sense of being dictated by objective, irreversible causes) and sees in consequence only the following alternative: changes *will* occur either with the active cooperation of men like himself, who will spare whatever can still be preserved from the past, or by radicals, who will frequently go much farther than necessary in destroying the ancien régime and will place no value whatsoever upon maintaining the maximum possible historical continuity. The lot of the conservative reformer is a hard one: champions of the party of movement accuse him of being half-hearted in the pursuit of the "good society"; other conservatives suspect him of unchaining sleeping dogs, and if he comes from the upper classes he is hated with special bitterness as a "traitor to his class." He is frequently forced into an ad hoc alliance with the radicals of his day, one in which it is not always clear who is using whom.

The reform conservative can (in theory, not always in practice) be clearly differentiated from the radical reformer both by his methods and his ultimate aims. He prefers gradual reform, if possible within the existing constitutional framework, to violent and rapid change; he reforms only what is necessary when it becomes necessary, instead of seeking to implement a theoretically conceived blueprint in toto; and he seeks above all to maximize continuity in institutions and ideas. His cautious method is closely connected with his overall conception of what constitutes a good society: he values the colorful variety of life as it has evolved historically, has reverence for the past even as he removes surviving anachronisms, and is free of the illusion that utopia can be achieved in a necessarily imperfect world. He has, in short, what Burke called "a tendency to preserve with an inclination to improve."

It may be added that the successful reform conservative usually receives from historians the acclaim denied to him by contemporaries. There is danger, however, in looking for reform conservatives in every modern historical situation as dei ex machina to solve the massive problem of adaptation to modernity without any violent break in continuity. It should be stressed, therefore, that reform conservatism is feasible only where two far from universally prevalent conditions exist: 1) an overall structure of society capable of adapting to new needs without altering its fundamental structure; 2) the availability of constitutional processes allowing for piecemeal changes, whether through parliamentary institutions or a reforming absolutism. Great Britain is the classic country for meeting both conditions, and it is no accident that it possesses the most successful record of any European country of conservative adaptation to new needs. The eighteenth-century parliamentary system, however encrusted with privilege, was not completely unresponsive to reform needs and did maintain a tradition of self-government; it was able to be democratized in the nineteenth century through a succession of reform bills. It is doubtful, on the other hand, whether the situation in France before the Great Revolution met either condition. The established structure of society was characterized by incompetent monarchical authority, intransigent aristocratic privilege, and intolerant clericalism. There is no warrant for the belief — advanced, for example, by Burke — that these basic evils could have been remedied by conservative reformers acting in a patient and reverential spirit; nor were adequate constitutional processes available for piecemeal reform. The theoretically absolute monarch lacked reforming vigor; the aristocratic Assembly of Notables proved reactionary in its outlook; the revival of the long obsolete Estates-General meant revolution. In these facts must be sought what little mercy the French Revolution is able to find in conservative eyes.

The third type of conservative, the reactionary, is, logically speaking, not a conservative in the strict sense of the term, since he does not wish to conserve what now exists, but rather to restore an earlier condition which history has passed by. He does not believe — like the status quo conservative — that the world is relatively static, nor does he wish it to be so; he knows all too well that it has changed, believes that recent changes have been for the worse, and wishes, therefore, to return to an earlier condition. He desires backward motion and insists that history does not know any irreversible unilinear movement. Man is not the prisoner of history: he can shape his social, political, and cultural world as he wishes. Reactionaries are usually bitterly hostile toward existing society and are logical in lacking reverence for historical development whose result has been a hated status quo. Their indiscriminate enmity toward the present is usually accompanied by a romantic transfiguration of some particular period of the past. Thus the reactionaries of the period of the French Revolution glorified the ancien régime or, going back further, the medieval *Ständestaat*; their picture of earlier social relations as patriarchal rather than exploitative did more credit to their romantic imagination than to their sense of historical accuracy.

The reactionary mind is rather at a loss when it seeks to explain how a glorious past developed into the miserable present. Legitimate grievances of the lower classes cannot explain the change, because the golden past excludes such grievances by definition. The responsibility cannot be ascribed to inevitable historical development, since this would lead to defeatist conclusions; the true reactionary is, on the contrary, an incorrigible optimist in his belief in the possibility of restoring a vanished past. The reactionary tends to ascribe all trouble to "damned agitators," that is, to demagogues who create imaginary grievances which they then exploit to serve their personal ambitions; the reactionary mind is especially prone to fall victim to the "conspiracy theory" . . . There is a perverse consistency in this reactionary view: reactionaries, who believe that they — a small elite standing above the masses — can turn back history, believe quite logically that a small group of agitators can push history forward. Reactionaries gain confidence in the attainability of their program from the belief that it is based not upon their subjective will, but rather upon the objective "nature of things." They believe that man must return — under reactionary guidance — to a "natural order" from which society has departed but temporarily due to ascertainable (and reversible) causes. What they cannot accept is the existence of "forward-moving," irrepressible historical forces, for to do so would lead to the recognition that the much hated "radical agitators" are more the symptom than the cause of the modern situation which dooms the reactionary program to quixotic futility.[7]

THE RECURRING CORE OF CONSERVATIVE ARGUMENT

Conservatives, though they tend to be better at governing than at arguing, are forced by the exigencies of modern political life to enter the arena of public controversy. They do so with heavy hearts, and their thinking is in fact a reluctant concession to the challenge of the party of movement. They know that conservatism is a way of life, not a complex of arguments, and that it flourishes best, as unselfconscious traditionalism, before it is compelled to justify itself as theory. As conservative thinkers are compelled to make a virtue of a necessity they are usually best at defending specific challenged institutions, worst at developing a comprehensive theory of conservatism.

Conservatives usually dislike abstraction and general argument, and they think system-building is a distinctive radical vice. One can discover, nonetheless, a core of recurring conservative argument which is quite independent of the defense of any particular status quo, and may be considered — when stated in systematic form — the general conservative answer to the general challenge of modern progressivism. This recurring core does not, however, constitute a set of substantive conservative principles concerning the "best form of government" or the "best order of society"; it defines only a framework into which the most variegated conservative defenses of the most variegated status quos can be fitted.

It may be added that even the greatest of conservative thinkers have hesitated — because of their instinctive hostility to *all* system-making — to state the general conservative case in a systematic manner; it must be extracted from the wealth of specific argumentation dealing with particular cases. Edmund Burke, to name only the most influential conservative, has almost all the elements of the general conservative case in his *Reflections on the Revolution in France*; but he embeds them somewhat inconspicuously within the rich framework of his colorful and highly specific defense of the eighteenth-century English constitution. It may nonetheless prove useful to outline this case as an "ideal type" to serve as background to the fragmentary voices presented [here], although it goes without saying that many German conservatives did not subscribe — least of all explicitly — to all of the propositions outlined here.

Since conservatism is primarily a defensive movement against the efforts of the progressives to change the world, it naturally seeks to expose the weaknesses of its enemy. It is easy to state what conservatism, in each of its three forms, is *against*. It is above all against rationalism and utopianism, since reason is the *method* and a secular utopia the *goal* of progressivism. Conservatives insist that the systematic application of reason to political, economic, and religious problems usually leads to disastrous results. To tear down existing beliefs and institutions through acid criticism is easy; to find satisfactory and workable substitutes capable of attracting broad consent, difficult. Hence it appears far better to "make do" with the legacy of the past, however imperfect it may appear in the light of reason. Conservatives believe that this legacy incorporates — usually, not always — a "collective wisdom" far more trustworthy than the opinions of any individual thinker: this wisdom is enshrined in custom, tradition, and even sheer prejudice. Rationalist criticism is purely destructive, as it seeks to uproot these society-preserving factors, though they are, fortunately, so deeply rooted in the instinctive needs of man as to be virtually indestructible. They are, furthermore, buttressed by established authority and consecrated by traditional religion, at least prior to the spread of democracy and secularism. The conservative rejoices in the fact that religious faith, civic loyalty, and the emotional needs of man constitute a formidable barrier against rationalism, and he expects that the triumph of rationalism will never prove more than ephemeral.

Conservatives believe that the modern goal of establishing an earthly utopia — that is, a society characterized by universal happiness — is intrinsically unrealizable. It is unrealizable because the main handicap to establishing the millennium is not some easily overcome external social obstacle, such as monarchy, aristocracy, or clericalism, but rather the internal obstacle which exists in each individual as ineradicable original sin. Conservatives consider it a typically modern illusion that mankind can start life de novo by the mere wish to repudiate the past; indeed, they rarely resist a feeling of *Schadenfreude* that the noble ideals of the party of movement tend to break down in implementation after every apparent triumph. They point to what happened to the ideals of 1789 in the course of the French Revolution: liberty turned into the tyranny of the Committee of Public Safety; equality provided the legal framework for the exploitation of the lower classes by the bourgeoisie; fraternity led to militant nationalism and a quarter century of destructive war. Liberty is always in danger of degenerating into anarchy, which leads easily to tyranny; the egalitarian creed is defeated from the start by the inescapable fact that men differ from childhood in important respects for hereditary rather than environmental reasons; and fraternity usually expresses itself through participation in a parochial "in group" marked by hostility toward supposedly less desirable outsiders.

Conservatives assert, moreover, that man's cumulative experience with rationalism teaches that its erosion of the traditional bases of civilized conduct — religion, habit, and reverence for established custom — has unintentionally unchained primitive human drives for wealth, power, and pleasure on a scale unparalleled in history. This unintentional unleashing of drives, when combined with the pursuit of intrinsically utopian goals, has made frustration and discontent the hallmark of the modern world. Even where modernity has achieved great things — as in the creation of higher living standards — the rise of expectations characteristic of the modern temper has increased faster still, the result being a net increase in dissatisfaction. The eternal facts of frustration and suffering, previously accepted as part of God's plan for maturing and regenerating man, are inexplicable to the impatient hedonism of modernity.

Conservatives question, furthermore, not only the attainability but also the desirability of the radical vision of utopia. They see it as but the final culmination of that secularist hedonism which was the basic value of the Enlightenment. Secularism meant the repudiation of all transcendental religious conceptions, including the view that man possesses an immortal soul whose salvation in the hereafter is at least as important as happiness in our brief earthly life. Many of the thinkers of the Enlightenment tended to view man as only a higher type of animal destined to seek and find happiness here and now; they tended to identify happiness too narrowly with material welfare and emancipation from "superstition" at the expense of "ideal" endeavors. The hidden recesses of personality remained a closed book to them. They tended to ignore certain uncomfortable facts — for example, that the attainment of material goals usually creates frustration rather than satisfaction, since material wants are almost infinitely extensible and our comparative position vis-à-vis that of our neighbors often affects us psychologically more than our absolute standard of living; that the jealousy and envy which accompanies status seeking creates problems as great as those of poverty and exploitation; and that the stress upon pleasure rather than duty, egotistic self-interest rather than altruistic service, usually proves self-defeating in practice. The personal "enlightenment" achieved through education solves some problems only to create new ones: familiarity with other ways of life breeds discontent with one's own; the opening of opportunity probably creates at least as much frustration for the many who do not advance in the social scale as satisfaction to the few that do; while half-education leads to the vulgarization of culture and threatens that religious faith which is psychologically comforting, regardless of whether it be "true" or "false."

These, then, are the flaws which conservatives denounce in the method and goals of the party of movement. But what are conservatives *for?* The answer has been largely implied in the previous discussion but may now be stated systematically.

In its mode of thought — its epistemology — conservatism rejects rationalism; although conservatives do, of course, use their heads exactly as do men of other political persuasions, they warn against the excessive or exclusive use of speculative reason. They praise experience as a more reliable guide to truth than a priori conceptions and assert that, at least when dealing with human affairs, cautious induction is preferable to the deductive reasoning beloved by too many radicals. Above all, they insist upon the necessity of balancing the use of reason by listening to the voice of natural emotion and supernatural faith, and they believe that the individual reasoner should humbly subordinate his personal opinions to the collective wisdom of the race as expressed in customs and traditions. The habit of deference to what exists and reverence for what has developed are deemed more valuable human qualities than intellectual skill at constructing syllogisms.

Conservatives differ from radicals not only in their epistemology but in their view of what is most significant in the world. They tend to emphasize the importance of variety, whereas their opponents stress general norms; they proclaim the need for compromise in a pluralistic universe, whereas their opponents seek the triumph of "right reason" everywhere and at all times; and though willing to acquiesce (albeit reluctantly) in natural historical changes, they insist that the artificial human manipulation of history can only affect society for the worse.

Conservatives not only emphasize variety, they also love it. The spontaneous development of human society has led to a colorful richness which conservatives find emotionally and aesthetically satisfying. They do not bother to rationalize this preference in terms of any metaphysical system, for they consider it to be simply "natural," that is, in accordance with the "real" needs of "uncorrupted" human nature. Conservatives usually accuse radicals of wishing to destroy existing variety — expressing what is old and familiar — by implementing the precepts of an abstract and uniform rationalism. The conservative love of the customary is usually accompanied by a fear of the unknown — two of the taproots of what may be called the eternal appeal of conservatism to at least part of every man.

The conservative view of the world affirms in theory (not always in practice) the existence of a plurality of competing values. We have seen above how the conservative epistemology rejects rationalism but accepts the use of reason when balanced by the equally valuable — but partially incompatible — dictates of emotion and faith. This outlook of "yes, but — provided that" is characteristic of conservatism; it likes to criticize the party of movement for its frequent tendency to absolutize some single good, such as liberty, and to apply it ruthlessly and one-sidedly at the expense of other equally important values. Burke stated this point in a classic fashion when he replied to a French critic who accused him of being insufficiently enthusiastic about the progress of French liberty: "I should suspend my congratulations on the new liberty of France, until I was informed how it had been combined with government, with public force, with the discipline and obedience of armies, with the collection of an effective and well-distributed revenue, with morality and religion, with solidity and property, with peace and order, with civil and social manners.

115

All these (in their way) are good things, too; and without them, liberty is not a benefit while it lasts, and is not likely to continue long." [8]

The conservative affirmation of a plurality of values calls for an equilibrium between liberty and order, equality and hierarchy, individualism and collectivism, self-government and authority, cosmopolitanism and nationalism, material goods and ideal aspirations, pleasure and asceticism, reason and emotion, secularism and religion, dynamism and stability. It is true that the actual conduct of conservatives (especially reactionaries and defenders of the status quo) is often motivated by a single-minded emphasis upon the latter of each of the above antinomies (order, hierarchy, collectivism, et cetera). This conservative one-sidedness usually parallels and neutralizes equally one-sided exaggerations of progressivism on behalf of liberty, equality, individualism, et cetera; the difference between these two "lapses" is, however, that conservatives generally acknowledge the principle of pluralism, while progressives too often deny any value to at least some of the above-mentioned elements. One can also say that the existence of progressivism makes the disturbance of the intraconservative equilibrium of values necessary to serve the interests of the equilibrium of society as a whole. Hence moderate conservatives (or moderate progressives) often admit that progressives and conservatives are both essential for the best functioning of modern society — an insight which sometimes leads to the tolerance which we associate with civilized political conduct.

A constant danger confronting conservatives is that they will too easily get angry at history; only reform conservatives are free of this danger. Yet even the latter tend to deplore the dynamism of the modern world, and more especially the velocity of its changes. They inevitably resent the progressive habit of never taking the foot off the accelerator as mankind drives into the future. Conservatives — if the automobile analogy may be continued — keep their foot constantly on or near the brake; they attach the greatest importance to enforcing speed limits and safety regulations; they view the road ahead as bumpy and do not mind occasional road obstacles; above all, they see no reason why the approaching terra incognita should necessarily be superior to the familiar landscape being left behind.

The conservative function is one of avoiding unnecessary journeys and slowing the pace of those that are really necessary. It is the belief of reform conservatives, however, that this negative work must be accompanied by the positive work of adapting the old to the new. Old institutions are revitalized by eliminating anachronistic abuses, even as the life of a tree is prolonged by careful pruning and removing of dead limbs. The problem to be solved by the reform conservative is to differentiate between what is still viable and what is inevitably doomed to die. He must then select the proper method for strengthening the former while not hesitating to be ruthless in eliminating the latter. The precise method of action of the reform conservative will always depend upon time and circumstances, but certain general guidelines are nonetheless clear. The reform conservative will always seek to maximize continuity; when encountering a defective institution, he will try reform before consenting to its abolition; he will, if possible, pour new wine into old bottles rather than create completely new institutions to cope with new needs. His action will always aim at rearranging the elements of the existing structure of society instead of aiming at a total reconstruction de novo; his reform work will be done in sorrow rather than in anger, in a spirit of reluctant bowing to necessity rather than joyful triumph. He will view with reverence what was valuable in the past even though it must be eliminated for the sake of the future; and he will seek to maintain an overall pattern of society where the old always overbalances the new. The social engineering done by reform conservatives is always of a strictly prophylactic character. They do only what is necessary, as it becomes necessary, and with a primary view to preventing worse things being done by the party of movement. They never forget that society ought to be considered primarily as a *given* whose fundamental structure is shaped by God, or history, or the essentially unchangeable nature of man — not by any deliberate manipulation following man's subjective will. The reform conservative emphatically repudiates any kind of subjective caprice as he goes about his reform work; he only does, humbly and reverently, what he believes is objectively necessary to adjust the old to the new in the inescapable stream of historical development.

The question arises, Is reform conservatism only a doctrine of adjustment to the inevitable? Is it only an attitude and a method which seeks to minimize the evils of modernity by maximizing continuity, and by preventing revolution through timely reform? As adjustments accumulate quantitatively, the entire quality of society changes despite the absence of any sharp break in continuity at any particular point. Thus England has been changed in the last two hundred years from an agrarian to an industrial, an oligarchic to a democratic, a religious to a secular society, without any political revolution — a smooth record of adjustment of which Englishmen have reason to be proud. Today's English conservative champions and defends positions on liberty, local self-government, progressive income tax, et cetera, which would have done honor to any eighteenth-century radical. Should the conservative be considered, therefore, a mere opportunist who lacks any substantive principles which may not be compromised at any price? Or are there certain unchangeable conservative substantive principles, or at least ways of looking at the world?

For the Catholic conservative there is, in the religious field, the clear-cut case of revealed dogma: he obviously cannot compromise the slightest part of the infallible teachings of his church (though the possibility of differences in emphasis to meet differences in situations allows Catholics, in practice, to act far more flexibly than the statement above would suggest). Are there in the fields of politics and economics any absolutely valid beliefs, institutions, or patterns of life which possess the same sacrosanctity as revealed dogma in religion? Many conservatives have thought so at specific times with reference to specific institutions. In politics they have believed in the absolute value of monarchy or oligarchy or (some particular interpretation of) the American Constitution; in economics, in mercantilism, the free market, or some type of state socialism. Yet the very diversity of ideals which have evoked absolute loyalties indicates that all possessed but a relative, historical, and — philosophically speaking — ephemeral character. It follows that conservatism per se cannot be committed to any specific form of political or economic organization, and that there is, therefore, in principle no limit to conservative adjustment to modern political and economic forces.

One is tempted to say, somewhat paradoxically, that conservatism is static in aim but dynamic in character, since it constantly adjusts to historical development; while progressivism is dynamic in aim but often static in the character of its unchangeable goal. We have seen that conservatism cannot be identified with any absolute allegiance to any particular social or political order (though individual conservatives have, of course, such allegiances). One can, however, identify an underlying general conservative conception of society which remains constant in the midst of the unending process of adjustment to historical change. This conception is based upon the belief that human nature has remained essentially the same, at least insofar as its fundamental needs and some of its essential qualities are concerned. These needs can be met, these qualities can be taken into account, only by a general framework of society as constant as human nature itself and hence dictated by God or, if God be not allowed, by Nature. Its constituent elements are defined by the following basic needs of human nature: man requires society because he is, as Aristotle said, a social animal; the maintenance of society requires some kind of government authority which enforces law and order and a degree of social differentiation (hierarchy) which guarantees the performance of all socially necessary tasks. The social needs of man seeking to live a good life are, however, so diverse that they require far more than just satisfactory political institutions. Man requires a family which fulfills biological needs (not to mention the needs of the young); property, to provide security and independence; and some local roots in his place of birth or neighborhood to avoid becoming an unhappy nomad. All these relationships can be maintained satisfactorily only where moral codes and customs establish a tradition with a certain degree of continuity. Since man is more than a customary animal, he also needs some measure of freedom and opportunity for personal development. He is, finally, a religious creature who will never cease to wonder from where he has come and to where he is going and what the significance of his earthly life is. He needs, therefore, religion or some modern surrogate which performs most of the functions of traditional religion.

These dictates of Nature, as seen by conservatives, are at once inflexible and flexible: inflexible in the sense of being necessary (or at least desirable) at all times and places; flexible as regards their substantive content. Authority can be embodied in many different kinds of institutions; law is not simply the embodiment of "natural justice" but the reflection of changing social circumstances; order is a relative thing in view of the sinfulness of human nature and man's irrepressible (though variable) desire for freedom. The elements of social hierarchy vary from one society to another, both in their content and the permissible degrees of social mobility. The structure of families has changed throughout history; the forms of property are as heterogeneous as societies and their laws; and neighborhood roots are infinitely variable both in their intensity and substance. Codes of morality, customs, and traditions and the extent of their continuity differ from place to place, as do specific religions. The important point is, however, that all these elements must be present in *some* form at all times if man is to lead a satisfactory life. Conservatives point an accusing finger at progressives for ignoring this fundamental fact, as in their frequently intransigent hostility to authority, hierarchy, and traditional religion; and for likewise failing to understand that the value of all these elements is greatly enhanced if they are relatively stable, deeply rooted in the past, and comparatively noncontroversial in substance. They deplore the radical habit of throwing everything into controversy, despising the legacy of the past and delighting in the dynamism of the modern world.

Reform conservatives, however willing to adapt themselves to the continuous needs of historical development, will always keep in mind the eternal needs of man in society stated above; this will put some limitation to their adaption and opportunism (a word which need not have a negative connotation). The essential characteristics of conservatism per se are adherence to this eternal framework, dislike of unnecessary social change, and a propensity to find satisfaction in the status quo. Conservatism as thus defined has existed throughout recorded history, but it has become self-conscious, argumentative, and explicit only since it has been forced, beginning with the late eighteenth century, to meet the challenge of an aggressive progressivism operating within an ever more dynamic society.

It may be well to round out the picture by pointing out some of the characteristic vices of conservatives: complacency, callousness, and short-sightedness. Defenders of the status quo emphatically, reform conservatives and reactionaries to a lesser degree, feel very much "at ease in Zion." Their recruitment from the upper classes (with the corollary possession of wealth and power) make them too frequently indifferent to the condition of the less fortunate part of the human race; even reform conservatives tend to patronize the lower classes and to promote reforms more from prudence than genuine sympathy with human suffering. When defending the existing structure of society, conservative theorists too often stress the beauty of its overall configuration while ignoring the ugliness of many of its component parts. To give only one example: the conservative sympathy for the principle of hierarchy expresses an aesthetic appreciation of its resulting colorful variety — an appreciation marked (like all aesthetic appreciation) by a detachment often incompatible with a sense of social responsibility. A society headed by landowning aristocrats will naturally have more color and variety than a "leveled" Jeffersonian democracy of small farmers, but the aesthetic beauty of the whole is marred — at least to observers not captives of conservative phrases — by the monotony and squalor of life seen from the bottom of the pyramid. Conservatives like to assert that they are defending concrete society against radical abstractions, but in fact their idealization of the Whole amounts to an aesthetic appreciation of a pure abstraction which becomes amoral when it ignores the very concrete sufferings of the poor. There is justice in Paine's response to Burke's lament on the fate of the French aristocracy: "He pities the plumage, but forgets the dying bird."

Callousness toward the sufferings beneath them is often accompanied — even among reform conservatives — by shortsightedness in the face of the problems ahead of them. Since the irresistible character of the modern forces which are transforming the world is either denied or their impact minimized, conservatives have little incentive to analyze the long-range needs of society. Conservatism easily becomes a philosophy for doing tomorrow (or not at all) what should be done today. Thus conservative reforms are rarely introduced in time, and more rarely still do they suffice to set a controversy even temporarily at rest. Complacency toward existing conditions — even worse, nostalgia toward the past — is poor equipment for coping with the problems of the dynamic world of the last two centuries. The conservative penchant for belated stopgap measures bears a heavy share of responsibility for that chronic maladjustment between old institutions and new needs which is the source of much of the turbulence of modern history.

4. THE REVOLUTIONARY USES
OF REPRESSION

Michael Walzer

In most studies of revolutionary repression it is possible to detect a fairly simple political strategy lurking behind the intellectual effort, a strategy either of condemnation or apology. On the one hand, some writers have jumbled together different sorts of repression — enforced by different groups, by different means, against different people, for different reasons — in order to condemn them all.[1] On the other hand, other writers have maintained, for essentially apologetic purposes, a purely abstract and mechanical distinction between the repression of "reactionary" and "progressive" elements.[2] Both groups have tended to identify revolutionary repression exclusively with state-organized violence, using as models the brief year of Jacobin terror or the Stalinist purges. Now it is certainly true that such events ought to be condemned or justified; the victims demand that much at least; and I think it clear that they ought to be condemned. But whatever judgments we make, these need not and should not be extended (as they generally are) to revolutionary radicalism as a whole. This is so for two reasons: first, because the terrorism of the revolutionary state is only one example of state terrorism in general and not necessarily the most important example; secondly, because the kinds of repression most typical of revolutionary radicalism usually take shape before the seizure of state power and do not require state-organized violence.

The second of these points is perhaps best argued from Puritan rather than Jacobin or Bolshevik history. For though Puritanism has become virtually synonymous with repression, the Puritan revolution never produced a Puritan terror. I want to suggest that the patterns of repression developed by the Puritans *before* their own revolution have been redeveloped, in new vocabularies, with shifting emphases, by each subsequent group of revolutionaries. And these patterns have been more important, more central to the radical or revolutionary perspective than the reigns of terror have been. Puritanism is functionally necessary to every revolution; state terrorism is not.

The first point requires a more elaborate argument. It is necessary to sketch a very rough and doubtlessly incomplete overview of the modern history of politically organized repression and try to place revolutionary activity in that history. For this purpose I need to distinguish three different historical moments, which occur and recur in no necessary chronological sequence, but which together reveal the character of that long and complicated process whereby modern forms of social discipline have been learned. Only the last of these, I should add, applies in any complete sense to the United States; the first two belong to our European past. For if, as Tocqueville says, we were "born free," we were also "born repressed" — without ever having, as a culture, to go through the tortuous processes that produce promptness, self-restraint, method: the key ingredients of modern rectitude.

I

The first moment can be called, simply, state terrorism. I mean to indicate by that phrase all those activities that the state undertakes in the name of its sovereign and exclusive power (or rather, that the rulers of the state undertake in the name of their sovereign and exclusive power) and for the sake of one or another sort of "law and order." Obviously, the list is long, but a few examples from early modern history ought to make the notion clear enough.

The repression of rebellion: like that of the Great Northern Revolt by Queen Elizabeth I, with its terroristic aftermath when hundreds of peasants were tortured and hung.

The persecution or destruction of religious minorities in order to establish national or political unity: like that of the Huguenots in France, perhaps the classic early modern example of state terrorism, involving the quartering of troops on a civilian population, the use of spies and informants, brutal punishments, forced conversions, the torture and massacre of men, women, and children — a barbaric episode far exceeding the reign of terror of 1793 in its traumatic effects upon French life if not upon French literature.[3]

The savage suppression of vagabondage and crime: as in sixteenth-century England where Henry VIII is said to have hung 17,000 vagabonds, which (though the figure has been disputed) surely suggests one of the typical ways of dealing with the problems caused by the breakup of the traditionalist rural economy.

The use of force and violence to establish new patterns of work: Marx has described well the terroristic processes whereby peasants, driven from the land, were "whipped, branded, tortured by laws grotesquely terrible, into the discipline necessary to the wage system."

The use of force and violence to establish new property systems: as is evidenced best by the penal codes of the sixteenth to eighteenth centuries and especially by the extraordinary increase in the number of capital crimes.[4]

All these things constitute state terrorism, and to them must be added the random and routine sadism of powerful men which putatively serves the purposes just listed. It can hardly be denied that the state, not the revolutionary state but the state itself, has been the great agent of terror in modern history. This is so even when it has not been, even when it could not yet be, totalitarian. In the early modern period, at least, state-organized terrorism was rarely either pervasive or sustained; both its incidence and its effectiveness were radically uneven. Moreover, it was often directed against various sorts of locally organized violence; and it is probably true that the general level of internal violence was reduced as the state gradually acquired its monopoly over the use of force.[5] Nevertheless, both for the sake of this monopoly and of its real and presumed purposes the state has functioned as a terrorist organization. And whatever progress it has achieved has been achieved at the expense of large numbers of people — feudal aristocrats, religious heretics, uprooted peasants, new workers — who were unwilling to sacrifice their power, or their faith, or their simple human rights, and who therefore "had to be" coerced.

So the whip and the gallows became the central symbols of the modern state. The state inspires fear, the state takes human life — and only in these ways does it maintain order. The sword of the ruler must always be red with blood, wrote Martin Luther. The point was often made more euphemistically, but it was one of the central points of early modern political theory. To say order, however, is to say too little. The purpose of the sword was a new kind of order, appropriate to the developing society and economy of the modern world. And a new order implies a new subjection. What the modern state requires is not simply that its laws be obeyed, but that they be obeyed promptly, predictably, and in detail, and that the obedience be absolutely independent of private whim and emotion. This is not a subjection that has anywhere been easily enforced or peacefully maintained.

Indeed, it is not at all clear that state terrorism by itself can produce the kind of obedience that modern social and economic systems require. That it cannot do so has been the central claim of all reformers and revolutionaries. For the bloody sword is utterly external to the wills and the consciousness of men, and so it is incapable of inspiring an obedience that is willful and conscientious, which is also to say, it is incapable of inspiring an obedience that is prompt or dependable or detailed. The only kind of social order that the sword can produce, wrote John Milton, is "the forced and outward union of cold, neutral and inwardly divided minds." [6] The danger of *coldness* is one of the most interesting themes of revolutionary literature. It appears most poignantly, perhaps, in the last writings of the Jacobin St. Just, who had himself experimented with state terrorism. "The revolution is frozen," he wrote shortly before his death, and he went on to admit that the terror had failed to evoke that lively willingness, that warm and eager compliance that was one of its goals.[7] Of course, state terrorism does not entirely fail — we would all live differently if that were true — nor however does it entirely succeed. It produces a "cold" conformity, a forced unity, a gross kind of obedience. It produces what one Puritan minister called "easy, dull, and drowsy performances." And it gives rise at the same time to new patterns of private escape, evasion, fantasy, and crime.

The second moment in the modern history of terrorism can be called revolutionary repression. I mean by that all the efforts of political and religious radicals to develop some sort of mutual control and self-restraint as an alternative to state terrorism, and so to generate a warm and conscientious obedience, at once making force unnecesary and blocking off the avenues of private escape. Freud's *Civilization and its Discontents* is helpful in suggesting a description of radicalism that takes into account this drive toward self-control. Revolution, in the light of his argument, may be seen as the sharing of instinctual deprivation (in the name of justice), the willing, even the willful, acceptance of repression by new social groups. "Liberty has undergone restrictions through the evolution of civilization, and justice demands that these restrictions shall apply to all." Revolts against injustice, Freud goes on, may thus prove favorable to the further development of civilization. "The end result would be a state of law to which all . . . have contributed by making some sacrifice of their own desires and which leaves none . . . at the mercy of brute force." [8] What is revolutionary about this "sacrifice" is that it calls into question the very necessity of government, that is, of the whip, the gallows, and the bloody sword. It suggests that all these be replaced (or at least partially replaced, or replaced for some part of the population) by self-government. "Sovereign power is necesary for social order," announces the ruler of the early modern state, "therefore I will repress you." And to this the reformers and revolutionaries reply: "Holiness or virtue is necessary for social order; therefore we will repress ourselves."

This is a dramatic announcement. It means: we will free ourselves from the inert state of subjection to a sovereign; we will find one another; we will create obligations and pledge ourselves to fulfill them; we will give to our brethren or comrades what we have never freely given to the sovereign — the right to punish us if we default on our pledge. "The pledged group," writes Sartre, "is a common product of reciprocities mediated under the statute of violence." [9] The pledge or covenant creates a kind of mutual terrorism, which frees men from the coercion of the state but subjects them to that of their fellows. The act of union is the first act of self-control, but this is always self-control-with-the-others, for alone the individual remains passive and subject. And the first act of self-control, or mutual control, is also the first act of revolt. The claim to control oneself is the claim of revolutionary right, the claim to be free. Thus Oliver Cromwell was able to challenge the king and wage war against him, writes Milton, only because he had already conquered himself: "it was over himself he had most learned to triumph." [10] This triumph brings Cromwell into "the congregation of the first-born." It gives him brethren; now he no longer needs and can no longer endure a master. He no longer needs a lawgiver; he and his brethren give the law to one another. He no longer needs a law-enforcer; he and his brethren enforce the law upon one another. This mutual lawgiving and lawenforcing is the primary meaning of revolutionary repression.

These first two moments can be summed up as terrorism from above and terrorism from below. They are, at least in certain crucial respects, precise opposites. State terrorism depends upon the customary inertia or the coerced passivity of masses of men, and upon the activity and power of a relatively small number, assisted by a more or less efficient organization of spies and informers, torturers and hangmen. It exploits the human fear of violent death — as Hobbes so well understood — and it offers to its subjects in exchange for their passivity and obedience security against all violence except its own. The great and only pleasure of its members, wrote Rousseau of modern society, "is the pleasure of not being dead." [11] In order to enhance this single pleasure, the state is committed to overreact to the slightest suggestion of crime or rebellion. It brings death in its most violent and gruesome forms to every recalcitrant subject.

Revolutionary repression, on the other hand, requires the activity of as many men as can be roused to action; it depends on their voluntary participation, on the widespread sharing of power and government. Every man is its agent. Thus spying is replaced by mutual surveillance — by what the Puritans called "holy watching" — which is probably far more effective than state-organized espionage in breaking into private life. The lay elders of Calvin's Geneva, chosen with the consent of their congregations, were supposed "to watch over the life of everyone . . . to have an eye everywhere." [12] Rousseau's goal was to render all men "transparent," which is something the torturer and the hangman never achieve. It is achieved, perhaps, when citizens consent to be watched. (Jacobins and Bolsheviks sometimes talked of turning men into steel rather than into glass, but the effect would be more or less the same: one knows with certainty the internal constituency of steel.) In communist society, wrote Lenin, there will be "no police force distinct from the people" — an arrangement more equalitarian than Geneva's and potentially even more repressive. It does not mean that there will be no police, but rather that there will be more police than ever before, and they will not wear uniforms. [13] Finally, to complete the comparison, the threat that underlies revolutionary repression is not death but ostracism: excommunication from the congregation, expulsion from the party, exile from society. Then the holy watchers look the other way; neighborly surveillance ceases, for one has no neighbors; one is thoroughly opaque. It is a fate worse than death. And the reward that the collectivity offers to willful and obedient members is not mere security, but approbation and honor, even glory or, as the Puritans would have said, eternal life.

It is important to stress once again the radical and revolutionary character of what I have called "terrorism from below." Its bias is consistently democratic, equalitarian, and activist. Conservatives, of course, might also oppose state terrorism, as Edmund Burke did, but they cannot defend an equalitarian and activist self-government. Burke wrote angrily against the theorists of the modern state, against Locke above all, insisting that theirs was a "barbarous philosophy, the offspring of cold hearts" (thus he touched a radical theme) "and muddy understandings . . . In the groves of their academy," he went on, "at the end of every vista, you see nothing but the gallows." [14] Burke's alternative to terrorism was a romantic evocation of the traditional social structure in which men did not control themselves or one another, but rather were passive and faithful members of an authoritarian church, loyal participants in a hierarchical order or, less romantically, degraded and deferential peasants. He raises customary, habitual, emotionally smooth obedience above the "cold conformity" of the modern world. But the revolutionaries have as little patience with habit, custom, deference, and passivity as they do with coldness and conformity. All these, they would say, are simply ways of avoiding conscientious work and willful self-control. Revolutionaries are always "stirring themselves up" to greater and greater efforts and their ultimate bias, perhaps, is that there is no one incapable of being stirred.[15] They do not assert an equality of wisdom or of strength, but an equality of willfulness. Everyone, they say, is capable of making and honoring the pledge. And this assertion poses a threat greater than any other to established authority. Even among the Puritans, whose doctrine of predestination would seem to make inequality permanent and inevitable, the actual practice of collective repression in the congregation could produce the extraordinary hope that all men join in the good work and England become "a land of saints, and a pattern of holiness to all the world . . ." [16] Lenin's vision of a future communist society in which every cook would be a bureaucrat and every citizen a policeman sounds very different from this, but it is fundamentally the same. It implies the same equality, the same activism, the same sharing of political functions previously usurped by lords and kings, autocrats and officials.

These first two moments in the history of modern social discipline are, I think, both analytically and historically distinct. Nevertheless, revolutionaries do seize state power and use it against their opponents and also against those passive, withdrawn or simply fearful people whom the Puritans called "neuters." [17] They use the state, or try to use it, to short-cut those long and difficult processes by which men are brought to pledge themselves to collective repression; they use it to reinforce the new and generally underdeveloped mechanisms of mutual surveillance. But when revolutionaries do this, they "freeze" the revolution, as St. Just realized too late. They themselves deny the possibilities of genuine self-government; they reestablish an older pattern of public conformity and private vice, and then the committed conscience of the saint and the virtuous will of the citizen become once again the "neutral and inwardly divided mind" of the subject. Revolutionaries in power justify their terrorism by statements which are perhaps true. They point out that the majority of people in their country have not yet committed themselves to self-control and mutual surveillance. For these people, they argue, external coercion and the bloody sword continue to be necessary. The revolution needs time to win the hearts of its people, but until hearts are won, bodies must be constrained; there is no choice. All this may be true. But the truth or falsehood of such arguments has nothing to do with the effects of the terror. These are always the same: a frozen revolution, a failure to win the heart.

Perhaps the effects are worse. For a brief moment in time the terrorism of a revolutionary state may be more far-reaching, more ruthless, more terrifying than that of the conventional state — in a word, more total. This is by no means necessarily the case, and it is characteristic of many of those who suggest that it is that they drastically underestimate the violence perpetrated by conventional states. Still, revolutionary radicalism does raise the possibility of a totalitarian politics. For one of the things we mean by totalitarianism is the coming together of a creed that justifies mutual repression and an organization that practices it with a state possessing a monopoly on the use of force. In the long run, probably, the combination is unstable; the use of state terror converts the revolutionary creed into a conventional ideology and the revolutionary organization into a conventional elite. In the short run, it can be very frightening. There are always revolutionary groups to which one wishes every success — short of the seizure of state power.

The third moment in the history of modern discipline depends to a considerable degree on the success, or relative success, of the first two. It involves what might be called the routinization of terrorism, or better, the transformation of terror into a routine anxiety. It is the liberal theorists — from Locke to Smith and Bentham — who provide the best descriptions of this stage. They replace state terror with state regulation, the torturer with the night watchman. And, more important, they replace mutual repression with the pressures generated by social and economic competition. The results are perhaps best exemplified in America, where, as Tocqueville noted, the citizens are not virtuous, yet they are free. The morality produced by a strenuous public life has given way to the morality produced by a strenuous private life; commitment and zeal have given way to enlightened self-interest. The citizens do not repress one another, at any rate not in the ways envisioned by Puritan or Jacobin radicals, but their endless competition forces every individual to repress himself. The result is a lesser morality, but still a morality that each individual imposes "upon himself." [18] Hence state violence is unnecessary, or only minimally necessary. All this was foreseen by the liberal theorists. It was their great discovery that the fear of falling behind in the race for worldly goods was an entirely sufficient basis for socially acceptable behavior. Constant comparison of the self and the others — not brethren now, but competitors — makes "holy watching" needless; keeping up with the Joneses requires a sufficient degree of self-control.[19] But whereas living in the public eye — in theory at least — stimulated devotion, discipline, and even heroic endeavor, living under the nervous scrutiny of private eyes is most likely to produce only conformity. But I need not say anything more about this third moment; it is our own moment in world history.

II

Puritanism is undoubtedly one of the more successful attempts at revolutionary repression, one of the best examples of terrorism from below. Repression of this sort, as I have argued elsewhere, represents a very immediate and personal (or group) response to the same experiences that produce terrorism from above: The disorder, the rapid social and geographic mobility, the normative uncertainty and confusion that occur as a result of the breakdown of traditionalist patterns and institutions.[20] Sainthood is a way of coping with these problems, of proving oneself a competent man, in control, capable of freedom. But it is not an easy way, for it requires a radical reconstitution of the self —

the saint is a man whose obedience is conscientious, whose performances are never dull or drowsy — and also of all those social settings within which the self lives and moves. The saint depends on the others; he requires a whole gamut of supportive communities. These communities must repress him, but at the same time involve him in the hard work of repressing himself and others — involve him, that is, in self-government. I want now to describe some of the ways that involvement and repression actually worked.

The congregation was the crucial institution within which Puritan repression was carried out. For the congregation, far from being a "forced and outward union," was founded precisely on the willingness of the saints; it was, at least in theory, a voluntary association. A man joined it, and so submitted himself to its discipline; he pledged his faith; he agreed to watch and be watched. And this was a moral commitment, above all, a commitment to hard work. Self-government takes a lot of time; mutual repression is an exacting business. Studying the day-by-day, week-after-week functioning of the Puritan congregation I was often reminded of Oscar Wilde's aphoristic warning about socialism: "Socialism would take too many evenings." That is equally true of all the forms of revolutionary self-government and certainly of Puritanism, the earlist form. The schedule of Puritan activity was vastly different from that of a Catholic parish, different not necessarily in the number of events, which may well have been high in both cases, but in the intensity of participation required. There were three-hour sermons on Sundays and lectures, often twice a week, on weekdays in between; there were catechisms for the young before lectures and discussion groups for adults afterward, "to resolve doubts"; there were congregational meetings to elect ministers (or to confirm decisions arrived at by previous meetings of the elders) and more meetings to argue about their performance; there were meetings of the consistory to take up matters of "moral discipline" and perhaps to reprimand or punish sinning members; there were meetings for new mothers and for boys about to be confirmed; there were private conferences for especially conscientious families; and, finally, there were public disputations among neighboring ministers. It was an exhausting round and served as a bar to privacy and withdrawal. Attendance at meetings is a significant form of social control. And yet, as anyone active in nonconformist religion or left-wing politics can testify, there are few people who love meetings more than dissenters and revolutionaries.

131

Above all, for committed Puritans, there was the hard work of "holy watching." Richard Baxter, from whose autobiography I have collected the list of meetings just given, writes that in his congregation the enforcement of the moral discipline was made possible "by the zeal and diligence of the godly people of the place, who thirsted after the salvation of their neighbors, and were in private my assistants." [21] It is impossible to guess how effective that zeal and diligence ever was, though even its routinized forms, which we still encounter, are a fairly efficient means of social control. "How many public scandals are prevented for fear of these severe observers?" writes Rousseau of gossiping women.[22] Sometimes, of course, scandals are not prevented and so must be deliberately made public — for the moral good, presumably, of all concerned. Thus, among the Puritans, there were public accusations and confessions at special sessions of the consistory or congregation called "experience meetings."

The Jacobin clubs offer a similar spectacle, first developed, it may be, in imitation of the French or Swiss Protestants. The *épuration*, or purification, is described as follows by a contemporary writer: "This tribunal of conscience . . . is terrible indeed, but it is also just. The most practised audacity, the most refined hypocrisy disappeared before the watchful and penetrating eyes of the sound members of the society and the numerous citizens who filled the galleries." [23] The "sound members" of the Jacobin clubs and the "godly people" of Baxter's Puritan congregation are obviously similar sorts of persons. They are not agents of the state, uniformed police or paid officials; they are conscientious saints and citizens; they are doing a job, but they are amateurs in the root sense of that word, who love their work. I don't think, however, that it is unfair to call them terrorists; certainly it was their intention that the men who stood before their tribunals be terrified. But it has to be added that they are not like torturers who torture only other men. As a glance at their diaries will suggest, they are self-tortured too.

Mutual surveillance and self-watching go closely together. An argument as to which comes first in time would be foolish. It is easier simply to repeat the conventional wisdom and suggest that, for most people, the vigilant eyes of the godly others are internalized to form conscience, and the public accusations of the godly others transformed into private guilt. In these two processes the Puritan family undoubtedly plays an important part, perhaps a far more important part than does the congregation. But the family was generally described in Puritan literature as a "little congregation" and the patterns of repression in the household were consciously modeled on the congregational discipline — except, of course, that the willingness of children was not required. Children were subjected to the vigilant eye of an authoritarian father, to a kind of paternal terrorism, modified only somewhat by maternal solicitude. In the interests of both surveillance and solicitude, Puritan writers often attacked both the feudal household and the extended family: they were aware of the many ways by which children might escape repression in both, receiving protection, so to speak, from an uncle, a grandmother, or a sympathetic servant. A godly father must watch his children, full of anxiety for their wayward souls. Nor was love a sufficient guarantee of vigilance. Parents must be "wary and circumspect," wrote one minister. And another: "Fondness and familiarity breeds irreverence." [24] But these are warnings against simple affection, not against the most passionate concern. Indeed, the extraordinary closeness of the modern family is at least in part the product of Puritan watchfulness — and also of that "thirst" for the salvation of our children's souls, in which, however secularized it has become, something of Puritan zeal can still be discerned.

I was especially struck by the importance of the Puritan family when I first came across the letters of a Puritan mother to her son at Oxford, written between 1638 and 1643. She sent him medicinal syrups and Puritan pamphlets in the same packages and in her letters endless advice: "My dear Ned, keep your heart above the world . . . be careful to improve your time . . . tie yourself to a daily self-examination . . . think over the company you have been in . . . be careful to keep the Sabbath." And then, after Ned had joined the parliamentary army to fight the king: "I pray God bless you, that you may be very able to do your country service." [25] Here is a saint and citizen being trained. Parental watchfulness follows him even away from home — "my thoughts are much with you," wrote his mother — though it is gradually replaced by self-examination and also by new forms of collective repression, as in the New Model army.

Self-control, the ability to lead a holy or virtuous life even when out of range of the public eye, is the finest product of revolutionary repression. It opens the way for perfect trust among men, making even the consistories and "tribunals of conscience" unnecessary. Few Puritans thought it possible except for a small minority, God's elect. Among them it was achieved and maintained in part by a kind of constant nagging at the self, a stimulation of anxiety and guilt that had at first to be deliberate and willful and only later became habitual.[26] The agent of this stimulation was conscience and its key expressive form was the diary. The Puritan diary is not filled with romantic musings and not often with imaginative introspection; vivid personal experiences are rarely vividly recorded. Rather, it is given over to a peculiarly intense version of that moral bookkeeping recommended by Ben Franklin to the readers of his autobiography. There is no reason to multiply examples, for the best of them tend to be similar in style if not in content. Here is a minister warning himself against sexual fantasy (he has been daydreaming, quite properly one might think, about his wife, Barbara): "ceasing but a little from good doing . . . I began to wax cold, which grew upon me by reason of lingering after Ba . . ." And here is a woman reprimanding herself for some hasty words: "I talked of some things not so as I ought when I had considered of them . . . but this is my comfort, that my heart is settled to be more watchful hereafter . . ." Finally, a semiautobiographical passage from a published book; the author is worrying about lost time and readily falls into the bookkeeping style: "If a man should at every week's end consider how he hath spent it, how many hours might he reckon up which he cannot tell how he bestowed . . . ? How many needless items would he find given to sleep? Item, seven nights; item, perhaps seven half-afternoons, beside half hours and quarters at unaccustomed times . . ."[27] Now it would not be difficult to list state laws from many countries directed against careless speech and wasted time (though not, I suppose, against sexual fantasy), and such laws have undoubtedly inspired a great deal of fearfulness and caution, silence and punctuality. Puritan vigilance would make such laws unnecessary.

Not entirely unnecessary, of course, for I do not want to suggest that the Puritans were early and hitherto undiscovered advocates of the withering away of the state (though it is true that the thrust of "holy watching" was in the same direction as communist discipline). Puritans were perfectly willing to use the state to reinforce the congregational system and to control all those who did not join a congregation and attend its meetings. Though they never organized a full-scale terror and never set about to kill suspects and enemies, they did use the power they briefly seized — in two ways not entirely unrelated to its former uses. First, they punished individuals: free-wheeling, loose-living men and women, idlers and vagabonds, and also free-thinking men and women, heretics, atheists and protestant autodidacts who invented their own religion. Secondly, they banned activities: privatizing, stimulating, releasing activities that imperiled self-control and communal surveillance — fornication, maypole dancing, theater-going, "dawdling in taverns." Now this sort of thing evokes from worldlings, as one might expect, a "cold" response: public conformity and private evasion. And since the hopes of the revolutionaries, and their demands, are so much greater than those of the more conventional rulers of the state, their failure is greater too. Congregational discipline can produce saints, but a purely external coercion cannot.

But the revolutionary state, like the revolutionary politics that precedes it, is not simply coercive. It also involves an attempt to mobilize the whole society for the hard work of self-government, and its most immediate and significant, if not lasting, effect is to activate thousands of previously passive, resigned, sullen or deferential individuals. Rates of political participation leap upward during revolutionary periods, and this participation, though it may seem chaotic, disorderly, unlawful or seditious to the old (and soon enough, sadly, to the new) rulers, is in fact rooted in new patterns of sustained commitment and communal responsibility. If the worldlings are antagonized and coerced, the saints, at least, come into their own (and anyone who chooses can be a saint). This is the climax of the second moment in the history of control and self-control. It is not, or at any rate has not yet, been sustained. At some point the political effort to universalize sainthood collapses, revolutionary repression, sometimes gradually, sometimes very quickly, is routinized, and activist self-government replaced (so far as the state is concerned, not necessarily in other groups) by a more or less conscientious but essentially passive obedience to new rules and regulations. Later, perhaps, the same drama is reenacted, with different social groups playing the part of the saints.

It is not always reenacted at the level of revolutionary politics. For once certain sorts of political battles have been fought and won, organizations that encourage mutual repression (religious sects, trade unions, and so forth) can operate *within* society, tolerated by the authorities. Their activity is still implicitly radical — that is, they prepare individuals for self-government — but it may not be explicitly so. And insofar as opportunities actually exist for self-government (they generally do not exist in traditional societies), such organizations may serve, as English

Methodism did, to limit or divert revolutionary energy.[28] If the time for full-scale mobilization ever returns, however, their members are likely to be found in the ranks of the saints.

III

The whole of the argument I have just gone through might be regarded as a historical and theoretical gloss on that old cliché about eternal vigilance being the price of liberty. That means: revolutionary discipline is the price of an activist and equalitarian self-government. Or better, the two are opposite sides of an equation; when one is modified, liberalized, routinized, or whatever, so is the other. There cannot be a relaxed, permissive, privatized society of self-governing citizens. That is the lesson, I think, of Locke's political theory. For Locke's citizens, though they have many rights, are no longer in any significant sense self-governing. They consent *to be governed* and only function as political men when their government abuses them and drives them to revolt — which happens rarely. In general they are apolitical; unlike Rousseau's citizens they do not "fly to the public assemblies." They spend their evenings at home or in the office or the shop. They respect one another's privacy; they do not watch their neighbors except to judge their own relative position in the competitive race. Self-government requires an entirely different way of life.

I don't mean, of course, that self-government requires the reign of terror with all its brutality and sadism. Those two are contradictory indeed, and in that contradiction lies the great dilemma of the seizure of power. Ideally, state power ought not to be seized, but destroyed. At the same time it must be said that the destruction of state power, if it ever occurred, would not be the end of repression, but rather the beginning of "too many evenings" spent at meetings, of "holy watching," conscientious and sustained work, and all the rest. Refuse these and you refuse freedom; you submit yourself in one way or another to hangmen or bureaucrats. That is the revolutionary's message, repeated over and over again in different historical circumstances and in different cultural forms. It has not yet been disproved.

HISTORY

5. THE CHANGING PLACE
OF COLLECTIVE VIOLENCE[1]

Charles Tilly

Around the middle of the nineteenth century the character of collective violence in France changed rapidly, thoroughly, and definitively. The forms of violence evolved before and after that turbulent moment, but never so fast. Exactly how the change to newer forms of conflict occurred varied from sector to sector and region to region within French society, but it occurred almost everywhere. From a country in which local food riots, scattered machine-breaking, sporadic protests against such government measures as taxation and conscription, and mass trespassing in rural properties were the predominant varieties of collective violence, France transformed herself into a nation of organized demonstrations, bloody strikes, and sophisticated attempts at revolution. Despite the shift to apparently more formidable types of rebellion, collective violence became a less reliable means of seizing power or of changing public policy. It all happened in little more than twenty years.

Those twenty-odd years, moreover, spanned the country's first great surge of industrial expansion and urban growth. They included the knitting together of the nation by railroad and telegraph. They contained the advent of universal manhood suffrage, the emergence of political parties, and the formation of trade unions. They even saw a crucial and durable switch from high fertility toward low fertility.

In a short generation the quality of social life and the style of political life in France took on many of the features we customarily call "modern." What is more, in many parts of France the pattern of political action stamped in the mid-nineteenth century endured well into the twentieth.

Writing of the momentous changes in the political life of the Alpine region from 1848 through 1851, for example, Philippe Vigier says:

It is not just a matter of a political *prise de conscience* on the part of the rural masses (or at least a good part of them) as a result of the establishment of universal suffrage. That *prise de conscience* was accompanied by *prises de position* which have marked the population of these areas up to the present day: those four years were enough to create a republican tradition which . . . permitted the regime produced by the Revolution of September 4th to take a solid hold in the Alpine region in 1871 — thus aiding powerfully in the strengthening of the Republic in the country as a whole.[2]

It was a time of profound political transformations. The nature of collective violence changed in step with those transformations. In most of these respects the quarter century from 1845 to 1870 was more decisive than the quarter century of the great French Revolution.

Any student of modernization who happens onto such a cluster of changes can be expected to shout "Eureka!" To the extent that contemporary notions of modernization rely on fragmented memories of what happened in Western Europe (and that extent is large), the experience of France needs attention. At a moment when many scholars are elaborating theories somehow linking political instability, protest, and collective violence with modernization, the turbulent life of nineteenth-century France deserves analysis.

Despite an understandable tendency to consider violent protest a temporary and fruitless diversion from the main line of social change, students of various sorts of "development" have taken the study of collective violence with increasing seriousness in the last few years.[3] Twenty or thirty years ago, much to the amusement of most historians, the fashionable way to deal with it was to search for the standard life cycles of revolutions, protests, or social movements. (I should say, however, that a historian, Crane Brinton, did the most famous example of this kind of analysis.)[4] Not any more. Neil Smelser's *Theory of Collective Behavior* marks the transition — a scheme which still concentrates on stages and taxonomies, but which grows out of a larger analysis of the way large structural changes in societies produce strains and protests, and which poses more sharply than before the problem of specifying which strains lead to what kinds of protests.[5] Chalmers Johnson's codification of that line of thought and Barrington Moore's restatement of a quite different kind of argument both establish that the discussion is proceeding, and gaining in sophistication.[6]

Recently the chief efforts of sociologists and political scientists to deal empirically with this relationship between large-scale social change and collective violence have consisted of quantitative comparisons of considerable numbers of contemporary nations differing both with respect to the frequency of collective violence and with respect to level of industrial activity, urban concentration, and so on.[7] Most of the arguments, and most of the preliminary findings, point to some phase of maximum turbulence intermediate between very low and very high economic well-being and to a definitive calming of public order with advanced industrialization. But there are two contending ideas about how this happens:

1. The dissolution of norms, controls, and social attachments by large-scale structural change (for example, in the mass migration of rural people to cities or in the destruction of family solidarity by occupational specialization) creates personal malaise and facilitates its expression in individual or group deviation, the key words are "breakdown," "uprooting," or "anomie"; violent rebellion is simply one expression of that disorganization; in the longer run, new forms of association and of control grow up and reintegrate vagrant individuals and flagrant motives.

2. The improvements in communication, the extensions of political activity, the "mobilization" which accompany industrial growth inevitably create and disseminate aspirations or ideologies faster than the industrial and political apparatus can satisfy them, so the gap between expectation and reality widens catastrophically, especially at the moments of rapid reversal of political and economic advances; hence revolutions of rising expectations, of frustration, of disappointed hopes; advanced industrialization, however, eventually raises productivity enough to close the gap, enough to create a calm and sated public.

When applied to the contemporary world, either one of these general statements is plausible, although neither one has yet appeared in a sufficiently sophisticated form to account for the enormous range of collective violence — Biafra, Vietnam, Bolivia, Watts — now going on in the world.

For a number of reasons the students of collective violence are turning increasingly toward the study of the past. We can expect them to apply the same quantitative, cross-sectional procedures to historical materials that they have used with contemporary observation. But others, more deeply concerned with the whole process of political and economic change, will find themselves drawn into studying long-range transformations in economic activity and political participation very closely. In short, they will move into historical work, but with unconventional questions and techniques.

In history, all will not go well for contemporary theories of protest. The case of France, for example, raises some doubts about the tightness of the connection between rapid industrialization and collective violence, since the country's periods of especially fast growth were also periods of relative calm. It also suggests some more complex ways of viewing the relationship of collective violence to large-scale change. Over the last few centuries the predominant forms of collective violence had a political character and a political impact which neither of the major theories linking protest to large-scale change quite captures. Let me sketch an alternative line of theorizing which connects collective violence more directly to the political process.

Collective violence is especially likely to occur when and where new groups are acquiring membership in the political community or old groups are losing it.

This idea rests on an interest-group conception of political life.[8] The main elements of that conception are:

1. Every polity consists of a limited number of identifiable groups with known but shifting relations to one another. Collectively they control the principal organized means of coercion within a society.

2. Those groups — the "members" of the polity — do not include all identifiable groups within a society and need not include all persons within the society. For example, a Muslim longshoreman may belong to a political bloc in Pakistan by virtue of being a Muslim but not by virtue of being a longshoreman. Later, longshoremen may acquire membership in the polity — "political identity" — qua longshoremen, thus giving Muslim longshoremen two modes of participation in Pakistani politics.

3. Every polity establishes tests of membership. All polities include among such tests the ability to mobilize or coerce significant numbers of people.

4. Within the polity, members constantly test one another in partial ways; repeated failures of partial tests lead to fuller tests and/or to exclusion from the polity.

5. Membership in the polity gives important advantages to a group; exclusion is costly.

6. Members of the polity resist the entry of new members and use their control over the organized means of coercion to do so.

7. Groups acquiring the means of membership in the polity define their demands or aspirations as rights which ought to be recognized or extended to them.

8. Groups losing the means of membership in the polity define their demands or aspirations as rights or privileges which they should retain.

9. The entry of a new group into the polity tends to produce collective violence because: a) the existing members resist with the coercive means under their control; b) the aspiring members make or reinforce their claims to membership by the use of violence; c) each one defines the action of the other as illegitimate and as thus requiring and justifying extraordinary means of coercion.

10. The departure of a member from the polity also tends to produce collective violence because: a) among the fuller tests applied by other existing members are applications of violent coercion; b) the departing members state their claims to continued membership by the use of violence; c) again, each party defines the action of the other as illegitimate and as thus requiring and justifying extraordinary means of coercion.

11. Peaks of collective violence therefore occur when multiple entries into the polity and exits from it go on simultaneously.

12. The incorporation of smaller polities into some larger unit and the disintegration of a polity into smaller units both produce effects similar to the simultaneous entries and exits of several groups into the same polity, because they both shift the loci of important political identities. Powerful family-based factions in autonomous Italian cities, for example, lost their political identities as the cities merged into states. National party membership becomes less relevant to the struggle for power as a country like Nigeria breaks into linguistic or regional units.

13. Each entry into a polity and each exit from it redefines the criteria of membership in a sense favorable to the characteristics of the new set of members.

14. The structural conditions favoring multiple entries or exits therefore vary from society to society and period to period. In general, however, they include rapid changes in the means of political communication, in the groups defined by economic activity and in the society's coercive apparatus.

15. Every society also produces a significant amount of nonpolitical violence, which can for the short run of any particular society be treated as constant. However, long changes and international variations in the "culture of violence" — in the ways in which aggression is acted out and violence institutionalized — do produce important differences among societies in the level of collective violence. Furthermore, this nonpolitical culture of violence affects the form taken by political violence.

16. The mutual testing on the part of members also produces violence continuously, even when no exits or entries are occurring. Still, "testing violence" grows especially frequent around the entries and exits of members of the polity.

I cannot, of course, offer these abstract statements as a verified set of generalizations. Even leaving aside a number of ambiguities in concepts like "polity" or "culture of violence," the argument presented here suffers from the difficulty of specifying entries into the polity or exits from it independently of the conflicts which, by the hypothesis, they produce. Nevertheless, this argument points to a possible alternative to dissolution-protest or expectation-achievement theories, an alternative which takes fuller account of the political process itself as a shaper of protest.

If the line of argument has something to it, each society has a characteristic, irreducible minimum level of collective violence, but collective violence becomes particularly widespread when numerous groups are acquiring or losing political identities. These acquisitions and losses of political identity occur both when groups within the society are changing with respect to the criteria of membership laid down by the existing members of the polity and when the relevant polity itself is changing through an increase or decrease in the scale of political life.

I do not mean that when men burn tax rolls, heave rocks at policemen, or pummel their political enemies they usually do so coolly, with a calculating eye on the audience. The prevailing mood of collective violence in nineteenth-century France was more likely a blend of indignation and exhilaration. Yet men grow angry far more often than they rebel. Nor is it clear that the angrier they are, the more likely they are to rebel. My suggestion is that the situations of gaining and losing political identity produce angry rebels with extraordinary frequency. And collective violence establishes a claim to political identity, enough so that the mere threat of violence itself often starts the bargaining. It is not necessarily the sole claim, or even the essential one, but it is always an important one. An unrecognized entity like the Croix de Feu gains a place in national

political life through organized violence; a fading group of political participants like the *bouilleurs de cru* makes its demand to retain its identity
by mounting violent protests.

At the middle of the nineteenth century the basic conditions governing the acquisition or loss of political identity in France shifted rapidly.
The final crisis of a two-century process of centralization took place. The
great turning encouraged protest both from those who had their political
lives to gain through participation in a centralized nation-state and from
those whose very political identities its accomplishment would destroy.
Those political associations which had huddled underground until 1848
exemplify the first; workers in declining rural crafts illustrate the second.
To be sure, deep economic and demographic transformations were affecting the fates of these and other participants in mid-century protests: the
growth of a national market for agricultural products and cheap textiles,
the emergence of large-scale industrial production, the urbanization of
both industry and population. But instead of automatically and directly
generating protests where they struck hardest, those structural transformations stimulated collective violence principally where they affected the
structure and exercise of power.

The task of the remainder of this paper is not to sort out and confirm
this argument in all its particulars, but to show that it is not utterly
implausible.

In France the mid-century peak of violence was actually due to the
nearly simultaneous rise of two rather different kinds of collective violence: one backward-looking, local in scope, resistant to demands from
the center; the other forward-looking, broad in scope, taking the existence
of a central power as its premise. Tax rebellions, food riots, and machine-
breaking exemplify the first type. Violent strikes and demonstrations
belong to the second.

How should we label these types of protest? It obscures the point
slightly to call the first "prepolitical" and the second "political." They
were *both* political, in the sense that they expressed opposition to the
way power was being used and were seen by those in power as challenges
to the established order. Nonetheless, the second type did much more
regularly flow out of the activities of durably, even formally, organized
groups contending for power and did more frequently involve explicit
statements of allegiance to an articulated ideology or program.

Nor will it do to distinguish simply between "industrial" and "pre-
industrial" disturbances. That sort of labeling not only inserts an evolu-

tionary assumption into the basic definition, but also imputes a timeless, primitive character to the tax rebellion or the food riot.

To be sure, the earlier nineteenth century *did* see some collective violence in ancient forms — destructive panics in Poitou, brawls of rival groups in compaignons in Bordeaux, vendettas and mass banditry in Corsica, religious warfare in Albi and Nîmes.[9] These forms of violence better deserve the term "pre-industrial." But they were rare. They were far outnumbered by the food riots, tax rebellions, machine-breaking, and rural trespassing of the time. They resembled those characteristic disturbances in being local in scope, simple in structure, and largely rural in location. They differed in having virtually no political content and only a tenuous connection with the great changes sweeping over French society.

For these reasons we would do better to distinguish three types of collective violence: "primitive," "reactionary," and "modern." In nineteenth-century France none of the three was the work of masses uprooted by industrialization, although "reactionary" food riots or tax rebellions attracted many men whose livelihood the growth of an urban, industrial, capitalist nation was destroying. None of the three was intrinsically larger or more destructive than the other, although the "modern" violent demonstration or strike occasionally mobilized masses of men inconceivable in the heyday of the informal political disturbance. Yet it is roughly accurate to think of the primitive political disturbance as a standard response to local tyrannies and communal rivalries, the reactionary political disturbance as a characteristic form of resistance to the emergence of a centralized nation-state, and the modern political disturbance as the centralized nation-state's ordinary expression.

With these distinctions in place I can state a bit more clearly the nature of the change which calls for explanation: during the nineteenth century primitive disturbances were rare and becoming rarer; there was no apparent order to their fluctuations. In terms of frequency of occurrence, reactionary disturbances were by far the predominant form of collective violence in France up to the middle of the century. They were especially common in years of revolution, even if we exclude the events directly connected with the transfer of power. They reached their nineteenth-century height in the years 1847 to 1851. After that, this whole class of collective violence virtually disappeared.

Modern disturbances had occurred before the nineteenth century. They had, indeed, played crucial parts in the Revolution and other early struggles for power. But, proportionately speaking, they were exceedingly rare until a slow growth after 1830 gave way to a great spurt with the Revolution of 1848. By the 1860's the modern forms of collective violence were overwhelmingly predominant. The questions are: Why did the transition occur? And why the mid-century peak for both the reactionary and the modern forms?

Like England in the first third of the century and Italy in the last decade of the century, the France of the nineteenth century's middle years produced an incessant stream of violent disturbances. The understandable tendency of the largest and most influential of these disturbances to monopolize historical attention makes them seem much rarer and more like drastic breaks with routine political life than they actually were. On the whole the makers of collective violence were solid little people with strong social attachments rather than unstable individuals cut loose by industrialization or urbanization; their violent protests grew out of other less dramatic forms of political activity.

In the earlier part of the century France's collective violence took five main forms, four of them frequent and widespread, the fifth rarer but acutely important. The common forms were the food riot, the attack on machines, violent resistance to government controls (especially taxation), and the devastation of fields or forest. The rarer type was the urban rebellion. The first four were "reactionary," the fifth more nearly modern.

It may be helpful to sketch one of them. Let us consider the food riot. On the surface the food riot appears to be impulsive, purely local, unpolitical, irrelevant to modernization. In fact it sums up the essential features of the reactionary political disturbance.

Men have complained about shortages and high prices of food since food has been in the market. But the distinctive pattern of behavior we know as the Western European food riot seems to have taken shape during the sixteenth and seventeenth centuries. It remained the most frequent form of collective violence in some parts of Europe at the end of the nineteenth century. More exactly, it took two shapes — one urban and one rural. In the cities, at times when the bread supply shrank and the price of bread rose, men, women, and children would gather, grumbling, outside the shops of bakers or grain merchants presumed to be profiteering or hoarding. Often they demanded food at what they considered a just price — bread at ten sous — and reviled the city officials for their inaction. Sometimes they beat up the merchant. More often they broke into the shop, seized the grain or bread, then sold it publicly at the proclaimed just price. Later (if the troops had not already intervened) they went home peacefully.

A report from Auch, in June 1832, ran as follows:

Troubles of a distressing nature broke out last week at many fairs and markets of the department of Gers. A little riot broke out at Mauzevin on the twenty-eighth of May; it was quickly put down by the energetic cooperation of the police and the National Guard. Last Friday, fair day at Fleurance, the evil intentions of a few people produced a sort of uprising in the course of which a number of grain merchants were manhandled. A few wagons loaded with grain were dumped and sacks of grain opened or cut. The police of Lectoure . . . being too few to subdue the agitators, it was necessary to call on the National Guard to restore order. There were four arrests at Fleurance.

Finally, the market at Auch on Saturday the second of June was troubled by insults and threats to certain grain merchants, who were weak enough to give in to that violence and turn over their grain at the price of 25 francs the hectoliter, instead of the 27 or 28 francs which was its true price . . .

The mayor of Auch published the following proclamation Sunday morning:

Considering the report submitted to him the second of this month by the *commissaire* of police, stating that the sales of grain which took place at the market of that date were the result of the threats and violence of a public blind to its own interest; considering that such conduct cannot be tolerated by an administration which intends to be strong as it intends to be just.

Declares as follows: In no respect will the price of bread announced in the list of 26 May be changed this week, since yesterday's price list was not established by legal means.[10]

The mayor himself concedes that the municipality has the duty to set the price; the issue is whether it is doing its work properly and whether unenlightened people have the right to take the law into their own hands.

This predominantly urban version of the food riot sometimes occurred in the country as well, with the added fillip that the accused hoarder was then frequently a rich landlord. Many of the presumably antifeudal attacks on chateaux during the so-called Peasant Revolt of 1789 actually occurred in the course of organized searches for grain by town dwellers.[11] More often, however, the rural food riot began with opposition to the shipment of grain out of the community and ended with the grain wagon

emptied and smashed, the merchant manhandled, and the grain sold —
once again publicly and at an agreed-upon just price.

Throughout the country and small towns of the Sarthe, for example,
rumors spread in September 1839 that people were being starved to feed
the English.[12] (In fact considerable shipments of grain *were* going to
England.) Other rumors said wheat shipped to Paris was being dumped
into the Seine. Near Mamers, a crowd of men, women, and children
seized an outbound wagon from an inn where the driver had stopped to
refresh himself and carted the grain to the local market. They took other
sacks of wheat from the storehouse of a local flour merchant, tearing
down and smashing his sign in the process. At nearby Connéré "the
people" stopped numerous grain wagons and sold their contents in the
public square at the current price.

These disturbances were more or less rural, but that does not mean the
people were peasants. Mamers and Connéré were centers of rural spinning and weaving. There is every likelihood that hungry, underemployed
weavers played a large part in the food riots there, as they had in 1789–
1793. In fact, anyone who is familiar with the map or rural textile activity
in the West during the 1830's will notice striking similarities with the
map of grain riots, not to mention the geography of counterrevolution
then and forty years before.[13] The large mass of workers in declining
rural industries surely took a larger role in the rural disturbances of the
1830's and 1840's than our usual casual labeling of these disturbances as
"peasant" suggests.

The food riot, then, had not only an established routine, but a fairly
fixed geography. During years of acute subsistence crisis, such as 1829 or
1846, riots broke out with great regularity in a semicircular band of departments to the west and south of Paris.[14] They were not France's poor-
est departments, or those most liable to crop failure. Instead, they were
the areas which had to feed Paris when the capital's usual suppliers
(especially the Beauce) suffered dearth. Indirectly or directly, local
merchants felt the urgent demands of Paris and found it profitable to
heed them. Thus they gave substance to the indignant complaint that
famines were the work of hoarders and profiteers.

The ordinary people who rioted were not simply acting out their
hunger; starvation is silent. Instead of gradually falling into disuse as the
French food supply improved during the early nineteenth century, the
food riot reached a great peak in 1846–1847, only to vanish during the
next ten years.[15] During each of the nineteenth-century crises up to that

point, the rioters were outraged by profiteering, angry that the local authorities had not met their traditional responsibility to assure a supply of justly priced bread, soured on a regime which let such things happen, at least vaguely aware that collusion of local merchants with outsiders had helped produce their plight. When repeated over and over, the humble food riot took on local and national political significance. Demands from the center, rather than purely local misery, provided the incentive to riot.

The indignant response to pressure from the center shows up in the other forms of collective violence as well. In the case of direct resistance to exactions by the central government, the point is obvious; the recurrent resistance of winegrowers to the imposition of the metric system in 1840 and the widespread attacks on the census takers of 1841 all challenged the central government's right to intervene in local life.

I expect that when the histories of the food riot and the tax rebellion have been carefully examined, they will turn out to be closely intertwined. Just as the food riot came as counterpoint to the growth of hungry cities, the tax rebellion grew to an important degree from the exactions of an avid, expanding state. The expansion of the state and the growth of cities depended on each other. Both forms of protest became more serious and widespread with economic crisis — not because they were reactions to hardship as such, but because in times of hardship the pressure from the center increased exactly as the means to satisfy that pressure diminished. Before their abrupt disappearance, both swelled to a large scale during the prosperous nineteenth century, instead of gradually dwindling as the exactions of city and state became easier to bear.

The tax rebellion — at least of the sort which was to last into the nineteenth century — appears to have come into its own in France early in the seventeenth century. According to Jean Meuvret, it was only during the seventeenth century that the principle of royal taxation for the ordinary operation of government, rather than the extraordinary costs of war, began to gain acceptance.[16] Some of the sharpest debate over the "crisis of the seventeenth century," indeed, centers on the place of tax rebellions in the larger political and economic transformations of the time.[17] The triangular disagreement among Boris Porchnev, Roland Mousnier and Robert Mandrou about popular rebellion before the Fronde has to do especially with the extent to which the numerous tax protests of 1615 to 1645 grew out of deep misery, expressed popular opposition to the royal power, or resulted from the manipulations of self-interested elites.[18] But all agree that attacks on tax collectors, bailiffs and the like were extraordinarily common and vigorous in the period, that in fact they became the standard form of rural rebellion, and that whatever their origins they constituted a direct and conscious challenge to the authority of the central power. Despite the famous slogan "vive le roy et sans gabelle" resistance to the tax collector was an act of political opposition.

That was still largely true in the eighteenth and nineteenth centuries. One sign of it was the tendency of tax rebellions to flourish immediately after the major French revolutions. August 1830, for example, produced attacks on tax collectors, toll gates, and fiscal records throughout France. Most of them resembled the little outbreak in St. Germain (Haute-Vienne) on the fourteenth of August, in which, after customs officials had stopped a wagoner to inspect his load of produce, a crowd of men, women, and children "armed with hoes and rocks" surrounded them, shouted complaints about the duty the officials were hoping to collect, and forcibly dragged away man, wagon, and produce.[19]

As trivial as this sort of action was in itself, its multiplication effectively blocked the flow of tax revenue from large sections of the French provinces after the July Revolution. As the *procureur général* of Riom declared in his report to the Minister of Justice on 25 August 1830:

The memorable events of the capital caught the enthusiasm of the population here as elsewhere; but the people, thinking that the revolution entailed the legal suppression of all the indirect taxes (that is, taxes on production, consumption, and trade, as opposed to wealth), rushed to all the toll gates of the city on the evening of Sunday, 1 August, and broke them to bits. The impossibility of punishing all those involved kept me from taking any judicial action, and in any case it was simply a moment of excitement and error which it was more prudent to let calm down by itself. I hoped that mature reflection would bring people back to a sounder way of seeing things. However, all collection of taxes has been suspended up to the present and the administration, held back by the anger of the people, has not dared to set up the toll gates again, nor to start collecting the *octroi* or the indirect taxes again. That state of affairs harms the national treasury, the city, and public order, since the law is no longer respected.

Last Sunday, the twenty-second, two employees of the *octroi* were rather violently manhandled; and during the night, a National Guard patrol was attacked by a number of persons, and almost disarmed.[20]

Elsewhere in France the attacks on revenue offices were so widespread and effective that the authorities began to talk in terms of a political conspiracy. Many towns in the hinterland of Montpellier saw crowds break into offices, smash the furniture, and burn the tax rolls. A mid-August report said that "some people went in turn to the places of the director and of the receivers of indirect taxes in Béziers, forced their way into the offices, pillaged all the papers belonging to the administration and afterwards made bonfires of them in a number of public squares." [21] These scenes were reminiscent of 1789 and premonitory of 1848. They were like those other revolutionary disturbances in combining essentially personal or local resentments with a threat to the regime.

While tax rebellions sprouted in the shadows of revolution, they could also grow in the glare of political order. During the early nineteenth century the central government's attempts to establish new taxes, reestablish old ones, or simply to rearrange their administration quite regularly stirred collective violence. An outbreak at Libourne in 1833 illustrates the usual run of such events.

At the request of the city council of Libourne, two officials of the administration of indirect taxes came to the city last Saturday to help reestablish the beverage tax . . . these first attempts did not come off very well; the population gathered and displayed energetic opposition to the measures they proposed to take. Stones were thrown at the officials, who went away and pretended to desist at the request of the local authorities, who feared that the leisure of the next day (Sunday) would provide an opportunity for serious trouble.

Yesterday, Monday, they wanted to try again; but this time the opposition of the local residents was more threatening. In order to disperse the crowds, the National Guard was called three times, but in vain. The authorities sounded the general alarm, but the National Guard remained inactive. Only a few out of a force of 700 to 800 men actually turned out. Then the 14th cavalry regiment was given the order to mount, which it did at once. That order was the signal for grave disorders; stones were thrown at the troops and against the authorities; a number of soldiers were wounded. The cavalry charged a few times, but no one in the crowd was hurt.[22]

Under military guard the tax officials inventoried the drink on hand, but even then they found many cafés locked up and their owners uncooperative. Later the prefect of Gironde officially disbanded the unreliable National Guard.

The little rebellion of Libourne was an isolated event. Even outside of major revolutions, however, tax rebellions commonly traveled in families. Like food riots, they had their own favorite territories. In nineteenth-century France the southwest quadrant in general and the Massif Central in particular repeatedly threw up attacks on revenue agents. Gabriel Ardant has an interesting interpretation of this geographic concentration: "The typical areas for fiscal revolts were evidently those parts of the Massif Central which tended to live in a closed economy. The tax authorities forcefully told them to enter the world of the market but the government did not give them the means to do so, with the result that for these provinces any exaction, however small, was painful." [23] In other words, when the central government demanded cash payments from villages only slightly engaged in a cash economy, it forced them into the market; this in itself caused a good deal of distress, but when there was no market for whatever surplus the village might be able to accumulate, that was more distressing still. It led, in fact, to anger and revolt.

Tax revolts also grouped together in time, largely because the changes in national policy which commonly incited them affected many areas at more or less the same time. Over the period we are considering, the most emphatic burst of tax rebellions outside of a major revolution was the resistance to the special census of 1841. The new Minister of Finance, Georges Humann, planned the survey as a means of reforming the creaky, inequitable tax system inherited from the eighteenth century. However just his intention, Humann stirred up the dissident, secret political associations which were slowly coming to life throughout the provinces at the same time as he stumbled over the older and wider resistance to all the central government's attempts to taxation. As Félix Ponteil, the principal historian of the movement, puts it:

The opposition parties made a considerable effort during the months of July, August and September. All regions were not equally contaminated. According to the documents we have been able to consult, the Southwest, the Center and the North were particularly involved in the melee. The trouble crystallized around four main points, Toulouse, Bordeaux, Clermont and Lille. These four names symbolize the most violent and feverish thrust of the parties hostile to the government.[24]

His account gives pride of place to the section of France southwest of Clermont-Ferrand, which was, of course, the usual breeding ground for tax rebellion. Whatever success the opposition parties may have had in the region, they were building on a durable tendency of its people to resist the demands of the center. Ponteil himself speaks of the "federalism latent deep in the provinces." And he continues: "The struggle against the census was the form that the opposition of distant communes to the decisions of the central power took under Louis Philippe. The census was only the precipitant." [25]

As with the food riot, the tax rebellion broke out in one last spectacular burst shortly before practically disappearing from the French countryside. The "Forty-Five Centime Revolt" of 1848 responded, like the 1841 tax riots, to changes in direct taxes: imposts on property. That was unusual; the indirect taxes usually bore the brunt of popular rebellion. But the Forty-Five Centimes was only the most spectacular feature of widespread resistance to taxes after the Revolution of 1848. Rémi Gossez has argued that "by particularly touching the winegrowers, the extraordinary tax crystallized discontent which had been created mainly by indirect taxation." "The latter," he continues, "in the form of *octroi* or of liquor tax, struck especially at a winegrowing industry made acutely sensitive to the least exaction in cash . . ." [26] Later he adds that the poor mountaineers of France joined the protest as well.

Two features of Gossez's detailed analysis ought to attract our attention. First, regardless of the economic encitements to rebellion, the Forty-Five Centime Revolt frequently took on the tone of political opposition. The concerted (although relatively peaceful) resistance to the tax at the frontier of Gers and Hautes-Pyrénées produced its first confrontation with the authorities at Malabat (Gers), in April, when a retired soldier first refused to pay the surtax, then warned the collector not to try to get it from anyone else, and finally "at the market of Miélan publicly exhorted the inhabitants of city and country not to pay. He said that the taxes had been ordered without the participation of the legislature, and that no one should pay until they had been duly passed." [27] The resistance grew, and eventually led, on the sixth of June, to a faceoff between a subprefect, a judge, three brigades of gendarmes and a crowd armed with "forks, hoes, scythes, sabers, daggers, bayonettes on poles, halberds, rods and clubs."

According to the *procureur général*: "They made mad and menacing remarks about the government, the people and the workers of Paris. 'Death! A thousand times Death!' they cried. 'Death rather than pay the 45 centimes. We are overwhelmed by misery. We have no goods, or we can't sell what we have.'" And the movement spread so rapidly through the region that by the eleventh of June the lieutenant of gendarmes was writing to his superior: "Resistance is organizing on a large scale. More than 100 communes of the Gers, Hautes-Pyrénées and Basses-Pyrénées have joined together. At the first sound of the tocsin they are all supposed to go wherever the agents of the government appear. Emissaries are on the move continuously to recruit followers, and it seems that their recruitment is easy. Anyway, those who don't sign up of their own free will are threatened with death or burning."

The massive rebellion never occurred. Yet it should be clear that in the revolutionary year of 1848 the numerous incidents of resistance to taxation knotted strands of political opposition and economic discontent into a knout threatening the government itself. As Gossez says, "In many parts of the country, when it came to open resistance, it had the character of popular opposition to the National Assembly . . ." [28]

Gossez's analysis marks out one other striking feature of the revolt: its geographic distribution. For the tax rebellions of 1848 clustered very heavily in the triangle Bordeaux-Toulouse-Clermont — the area which had so regularly produced furious assaults on the agents of the central government. In short, despite their hints of increasing political organization and awareness, these last large revolts against taxation belonged, in form and locale, to the reactionary tradition of their predecessors.

This reactionary character, combining local grievances with resistance to changes promoted from the center and affecting the entire nation, also appeared in the other ordinary disturbances of the time. The innumerable incidents in which country people broke down fences and swarmed over fields or forests formerly used in common directly pitted the rural poor against the rural rich, but the incidents also expressed local resentment against a national forest code favoring private appropriation of public property and against the officials who enforced such a code. Even the men who smashed newly installed machines and sacked newly built factories in Lodève or Elbeuf sometimes shouted political slogans as they swung their clubs. [29]

Despite their sharp differences in other respects, the predominant forms of collective violence during the first half of the century embodied, to an important degree, angry reactions to the growth of a centralized nation-state organized around free markets, factory production, and capitalistic property. The men who made the collective protests came largely from established classes being squeezed out by the big change. As forging, spinning, and weaving concentrated in industrial cities, a vast number of artisans remained, workless, in the old towns and the deindustrializing countryside. At this very time land and property rights were becoming increasingly concentrated. Thus small landholders and tenants of many regions came to feel their livelihoods threatened. Firmly embedded in local life, they were not the uprooted, atomized masses that theorists of modernization have taught us to look for. But it would not be too inaccurate to sum up their actions as negative responses to modernization.

The rarer urban rebellions of the time do not fall into place so neatly. They were too various. Nevertheless, several important lessons emerge from recent studies of their character.[30] The rebellions, large and small, continued and extended peaceful political action in the cities; workers' rebellions in Paris or Lyon grew directly from a matrix of strikes, demonstrations, and nonviolent protests. Violence and nonviolence complemented each other. The largest, and politically most effective, rebellions brought out an alliance of bourgeois (as typified by the National Guard) and workers (as typified by the joiners, shoemakers, and stonemasons of 1830). In any case the most reliable recruits to rebellion were the established, ordinary craftsmen and shopkeepers of the city. The barricades sprang up in their own streets and were manned by men who worked, drank, and argued politics together every day.

The large urban disturbances often compounded several different types of collective violence while retaining the essential features of each of them. In Auxerre, in mid-October 1830, a crowd including a considerable number of winegrowers formed outside the gates of the city and tried to keep workers from going out to their jobs.[31] They hooted the mayor and the National Guard and forced them back to the city hall. Several hundred persons then sounded the tocsin, marched on the market, and sold off the grain supply at 8 francs instead of the prevailing price of 11. After the sale the crowd rushed to the home of a local grain merchant, broke in, and sold *his* stock publicly. The National Guard of Auxerre and reinforcements from nearby towns finally put down the rioters, but within the next few days smaller groups broke into more houses, smashed toll gates, and destroyed tax rolls. The authorities restored order after three days, making twenty-one arrests in the process. Here we see a conjunction between the food riot and the tax rebellion, with little obvious political *content*, but important local political *impact*.

But the character of urban rebellion was changing in the decades before 1848. In the insurrections of Lyon and Paris in 1831, 1832, and 1834, there were increasing signs of durable, formal, politically active working-class organization. Students, printers, turners, and other urban, politically active groups began to transform such ancient institutions as the *charivari* into true political demonstrations. In 1839 the Insurrection of the Seasons saw a political association deliberately, if unsuccessfully, organize a popular rebellion. During the same period, in Lille, Lyon, Saint-Etiénne, and Paris, the violent strike began to take on the prominence it was to have through the last half of the century. Under the July Monarchy the forms of collective violence which were later to predominate throughout France were already taking shape in the largest industrial centers.

The new forms displaced the old with extraordinary speed. In 1845 the old forms of collective violence ruled almost everywhere. Ten years later they had virtually disappeared. And during those ten years, rather than petering out, the old forms broke out in one last furious burst before subsiding.

What happened from 1845 to 1855? Politically, of course, France went from monarchy to republic to empire through a revolution, several insurrections, and a coup d'état. Economically, it experienced a crisis, a depression, and a great spurt of growth. Demographically, it felt a distinct quickening of the movement of people to the cities and a sharp drop in the birthrate. Everything happened at once.

The year 1845 was calm. The year 1846 started the cascade of food riots which rushed over the country in 1847. The year 1848 brought not only a revolution and a series of urban insurrections directly linked to it, but also a farrago of provincial disturbances: more food riots, anti-Semitic attacks in Alsace, panics in the Vendée, forest invasions in the Southwest, machine-smashing and attacks on the railroads through much of France, workers' protests in Marseille, Lille, Lyon and elsewhere, election disorders in numerous small towns, and the resistance to the 45-centime surtax on property. The years 1849 and 1850 were like 1848, but much less turbulent. Very little happened in 1851 until the December coup d'état, which set off an enormous burst of rebellions in city and country alike. After Napoleon III had put down the rebellions and his political opposition through a massive program of arrests and police control, the years 1852–1855 produced nothing but a last (and greatly attenuated) scattering of food riots in the traditional departments during 1853 and 1854, a few violent strikes, and an abortive workers' insurrection in Angers. By that time the old-style disturbances had virtually expired.

The rest of the Second Empire saw very little collective violence of any kind. But when violence revived at the end of the 1860's, its character had greatly changed. The Paris Commune of 1871, to be sure, explicitly operated on an anticentralist program and implicitly incorporated a reaction against the scale of the modern industrial state. But it occurred at a time when the central authority had virtually collapsed under the pummeling of the Germans, and the rest of France had in a sense seceded from Paris. From that point on, with few lapses, the modern forms of disturbance predominated in France.

Let us look more closely at the two most massive outbursts of violence during the pivotal decade: the June days of 1848 and the resistance to the coup d'état of 1851. The June days matter precisely because they have gained the reputation of marking a great shift in France's revolutionary style, the resistance to the coup d'état because it has so consistently been taken as evidence of the weakness of the republican and revolutionary forces outside of Paris.

The June days brought a moderate but significant shift in the kinds of people taking part in urban rebellion and an equally significant shift in the organization of rebellion. Unfortunately, no one has so far uncovered the crucial documents which could establish the degree of overlap between the membership of the National Workshops established to contain the Parisian unemployed and the actual participants in the June days. The government compiled splendid dossiers on the 11,000-odd persons charged with joining the insurrection, and they are available; the missing information once existed, and may still exist, in censuses and rollbooks of the National Workshops. As long as it is missing, the exact place in the June days of the National Workshops will no doubt remain hotly disputed.

Still, no one denies that thousands of men from the workshops took part in the titanic rebellion, or that a series of mass meetings and demonstrations largely manned by workshops' members led directly to the first outbreaks of violence. To a considerable degree the organization of the workshops continued into the insurrection; one of the first barricades to go up bore the banner "Ateliers Nationaux, 4e Arrondissement, 5e Section." [32] A police report of 23 June describes "A column of 1,500 to 2,000 workers from the National Workshops, banner flying, marching across Paris to shouts "Vive Barbès! Vive Louis Blanc! A bàs l'assemblée! Allons à la Chambre!" [33]

Who were the rebels? In sheer numbers the largest contingents were the 2,000-plus construction workers and the more than 1,000 men from metal-working industries, mainly mechanics and locksmiths.[34] In proportion to their place in the Parisian labor force of the time, the industries overrepresented in the June days were metals, construction, foods, leather, and printing, while textiles, clerical occupations and the innumerable knickknack industries of Paris contributed far less than their share. The quintessential cast of characters for the reenactment of the June days would feature a mason born in the Creuse rooming near the Hotel de Ville, a railroad workers from Reims living in La Chapelle, a turner from Lille (or maybe Brussels) settled in Quinze-Vingts, a laborer from Savoy living in la Villette, and a native Parisian printer lodged near the Sorbonne. The cast is a perfect combination of the old trades and the new.

The appearance of groups of workers new to urban rebellion, the apparently large role of political preparation in the National Workshops, the carrying over the organization of the workshops into the rebellion, and the preliminary sequence of relatively disciplined mass demonstrations all make the June days a considerable break with previous disturbances. In the short interval after the February Revolution, the coming of universal suffrage, the freeing of the press, the relaxation of restrictions on assembly, the proliferation of political clubs, the activity of workers' corporations, and the formation of the National Workshops provided the workers with an accelerated political education. Surely this rapid mobilization helped transform the character of collective violence.

If the June days somehow crystallized the newer type of rebellion, the insurrection of 1851 marked the disintegration of the old. The resistance to the coup d'état has been variously labeled a plot, a jacquerie, and a fiasco. In the more or less official history of the period, Charles Pouthas dismissed the insurrection with a sneer: "The resistance by force was even more pathetic than the resistance by legal means." [35] To Marx, it offered a classic illustration of the incoherence of the peasantry and the immaturity of the proletariat.

Yet it was a huge rebellion.[36] More than 100,000 men rose against the government. More than 500 died in the attempt. Armies of thousands went out to quell insurrections through large sections of France. In the aftermath, more than 26,000 people were charged and 20,000 convicted of participation in the rebellion. Though not so bloody as the June days or the Commune, the insurrection of 1851 ranks, by scale and geographic spread, among the great rebellions of the nineteenth century. Only the fact of its failure relegated it to obscurity.

In some places the rebellion even succeeded, at least in the short run. Some 6,000 rebels overran Digne on December 7, burned the tax rolls, established a governing Resistance Committee, and defeated the troops sent to quell them.[37] In la Suze (Sarthe), 300 workers seized the town hall, captured the local officials, and threw up barricades for defense. Although Napoleon's men quickly put the rebellion down in Paris, they had to kill some 400 rebels, and then make 3,000 arrests.

The local insurrections took two basic forms, both of them involving an interesting interaction of city and country. In the first, a group of republicans seized control of a regional capital or market center, then appealed to their country cousins for aid. In Marmande 800 insurgents set up a provisional government and then broadcast a poorly heeded call for men from the hinterland to join them. In Clamécy the *flotteurs de bois* and other urban workers took the first steps toward the seizure of power and were successful in attracting thousands of rural supporters to the city, where urban and rural rebels alike faced a deathly fusillade.

The second pattern consisted of the descent on the capital or trading center of crowds from the surrounding rural communes. Around 2,000 countrymen swarmed into Crest and attempted to seize control of the town, only to be driven out with 50 casualties. Another 5,000 occupied Aups (Var) and fought a pitched battle in which 80 or 90 died. Some 800 republicans from the area around Montelimar (Drôme) tried to take the city on the 7th, but 100 men of the line were able to turn them back. In appearance the insurrection was another Vendée — only a Vendée more futile than the original.

In actuality the insurrection was not nearly so agrarian as our standard histories say. True, some of the departments most heavily involved — Basses-Alpes, Var, Vaucluse — were largely agricultural and had produced frequent forest disorders or rural tax protests over the previous few years.[38] True, 7,000 of the 26,000 persons charged with taking part in the insurrection were agricultural workers. But another 7,000 came from the much smaller populations of merchants and free professionals. Considering their numbers in the general French population of 1851, the occupational groups contributing more than their share to the insurrection were the professions, commerce, metals, and "industries related to letters" — printing, journalism, and allied occupations. Proportionately speaking, agriculture contributed least. Furthermore, the two patterns of insurrection just described have a crucial common property: in both cases the initial call to action usually came from republican activists in the city and went to allies they had been recruiting in the countryside over the years of the Second Republic. The main difference was whether the urban insurgents were able to take over the city before the countrymen arrived.

The great rebellion of 1851 marked a transition in rural rebellion in something like the same way that the June days displayed the transition in urban rebellion. In Paris and dozens of smaller cities throughout France, the well-organized republican activists made a vigorous vain effort to prevent the coup. Being highly visible, they bore the brunt of the Napoleonic repression. Out in such departments as Pyrénées-Orientales and Basses-Alpes, thousands of peasants and rural craftsmen spilled out their anger in equally vain attacks on their local centers of government. The attacks were reminiscent of the tax riots of previous years, but they established a higher level of organization and a greater degree of rural-urban coordination than ever before. Then the countrymen were silent.

What happened? It is not just that France calmed down, although the country did subside into peace for close to twenty years. More happened than that. When collective violence returned at the end of the Empire, it was more highly organized, more regularly based on associations, more explicitly in pursuit or defense of a political program. It was modern. Rural rebellions eventually reappeared, but mainly in modern dress: as organized demonstrations or articulated criticisms of government policy. The old forms had ignored or resisted the influence of the center. The new forms took that influence for granted, but acted to change its character.

During the years 1845 to 1855 the center completed its two-century drive for control. The work of the revolution of 1789 was finished. In one respect at least, Louis Napoleon was his uncle's true heir.

Quickly the characteristic violent responses to demands from the center faded away. Only rarely thereafter did they reappear — when some neglected part of the work of centralization was taken up again (as in the inventories of church properties in the early 1900's) or when the central power itself temporarily broke down (as in the aftermath of the German victories of 1870). At the point of the great mid-century transition, violence shifted to struggles for control of the center. "If Paris, as a result of political centralization, rules France," said Marx at the time, "the workers, in moments of revolutionary earthquakes, rule Paris." [39] And from that point on, even the struggles in Nantes or Montpellier were ultimately struggles for control of Paris. Tocqueville placed the culminating moment of France's centralization in 1789; in fact, it occurred during his own time.

Other people have noticed how greatly the pattern of conflict changed

at mid-century. Marx came to see the June days as the first great proletarian insurrection, even if Louis Napoleon's seizure of power was proof
to him of France's unreadiness for proletarian revolution. (In a sense, the
Marx of before 1848, with his concern for alienation, his nostalgia for
primitive communism, and his admiration of American experiments in
communal living, was the spokesman of the older reaction against modernization, just as the post-1848 Marx was the prophet of the new forms
of collective violence.) Engels characteristically stressed the technological
side of the argument, concluding that government access to modern
rifles and railroads for troop movements had hopelessly outmoded the
rebellion of knots of workers behind urban barricades, and coming close
to an assertion which William Langer was to make a century later —
that only the slackness of the public authorities and the wavering of the
troops made the revolutions of 1848 possible anywhere in Europe.[40]

More recently, Albert Soboul has portrayed the provincial uprisings of
1848 through 1851 as the last protest of the independent peasantry against
the encroachments of capitalism.[41] And George Rudé has written that
"The Second Empire of Napoleon III saw another forward leap in industrial growth, in workers' organization, and in the relations between capital
and labor; and soon such manifestations as *taxation populaire* and "Luddite" attacks on machinery, which still survived in 1848, would be almost
as dead as the proverbial dodo." [42]

All of these statements have considerable truth to them. Other analyses
identify still further factors that a complete account of changes in the
character of collective violence must take into consideration: the new
prosperity which finally reduced the number of people vulnerable to subsistence crises; the rapid improvements in communications and transport
which facilitated the movement of grain, goods, people, troops, and
political ideas; and the increasing efficiency of the technology of repression.[43]

Yet the existing analyses just miss some crucial features of the mid-
century transition. The provincial disturbances of 1848 through 1851
brought out not only the dying peasantry, but also large numbers of
people — semirural semi-industrial workers whom the deindustrialization
of the countryside was driving into oblivion. After the failure of their
last great protests, they gave up. From that point on, the surplus rural
population turned to migration toward the big cities. More so than we
have realized, the midcentury provincial disturbances recorded the final
outraged cries of whole classes whom the growth of a centralized, capital-

istic, industrial nation-state was stripping of political identity and means of existence. Those who held on longer, like the Poujadist *petits gens* of the 1950's, mounted their petty protests later. But most of them had voiced their rage and then expired by 1855.

At the same time, their very classes created by the growth of a centralized, capitalistic, industrial nation-state were acquiring political identity by means of collective violence, if not by that means alone. Like their basic conditions of existence, their forms of violence were shaped by their willy-nilly implication in such a nation-state. Hence the fundamental traits of the new forms of collective violence: complexity and durability of organization, growth from formal associations, crystallization around explicit programs and articulated ideologies.

If this analysis is correct, it means that neither arguments about the gap between expectation and achievement nor notions of sequences running from change to breakdown to protest produce convincing accounts of the loci, participants, or forms of collective violence in industrializing countries. Yet it suggests that each of the ideas gets at one part of the reality. Each applies, in its way, to a different type of collective violence.

The expectation-achievement line catches some important features of what we have met as the modern forms of violence in France: their emergence from newly developing aspirations, their frequent ideological character, their recruitment of groups just acquiring political identities. The dissolution-protest argument, on the other hand, does some justice to the older forms, at least by suggesting that men become distressed when established guarantees of their social positions break down. Both lines of reasoning are excessively individualistic, underestimating the extent to which violent protests represent collective responses to collective experiences.

Although it is quite compatible with the idea that collective violence tends to peak early in the course of industrialization, the case of France also suggests some modifications to the conventional explanations of such a peak. If the sequence of events which occurred in nineteenth-century France were a frequent one, it would be more appropriate to speak of two merging peaks of protest, differing from each other in form, content, and personnel, but growing in response to the same crucial transition in the political and economic structure of the nation.

Even if it does have a wider application, to be sure, this analysis of the transformation of collective violence in France leaves unpleasantly unresolved some of the fundamental issues: To what extent were the mid-nineteenth-century protesters responding specifically to capitalism, or to industrial life, or to the influence of cities, or to another of the multiple changes which were occurring together? Can such major transformations in the shape of collective violence occur more than once in a nation's life? Is the crucial transition necessarily rapid and decisive? Must we think of the nineteenth-century transition as a continuation, or culmination, of the work of the great eighteenth-century revolution? Closer analysis of France's experience can bring us somewhat nearer to the answers to these questions, but international comparisons are obviously essential.

The case of France has one more contribution to make to the general discussion of protest in modernization: it illustrates the deeply political character of collective violence. I say "political" not only because violent incidents shook many French regimes, but also because they grew so regularly out of peaceful attempts to change local or national arrangements of power, because they so frequently expressed the moral indignation of ordinary people at what they considered to be violations of their rights and because the central government itself watched collective violence so intently and sought so jealously to maintain a monopoly on violent means of coercion. If so, the common sociological portrayal of collective violence as passionate irrationality misses its most striking features. Hannah Arendt's dictum that "Violence is dumb" does not apply to her principal case, France itself. There, collective violence found its tongue. Martin Luther King's phrase "Riots are the language of the unheard" comes closer to the truth.

With great regularity new political actors in France won their memberships in the national community through struggles which wreaked death and destruction, only to settle into peaceful ways so long as their memberships were unthreatened, while actors losing their identities likewise struggled indignantly and violently as they were forced out. Obviously urbanization and industrialization transform the basic divisions within societies and change the means different groups have of acquiring or maintaining political identities. Less obviously, but not less surely, urbanization, industrialization, and the emergence of a powerful state transform the very character — the form itself — of collective violence.

6. COLONIAL RHODE ISLAND
AND THE BEGINNINGS
OF THE LIBERAL RATIONALIZED STATE[1]

Sydney V. James

Colonial America, for some time prior to the American Revolution, had in practice (if not clearly in theory) adopted within the colony unit the variety of authority that Max Weber described under the ideal type of "legal" or "rational." [2] Accordingly, the American Revolution, unlike the French, did not have occasion to install or perfect this mode of authority by replacing prerevolutionary institutions on a massive scale. Moreover, the colonies had proceeded much more rapidly toward rationalization than had the mother country. Historians have paid little attention to this phenomenon, and I have investigated it only in a limited area which may have been atypical. Only after much more work on the situations elsewhere will it be possible to judge whether Rhode Island was a representative or eccentric case, but some speculations on this point may be in order.

I

Legally rationalized authority, accompanied by an appropriate rationale and social order, has become prevalent in the modern world. It has its key characteristic in the role of the central government, through which all agreements with foreign governments and all decisions about the use of coercive power must be made, whether the role is filled by a direct and substantive centralization or by a delegated distribution of powers and merely formal centralization. The central government, however constituted, has a monopoly of legislation and the use of force. It may make and unmake laws as changing circumstances suggest, with no more regard to tradition than expedience or sentiment may inspire. It operates through officials whose power is limited by law and formally conferred in a fashion that gives them an official capacity while leaving to them a private capacity in which office carries no legal privileges. The central government lays down the conditions under which all other institutions exist, if allowed to exist at all. Ordinarily, the machinery of government, and of other major institutions, has a bureaucratic nature.

The legally rationalized state may act in anything from a totalitarian to a liberal fashion. At the one end of the scale, individual and collective action is extensively prescribed by law, while voluntary association is all but forbidden. In the extreme case all institutions are treated as functions of the state. At the other end, the area of prescribed action is minimal, while nongovernmental institutions are of various sorts, some with legal rights and obligations specified in general laws, others entirely voluntary and self-governing, and only a few types declared illegitimate, such as political conspiracies or religious cults devoted to practices inimical to public safety. A wide range of action is defined as a private sphere, subject only to laws designed to prevent private actions from interfering with the liberty of those unwilling to be affected.

The United States has always had a legally rationalized government and social order of a sort near the liberal end of the spectrum. The situation has been taken very much for granted, and historians have rarely thought of mentioning it or inquiring how it came into existence. Indeed, when concerned with the basic pattern of authority, they have devoted inordinate attention to that feature which most impairs the clarity of legal rationalization, federalism, which they make the object of scrutiny and veneration for its own sake, as though it possessed some magical power to further the general welfare. They have also lavished great pains on individual institutions, looking for the origins of modern forms. One way or another, they have ignored the main features of legal rationalization.

Not so in the study of France, where legal rationalization figured so conspicuously in the Revolution as to defy historians to ignore it. Though the way was prepared for it by centuries of advancing centralization under the monarchy, there is no denying the magnitude of the final steps begun in 1789 which abolished private property in public office, put an end to the old forms of local government and courts and corporations, and introduced new institutions fully controlled by laws made in Paris.

Not surprisingly, an expert on the French Revolution, R. R. Palmer, looked for something similar in the American Revolution, when seeking to define a common democratic revolution. He described the overthrow of colonial governments as the abolition of power held by what might be called de facto privilege or inherited right, but historians of the American Revolution have thought this formula fit the facts rather badly and preferred to deliberate over other points he raised.[3] Palmer was wise in not claiming to have found a comprehensive legal rationalization: the American Revolution resisted centralization of authority in London, and, to the dismay of some of its French friends, supported a diminution of centralism in framing the organs of the United States on a federal pattern.[4]

The Revolutionary period, as Palmer conceded, was not one in which American institutions were much reshaped; rather, he insisted that a momentous change was made in their foundations by the adoption of popular sovereignty expressed in a constitutional convention as the basis of public authority.[5] Louis Hartz, by contrast, argued that America, lacking what he called feudalism, was the autogenous product of bourgeois values and so had only a trivial amount of incongruent institutional baggage to jettison in 1776 when "the bourgeois spirit of the nation [that] had for years been piling up a silent hostility to the rationale on which . . . [monarchy] rested" finally came out openly against the king.[6]

Hartz was not greatly concerned with institutional forms though his argument implied a supposition that from the outset they manifested "bourgeois" values in a peculiarly pure way. Thus, he suggested the puzzling view that men who knew only the social organization of seventeenth-century England or Holland proceeded to create a new one as soon as they had crossed the Atlantic Ocean, even though few had reformist aspirations and in most cases they had brought with them a set of instructions conceived and written in Europe. His argument requires the belief that "feudal" institutions had to be physically near, not just remembered or felt when exerting control from a distance, to influence the bourgeois spirit. Otherwise he could not defend the proposition that a bourgeois offshoot or "fragment culture" lacked the bourgeois class involvement in the dynamic antagonisms seen in Europe. It would be more plausible, perhaps more logical, to expect the emigrant bourgeois spirit to remain preoccupied with finding means to combat its traditional opponents, to create a social organization corrective of a "feudal" order, not heedless of it. Broadly speaking, such was the case. Americans disdained Puritan radicalism, available on import during the Civil War and Interregnum and only in the eighteenth century became fond of a version of Restoration liberalism that put it at the service of liberty, equality, and constitutionalism, rather than of privileged safety from royal prerogative.[7]

Hartz, then, left us with the mystery of a bourgeois spirit operating unconsciously, creating a social order without any awareness of its basic principles, until Tom Paine snapped it out of its trance in 1776. Palmer left us with the mystery of a great change without much tangible effect: the overthrow of de facto privileged elements in society and the installation of a new foundation for authority carried out by men who wanted to keep the old style of government with minimal change. The puzzles can be unraveled by resort to concepts which distinguish an Old Regime or corporative social order from a feudal one. Hartz considered and rejected this approach.[8] Palmer used it, only to arrive at the misleading equation of colonial legislatures of the eighteenth century with such things as the Estates General, under the general term "constituted bodies." However, one institution with only a de facto element of hereditary privilege does not make an Old Regime; especially not in this case, where even that much privilege is hard to find. Examination of seventeenth-century America though reveals any number of better cases. In the example to be examined here, moreover, a clear change set in at the end of the seventeenth century toward a different sort of social organization. Throughout English America by 1776 there were in the colony units the essentials of a legally rationalized use of authority, well established for a couple of generations, but not present at the founding. Hartz was right in describing the repudiation of monarchy as easy, wrong in explaining it by a total exemption from the past. Palmer was right in looking for the overthrow of an Old Regime, but looked at the wrong time period and so unduly magnified a small change while missing a great one.

Émile Lousse has pointed out several traits of the Old Regime in the sixteenth and seventeenth centuries that distinguished it from feudal society in ways that are pertinent to early America, provided that an appropriate selection be made from his concepts.[9] Where the feudal order had consisted of ties of personal dependency linking superior to inferior, the Old Regime at this time consisted of "corporative bodies" constructed of people having types of equality — shared functions or identical rights. Lousse perhaps gave too little attention to institutions that supervised people in different ranks, such as craft guilds, or which regulated unequal quantities of the same sort of privilege, as in joint-stock companies. He was principally concerned with the relations between a monarchy and other institutions within the realm. Although he pointed out that corporative bodies expressed and preserved inequalities in their special domains, he sought to differentiate the ways in which they did these things from the ways used in the Middle Ages. Whereas the feudal order emphasized the unclassified particular relationship, the Old Regime zealously classified people, organized them accordingly, and created representational devices within and between organizations. Means were invented to empower representatives to make decisions for their organizations, a practice that ran against the grain of medieval attitudes.

In the Old Regime all relationships between people — and between people and property or power — tended to be expressed institutionally. The extreme was never attained, of course, but people almost instinctively formed collectivities on the basis of shared rank, occupation, church duties, and so forth, and used them to explain and require good conduct in the social roles they embodied. Homiletic literature delighted in dissecting social duties role by role, including the various roles in the family, an institution often regarded as the basic unit in society.

The corporative bodies which so overshadowed individuals ranged from the orders of the realm and chartered corporations down to small groups with inherited rights and duties to control land or trade or religious observances or local government. They enjoyed rights that often included the use of coercive authority (even over outsiders), self-government, and admission of new members and exclusion of others. Their duties were generally to ensure the performance of a function such as government, education, or prayer, though some corporative bodies dropped their functions in favor of simple enjoyment of their rights. Only with great difficulty and overwhelming justification could rights and duties be taken away by a monarch; a king ordinarily had to reckon corporative bodies as permanent curbs on his discretion,[10] though Lousse points out that kings actually gained power initially by conferring privileges on collectivities which as a result became responsive to more royal demands than before.

In legal form corporative bodies frequently received their rights from a king, pope, or bishop. In fact a royal grant often confirmed the powers of an existing institution; and on the humbler levels of social action corporative entities looked only to tradition to justify their rights, as was true of English proprietors of common fields or secularized vestries or most manorial institutions. Lousse, being primarily concerned with monarchies and the institutions closest to them, stressed the importance of grants of privileges, which mattered most on what may be called the "high-life" level of Old Regime society. To frame concepts applicable to colonial America, it is preferable to dwell on the attributes of the "low-life" level, where usage developing through time, unregulated by sovereign power, mattered more. This distinction is worth bearing in mind because colonial Americans quite naturally drew first on the "low-life" practices with which they had been familiar in England (except as they used the forms of chartered trading companies), when they set up governmental and social institutions of their own across the ocean.

Shifting the point of view away from the monarchs also makes it easier to abstract some assumptions about institutions which went with the characteristic forms of the Old Regime. These attitudes, of course, were not held exclusively in postfeudal Europe; rather, they constituted a special case of Weber's ideal type of authority legitimized by tradition. They included the following:

1. Institutions had collective responsibilities to the prince and to society as a whole. They regulated and spoke for their members; they saw to the performance of a socially valuable function; some exerted power over outsiders.

2. Institutions made social relationships knowable — in the family, shop, church, fair, nation, or whatever.

3. The past was authoritative. Property — in power or land, economic monopoly or ceremonial acknowledgment — could be vindicated by proof of long enjoyment. Ideas also could gain validity by age: from proverbs to Scripture, antiquity or freedom from known human authorship gave authority to ideas and the specific phrases which expressed them. Novelty had to pose as restoring the old.

4. Institutions were "spiritually" real. A municipal corporation was an actuality, not just a device which served a purpose. It had powers and officers, perhaps like no other, which were as essential to its being in every detail as was carrying out its functions. Even the disappearance of the population did not impair the factuality of the borough of Old Sarum. In a different way churches were even more real: divine decree created a Church of Christ, while Scripture and tradition gave clues to its inner nature and rules. Christians had the duty to make the visible form of the church on earth conform as nearly as possible to the divinely created invisible corporation. In a similar way the family had an eternal pattern which automatically provided the members with their roles, united the living with former and future generations, and governed the extension

of kinship links beyond the nucleus of parents and children — all this, even though marriage had a strongly contractual quality.

5. Institutions benefited from contractual and quasi-constitutional statements of their privileges, duties, and regulations. A charter, a book of customs, or some such document, especially if signed by the members, proved an organization real and authoritative by specifying its rights, obligations, and procedures in detail. Form and function, in other words, were inseparable and together confirmed legitimacy.

The assembled traits of the Old Regime may conjure up a vision of a world operating with cumbersome and self-jamming machinery. Still, it was a world from which came such cherished American devices as checks and balances, judicial review, and the bicameral legislature. More important, the Old Regime pattern, not the feudal order or the rationalized legal order, was that from which English colonists derived their norms for society and government in the seventeenth century. It is hardly surprising, then, that they behaved accordingly. The case was clear in Rhode Island, where for twenty-seven years people organized their own affairs without a significant external direction, either from a charter or from a well-articulated set of ideas voiced by an authoritative group in the population, such as Puritan preachers provided in neighboring colonies.

II

No complete formation of an Old Regime took place. Initially, of course, there was no past to which the Rhode Islanders could be literally faithful. Between 1636 when Roger Williams fled Puritan justice and 1644 when Samuel Gorton was released as unfit to occupy even a jail in Boston, refugees from Massachusetts set up a few simple churches and four towns — Providence and Warwick on the mainland at the head of Narragansett Bay, Portsmouth and Newport on the island of Aquidneck in the mouth of the bay. Until 1663 they performed the remarkable feat of improvising a social order according to standards which supposed a past. This was not hard in ecclesiastical matters, where the past was thought of as omnipresent and the ultimate authority absolute, if tricky to understand; nor in the practical side of agricultural community affairs, where tradition showed the way. But finding the basis for authority in town government was hard; the consent of the householders or landowners, who seemed designated by nature to exercise control, was the best makeshift, but it did not satisfy everybody. Confidence in the reality of rights made land ownership, conveniently, seem an actuality independent of an enforcing government. The family was apparently regarded as a fact of nature and divine will, and so likewise independent of a civil community's sanction.[11]

When the spontaneous social solidarity of the early years evaporated, only land ownership seemed a sure foundation for collective social action. By 1657 or 1660, even before the royal charter of 1663, Rhode Islanders began to create on this basis a more elaborate panoply of institutions. They established new ones and revised existing ones along lines approaching the style of Old Regime Europe. The process continued vigorously until near the end of the seventeenth century, when it was slowed and then denatured by the beginnings of rationalization, which fundamentally transformed the outcome by about 1730. In both the upsurge and frustration of the corporative institutions, ambitious land speculators played conspicuous roles; the failure of the corporative techniques to serve speculative interests goes far to explain why legal rationalization was attractive and acceptable. In addition, however, problems of creating internal order, of protecting real and commercial property in ways conformable to English law, and — even more obviously — of safeguarding the colony from intrusions of royal power, all promoted the changes.

The governmental framework of the colony, superficially centralized and orderly (especially after the promulgation of the royal charter), was actually quite otherwise in the seventeenth century. The colony government proper was a corporation consisting of the officers and freemen, chartered first by a parliamentary commission and then by Charles II. As such it had defined powers and responsibilities to exert control within the province, but it was not accountable to the monarchy in any clear way. The first charter allowed the preexisting towns to erect a colony government to suit themselves. Under the second charter the basic officers were specified: the governor, deputy governor, and ten assistants or magistrates — all elected at large annually by the freemen; and deputies chosen by each town whenever the legislature was summoned.[12] Though the colony officials partly took control of the judiciary from the towns and passed some laws affecting internal affairs, for the most part they handled business outside the sphere of the towns — chiefly relations with other colonies. Significantly, the defense of the corporation's land claims proved to be the objective that most effectively gave reality to the colony as a whole and began to make it something more than a loose federation of towns.

The colony government was connected to town government in a few ways only. Colony officers were elected in town meetings, the governor commissioned justices of the peace and militia officers in most towns, and the colony relied on town officers to collect its taxes and enforce the judgments of its courts, though it had no means to compel these officers to carry out such duties. The towns appealed to the legislature occasionally for laws to clarify town powers.[13] But colonial legislation in practice did not foster as much uniformity as it seemed to be designed to create in town administration.

Town governments varied widely, having begun on their own in most cases. The legislature in March 1649 granted charters of incorporation to at least three of the original four, allowing them self-government by majority rule within wide limits.[14] These grants of powers were of dubious legality and were treated seriously in one town only.[15] When new towns were established under the royal charter, they were granted powers under equally vague terms, in one case "all rights, libertys, and privileges whatsoever unto a towne appertaininge." [16] Uniform practice prevailed to the extent of having town meetings which conducted most business, with town councils to serve as interim committees and probate courts. Assorted other officers were chosen at the elections, which were usually annual. Town business, such as keeping records of deeds and earmarks, improving roads, licensing taverns, keeping order, or seeing that fences were maintained, was carried on haphazardly and by and large remained independent of actions of the colony government. On a few occasions controversial town actions were brought before the colony's General Assembly, which made some efforts to settle the disputes. As a rule, though, towns behaved like autonomous corporative bodies.

Beyond governmental functions, towns created rights that individuals held, and in so doing classified and specified the standing of their inhabitants. In the beginning the possibilities were few — Providence, for example, merely divided the heads of households, who held political rights on equal terms, from all the rest. As the seventeenth century progressed, the categories increased to the four usual ones: men with full voting rights, men who could vote in town government but not on common land business, people with a right of settlement only, and people without a right of settlement, who might be expelled at any time. The distinction between the two kinds of voting rights never became very important; when men were formally admitted to freemanship, nothing was recorded to indicate whether or not they could vote on land distributions. Nevertheless, the arrangement of common land rights created its own set of classifications. Starting with only two categories in Providence, full and quarter rights conferred by town vote, purchase rights gradually detached from their origin and were bought, sold, and inherited without restriction. They were subdivided in all conceivable ways. So when a purchasers' organization emerged from the town meeting toward the end of the seventeenth century, it consisted of a constantly fluctuating group of men, women, children, and estates with unequal rights in precisely quantified inequality. The purchasers behaved in a corporative manner, choosing officers, adjudicating claims to rights, hearing disputes over land between members, assessing the members, assigning land to individual ownership and exercising the power to generate a valid title, and even establishing public roads.[17]

The change in town structure which eventuated in the emergence of a proprietors' organization included a significant alteration in the view of what gave the town its existence. At the outset the townsfolk had justified their collective actions by an unstable combination of compact theory and tacit reliance on the obvious fact of the community's actuality. Between 1657 and 1662 Providence went over to a view that traced the town's origins to the purchase of the land from the Narragansett Indians by Roger Williams.[18] Uncertainty of the terms of succession to the land rights stirred up trouble for many years, until one woman vituperated "that this towne was a Cauge of uncleane birds . . ."[19] The separation of purchasers' meetings from town meetings, though it engendered an elaborate corporate institution, at the same time deprived the town as a political unit of a foundation as an autonomous collectivity, and thus cleared the way for absorption of the town government into a legally rationalized system by leaving the town to handle business in which the freemen were considered equal parties and on which a superior legislative power could act.

While the disputes were going on, subdivisions of the original purchase were made for various reasons. The roster of those holding share rights was different in each part. With uncanny regularity the shareholders of each part of the whole or "Grand Purchase" organized themselves entirely on their own volition as separate entities, even when there was no practical need to do so. Nothing shows more clearly the effect of Old Regime attitudes.

The situation in Warwick and Newport was much the same as in Providence; about 1660 the town's political foundations were reinterpreted as a function of partnership in land rights, after which there occurred a proliferation of intricately defined rights and privileges, culminating in a separation of town from proprietors of the common lands some time before 1700, with the proprietors' organization later undergoing further subdivision. Of the original towns, only Portsmouth deviated in part from this pattern.

Beginning in 1657 a series of land syndicates, based in Newport, reached for the Pequot and Narragansett Indian lands believed to lie in the colony's jurisdiction. The land purchases were made independently of action by the colony government until an act of 1658 required prior approval by the General Assembly; even after that change there was no regulation of negotiations or the forms of deeds. The promoters, however, anticipated the need for backing from the central government against rival operators based in Boston or eastern Connecticut. The need quickly arose, and the promoters accordingly had no choice but to cooperate with the government's requirements. Since the Newport syndicates saw no need to obtain permission to organize or carry on the quasi-governmental operations that they planned, it is safe to conclude that the central authorities were content with the arrangement. The first of these syndicates, that which developed the island of Conanicut (later the township of Jamestown), in most respects set the pattern for the rest. Organized informally until it was ready to make its purchases from Indian claimants, it then adopted a slate of "Articles of Agreement" which in the estimation of the signers created a Company.[20] The articles included provisions for assessments, the choice of officers, and enforcement of the decisions of the seven-man executive committee, called the Trustees. The signers had shares defined in fractions from 1/20 to 1/900. The Trustees made the intended purchases between 1657 and 1661 and prepared to divide most of the acreage into individual plots for the shareholders. Delays ensued, but eventually dividends were made and a resident population gathered on Conanicut, by 1678 large enough to warrant creating a town government.[21] The central colony government obligingly set one up, whereupon the moribund Company entrusted its remaining rights to the town's protection.[22] A small adjoining island was to be held in common for pasturage, and a 260-acre tract on Conanicut was reserved for a future business district.[23] In the early eighteenth century the use of these common lands required a revival of the proprietors' organization, which predictably turned into two, one for each tract.

Four other syndicates developed land on the mainland to the west of

Newport. Two of them did even more than the Conanicut Company to guide a future town. Only one was set up by the colony government, the one which acquired its land from the colony rather than directly from the Indians.

Very little can be discovered about other seventeenth-century institutions, but available information shows that they were self-formed and autonomous to an even greater degree than the towns and land companies. Sawmills, gristmills, and ferries generally had their origins in grants of sites for such purposes, made by towns or land syndicates.[24] Once the property rights had been transferred, however, the grantors seldom had anything further to do with the enterprises, which became individual matters or the business of small collectivities intricately specified in articles of agreement (sometimes woven into deeds).[25] This type of arrangement reached a culmination of sorts when a ring of counterfeiters in Newport specified their respective rights, shares, and duties in articles of agreement stigned in 1729 and subsequently produced in court.[26]

Churches were even more autonomous, and by the latter part of the seventeenth century, even more concerned with classifying rights and formulating rules. Religious bodies were apt examples of Old Regime attitudes in operation, but as most Rhode Islanders then and later opposed ecclesiastical establishment, the churches may be left out of consideration almost entirely in discussing the rationalization of authority.

All things considered, seventeenth-century Rhode Island had very promising beginnings of an Old Regime social order. Institutional frameworks had come into being to define, preserve, and regulate many kinds of individual rights. Shared rights, generally in some form of joint ownership of land, spawned organizational expressions with hierarchical ranks and neatly quantified definitions of inequality of shares. For some people, most of the major aspects of life were institutionally regulated; for others, very few. There were only the beginnings of (or raw materials for) a system of orders and privileges, however. Much of the activity of forming collectivities was probably defensive — broadly, to achieve security in the enjoyment of property or social orders; narrowly, to achieve strength which the colony government could not always exert in rivalry over land promotion.

III

Yet a corporative social framework proved unable to create secure rights or maintain social order in Rhode Island. Its inadequacy was demonstrated most tellingly when the English monarchy attempted to exercise control over the province. In fact the organization of proprietors of common lands led to English interference rather than preventing it. The disputes between subdivisions of the Providence Grand Purchase were appealed to the king's Privy Council several times, after a snarl of litigation had resulted in no clear decision and the town of Providence persistently refused to carry out unpopular decisions rendered by colony courts or royal commissioners and the central government proved powerless to do so against the town's will.[27] The dispute became intertwined with one between a Boston-based syndicate and the Newport-based ones in rivalry over the lands of the Narragansett Indians. A royal commission to examine their conflicting claims arrived in 1683, disposed to review all the land rights in the colony and nullify them on technicalities.[28] In a panic, the colony government rushed agents to London and declared the royal commission a riotous assembly and ordered it to depart.[29] This, however, was to no avail. The monarchy proceeded the next year to instigate legal action against the charter of the colony and decided on its inclusion in the Dominion of New England, which was to embrace all the northern colonies.

The Dominion did not last long enough to change much in Rhode Island, but for twenty-five years after its overthrow in 1689 royal officers badgered the restored charter government with considerable effect. The colony successfully resisted the king's orders putting its militia under the command of the Governor of Massachusetts, but put the militia under its own regulation.[30] It fended off attacks on its legislative and judicial competence by a wholesale revision of statutes to bring their provisions and the procedures of the courts into rough conformity with English law.[31] It docilely provided information to the king's Board of Trade, dutifully acknowledged that its powers had been delegated by the crown, and submissively answered charges of befriending pirates, disregarding the Acts of Trade and Navigation, and various other improper proceedings.[32] The colony had lost its separate existence once and did not want to lose it permanently or even accept a royally appointed governor. But to preserve the charter government the Rhode Islanders had to operate it in ways that would render groundless the objections royal officials raised against it. Moreover, if local disputes were to be prevented from creating disorder and inviting English interference, the central government would have to gain power to regulate all other institutions.

It is easy to say in hindsight that legal rationalization was the policy to pursue, and that in fact it was pursued. Yet there is little evidence that it was embraced as a policy or that any man in the colony had thought it out. Immediately after the overthrow of the Dominion of New England, confusion prevailed for a few years; some towns frequently sent no deputies to the legislature, a couple even seemed disposed to join Connecticut. The situation by itself certainly did not foster enlargement of the central government's authority.

Yet a course of action begun in 1690 fundamentally revised the social order during the following thirty years. If any man may be credited with giving it coherence it was Samuel Cranston, who was annually elected governor from 1698 until his death in 1727. Cranston was not only chief executive, but ex officio presided over the upper house of the legislature and the colony's highest judicial tribunals; in addition he was the Moderator of the town of Newport and prime mover in a swarm of civic projects, and also the active leader in at least four major organizations of proprietors of common lands. In all these roles his actions conduced to the ultimate result of legal rationalization, and where he was not involved, as in the affairs of Portsmouth, Providence, and Warwick, the reordering was slowest.

The central government of the colony enlarged and modified its authority most obviously. In 1690 it introduced a new system for apportioning taxes among the towns and boldly decreed that town treasurers were henceforward ex officio deputies of the colony treasurer — thus beginning the process (if it could be enforced) of ending one vital part of town autonomy.[33] In the next few years the central government stepped into disputed town elections and boundaries, asserting a right to act as final arbiter in such matters at its own discretion, not — as before — only when disputes were appealed to it.[34]

These were but preliminaries to further legislation during the Cranston administration, which gradually made town government uniform under colony law and made the towns administrative arms of the central government. After 1698 towns were given rights, powers, and duties, for instance, to provide standard weights and measures and to regulate the building of dams and weirs on rivers.[35] Some town authority was abolished, as when in 1702 the central government took charge of all the ferries.[36] A particularly important step was taken when the legislature gave town councils the duty to prevent townsfolk from harboring strangers without permission. To carry out this responsibility the councils were authorized to instruct one of the other town officers to prosecute the disobedient; for the first time a town could be represented in court without a decision by the town meeting.[37] By 1719 the General Assembly had gone far toward integrating town government into a uniform system of administration, had changed the powers of old town officers and required the election of new ones. That year the legislature, perhaps unwittingly, endorsed the cumulative result of thirty years of change when it approved the first printing of the colony laws. As arranged by Governor Cranston, Richard Ward, the Recorder, or secretary, of the colony, and William Frye, the clerk of the Assembly, the text omitted many statutes on record and included many others, attributed to years between 1663 and 1685, which had never been passed.[38] Several of these misrepresented laws provided for new interconnections between the central government and the towns or proprietors of common lands, entirely in keeping with recent legislation, but so far out of harmony with the times when they were said to have been passed as to allude to officers that had not existed then. This benign fraud, though details of it were detected and repudiated by the colony's General Court of Trials, produced valuable reforms and hastened rationalization. By 1730 town governments were almost completely standardized and accepted unquestioningly the duties and regulations given them by the central government.

The new approach to the use of law and central government provided ways to bring under the desired amount of regulation two other kinds of institution that had previously been autonomous: charitable trusts and churches. In the case of the churches the colony acted only to head off a suspected drive for privileges on the part of the Church of England. Fearing that the Anglican church at Newport would claim that it had been established by a colony law of 1700 declaring English law in force in fields not covered by colony statute, the legislature declared in 1716 that support of the ministry for any religion was to be "by a free contribution, and no other ways." [39] The General Assembly thus strengthened the charter freedom of religious association and implicitly defined the churches as voluntary associations under no governmental regulation, but without legal standing.

Charitable trusts were harder to deal with. The problem was brought to light in 1718, when the trustees of the oldest one were accused of mismanagement. The First Baptist Church of Newport, which expected more money than it had received from the estate of its first pastor, Dr. John Clarke, located the culprit, one William Weeden, but could not by persuasion or church discipline induce him to mend his ways.[40] He regarded himself and his two cotrustees exempt from accountability to anybody. The panel of three trustees set up by Clarke's will was to be filled in perpetual succession by the two survivors replacing the one who died or resigned.[41] The Town Council of Newport, as probate court, claimed some right to supervise, but Weeden refused to recognize it.[42] The council then prevailed upon the General Assembly in June 1719 to pass a law giving town councils jurisdiction over charitable trusts and specifying measures to enforce routine accountability on the part of the trustees.[43] Weeden still resisted, and a legal battle ensued, during which the legislature had to substitute a less drastic but more enforceable law.[44] By February 1723 the council had vindicated its powers to compel restitution of money misused by trustees, and Weeden gave up. Thereafter the trustees ceased their nefarious practices and presented annual accounts to the town council. Implicitly, an area of individual freedom had been marked out under central control: the government stood ready to enforce the provisions of any charitable trust and asserted no power to change the terms laid down by the donor, but gave to any trust a standardized position in law, with rights and responsibilities.

Town government, the courts, the militia, churches, and charitable trusts were brought under central legal regulation in fairly direct fashion, if not without controversy. The land syndicates required more delicate treatment. No direct attack was launched on those existing in 1690; as already mentioned, they continued for years after that date to divide and multiply and bring clarity to their organization. In all cases, however, where town government and control of common lands had been intermingled, the amalgamation of land and political rights was ended. In several towns this was done by creating an organizationally distinct proprietors' body; in other towns, though, the common lands were made the property of the town at the disposal of the town meeting.[45]

Samuel Cranston was a shareholder in four proprietors' organizations that acted as though they had decided to extinguish themselves by concluding their business. No evidence survives to disclose their conscious policies, but they took the obvious path to extinction by dividing all the remaining common land. Cranston figured prominently in steps taken in this direction during the first decade of the eighteenth century in New-port, Jamestown, and Westerly. Minor squabbles prevented final division for years, but the unsettled business concerned such tiny amounts of land as to leave the proprietary organizations powerless; more significantly, the proprietors stopped trying to resolve the conflicts among themselves and left the contentious partners to appeal to the courts. In Westconnaug not only did the proprietors divide up virtually all the land, but prior to doing so they worked through the colony government to clarify their rights: they obtained authorization from the General Assembly to erect a township on their tract, presumably to give their organization a legal basis in case it was needed, and they relied on this authorization in negotiating disputes over title with the town and proprietors of Providence.[46] Cranston took advantage of a dispute in Jamestown to bring the proprietary organization there specifically under legal regulation by the General Assembly.[47] In spite of the rage of one dissatisfied claimant, who tried to appeal the decision to the king, the legislature's authority over proprietary affairs held firm.[48] Potentially, the same authority could act on other land syndicates.

A subtler approach was much more common, however. Broadly speaking, the quasi-governmental aspects of proprietors' organizations were played down until nothing was left but partnerships in land rights. No evidence reveals how this effect was achieved; it is clear from the behavior of the proprietary organizations, though, that their leaders were very cautious about letting their corporative rights be scrutinized in court. They stopped trying to settle internal disputes except by persuasion and stern words; if a quarrel went to court, the organization's view, if one existed, was voiced only by members acting as private litigants.[49] Nor did the proprietary organizations often assess members after 1700. They did charge a fee for certifying title to lands divided into individual holdings, to pay the surveyors, but presently began to pay them in land and so avoid any occasion for demanding money from the members.[50] Proprietors stopped creating highways. The only quasi-governmental function they thought it safe to keep was certifying individual titles by majority vote, a procedure that the courts accepted.

Important as these alterations in the land syndicates were, a clearer indication of the direction of change can be seen in the fact that no new syndicates were formed when the colony sold "vacant lands" after 1689. The buyers, even when taking title as joint owners, rarely held rights in common for more than a few weeks. Instead, they proceeded at once to divide up the whole tract and grant quit-claim deeds to each other to generate individual titles.[51]

In a remarkably comprehensive way Rhode Island adopted a legally rationalized approach to authority by the time of Governor Cranston's death in 1727. Coercion and adjudication had become monopolies of governmental organs; a clear and recognized system of delegating authority from the central government had been set up; the legislative power of the General Assembly reached all aspects of colonial life and defined the scope within which towns might enact bylaws. The previously autonomous and often self-constituted collectivities had been subjected to legal definition and regulation and deprived of the quasi-political functions that earlier had seemed likely to increase and acquire legal recognition. No bureaucratic structure had appeared or was needed, but appropriate administrative arms had been contrived for the governmental organs. A private sphere had been roughly sketched along modern lines and legal safeguards applied to certain areas within it. Rhode Island had set up the basic framework of a new social order.

IV

Several observations can be made on the significance of the rationalization of authority in Rhode Island. The colony quickly began to enjoy beneficial effects, such as unprecedented internal order, in spite of a great variety of domestic conflicts over land and paper currency and the growing rivalry between Newport and Providence. Moreover, order was achieved without ruthless domination by some victorious group or interest. The central government followed a liberal policy, employing its powers to regulate subordinate institutions after 1700 at the request of the citizens, not taking the initiative in changing legal rights or creating nongovernmental collectivities.

The citizens apparently found the new system satisfactory and displayed ingenuity in using it. Working within the prevalent liberal policy and taking advantage of the implicit delineation of a private sphere, they contrived important new mechanisms for group action, notably the private corporation. Older forms of chartered corporations had been arms of sovereign power, differing from other corporative bodies not in their quasi-governmental character, but in the clarity with which their rights and obligations were specified and derived from an indubitable source of authority. Accordingly, there had been no bases for a classification of corporative entities into private and public corporations. With a private sphere in existence, however, and the older corporative bodies either deprived of quasi-governmental attributes or made into strictly governmental organs, it became possible in Rhode Island to conceive a truly private corporation. The first of them, the Company of the Redwood Library, was chartered in 1747. In a vague way it claimed to serve a public purpose, but above all else, this new institution was a private club, endowed with privileges which gave it a permanency and security unavailable to a voluntary association by enabling it to hold property in its own name and conduct business according to a system of basic rules which could not be changed at the pleasure of the members.[52] Several years later, religious bodies discovered that the same sort of institution could stabilize their existence without creating an ecclesiastical establishment.

The profundity of the change which had been wrought between 1690 and 1730 and the subsequent creation of the private corporation raise the question of what the Rhode Islanders thought they were doing. Regrettably they wrote nothing that has survived to show that they framed new ideas to guide or explain their new goals and behavior. Insensibly, ideas and attitudes appropriate to the new order appeared in actions, laws, and lawyers' pleas — only enough to indicate that the ideas and attitudes were there. The basic documents drawn up for the establishment of the Redwood Library indicate a deep uncertainty about the legal side of the event, suggesting that the founders were aware that they were innovating, but giving no clue to what they regarded as the novel or risky elements.[53] Modern liberal scholars, for all their sophistication, still thirst for evidence that an institution is the lengthened shadow of a great man, though they prefer an intellectual to a man on horseback. But no commanding figure stood at the founding of the Redwood Library, and in the almost complete absence of pertinent contemporary papers, it cannot be said with any confidence that Samuel Cranston took such a role at the transformation of the central government. Clearly, framing the abstractions with which to understand the rationalization of authority came long after the fact. Rhode Island had no more than a small learned coterie in the eighteenth century, which may account for the delay, but I believe that it is usual rather than exceptional to find ideas keeping up with events only on a minimal day-to-day basis during a time of radical change.

What took place in Rhode Island, of course, cannot be equated simply with what happened anywhere else. Even on the level of abstraction used in this description, a few unique features must be recognized — most obviously, no other colony had the same autonomy in its earliest years. Without charter or guiding ideology, Rhode Island was singularly "free." In this condition the settlers acted on attitudes which were the common property of seventeenth-century Englishmen — and probably very like those of contemporary Frenchmen or Dutchmen — with results only broadly comparable to those in colonies which received more guidance. The social order created around Narragansett Bay may well be viewed as a "fragment culture," in Louis Hartz's phrase, carrying into action the attitudes of middle-ranking Europeans with a few special quirks provided by the religious peculiarities of the persons who went to dwell there. External circumstances helped internal discord to stimulate change, but within a century Rhode Islanders found that their social order could not be stabilized on the original terms or even on a more fully corporative basis. The fragment culture had to change, and change it did. Modifications were made which compelled no sharp repudiation of inherited legal terms; in this sense the colony could remain within an English framework and even fail to perceive the extent of alteration. But the change was in directions which the mother country took later, indicating that the fragment culture had not been launched on a pattern of evolution basically different from that of its parent.

The importance of external threats as well as internal discord in fostering rationalization in Rhode Island raises the possibility that such a change in a corporative society is primarily a response, though not a necessary response, to outside interference. A preliminary examination suggests that although all the English colonies in North America had corporative characteristics, however diverse during the seventeenth century, their progress toward rationalization and uniformity can more readily be correlated with efforts to improve control from London than with internal processes. The later rationalization in England, which might seem sufficiently explained by industrialization, perhaps should be seen also as a product of international conflict. Poland, where rationalization was avoided and predatory neighbors demolished the state, offers a curiously apt example in reverse. There, those who enjoyed power by privilege and autonomous corporative rights chose to preserve their rights by blind assertion or intrigue with foreign powers rather than jeopardize the foundations of their rights by altering the central government.[54] Rhode Island faced a similar possibility in the last quarter of the seventeenth century, when land speculators frequently dabbled in projects to partition the colony in order to gain recognition of their real estate claims. Pursuing the alternative of rationalization apparently required willingness on the part of most influential men to surrender power based on privilege, a choice which was easier to make in Rhode Island, where privilege had not been firmly established and gains could be anticipated from progress toward security of rights on any footing, than in Poland, where any change threatened to undermine rights and no compensatory benefits were widely felt to be available from centralization.

Speculation about the implications of colonial Rhode Island, however, should remain exploratory until information is gathered to permit comparison between it and other colonies. Problematical features dot the seaboard: for instance, proprietary power in Pennsylvania and Maryland made those provinces special; the durability of the county court in Virginia and North Carolina suggests that corporative institutions there survived even the American Revolution; the nature of landlordism in colonial New York remains unclear; and so forth. Very likely, no simple correlation will be found between rationalization and centralization of power, and in this respect Rhode Island may be misleading. A corporative social order necessarily includes certain kinds of decentralization, but a rationalized one may also; they differ in the relations between authority-wielding officers and institutions, in the relations between a given man and his privileges and powers, and in the attitudes underlying the whole system. A review of revolutionary-period pamphlet literature, with a view to discovering the presence or absence of attitudes compatible with a rationalized social order, might help clarify the problem of generalizing on colonial America. This foray into the subject will have served its purpose if it provides some usable methods to understand one of colonial America's most striking achievements or provokes somebody else to find a better way.

7. AMERICAN VOTING BEHAVIOR
AND THE 1964 ELECTION

Walter Dean Burnham

An assumption which underlies much of the study of American electoral politics is that the mass base of our major political coalition has a high degree of stability over time. As V. O. Key, Jr., and Frank Munger have observed, most voting behavior most of the time is a continuing affirmation of preexisting political commitments which were forged under the pressure of a major social trauma. Looked at in terms of the party system as a whole, this profound linkage with the past often amounts to a "standing decision" which is only very infrequently subject to review by any decisively large part of the electorate.[1] Even in the contemporary period the findings of survey research, though documenting the significance of short-term factors in voting outcomes, emphasize that the most important single variable which influences the voter is still his party identification.

A tautology which emerges from this view is that an aggregate system of voting behavior will act like a system over time, that is, the system will be more coherently related to itself — especially in the short run — than to any extrapartisan social variables. Key demonstrated the plausibility of this argument by use of the standard correlation coefficient in his book *A Primer of Statistics for Political Scientists*.[2] The autocorrelation of pairs of contiguous elections tends to produce coefficients which are among the highest to be found anywhere in the social sciences — for example, the 1944–1948 r of $+0.98$ for the ten counties of New Hampshire. Such autocorrelations, which amount to saying that A_{1944} substantially equals A_{1948}, have hitherto been pretty well limited to the kind of methodological inquiries Key undertook, since reiterations of such state-

Note: Reprinted from the *Midwest Journal of Political Science* XII (February 1968) by permission of the Wayne State University Press.

ments are not of very great substantive interest once the equation is established.

Yet, paradoxically, the results of recent presidential elections — especially the 1964 election — point in an entirely different direction. As we shall see, two major and "unexpected" characteristics of these elections stand out with particular clarity. First, according to this mode of analysis and using states as components of the national voting system, presidential elections have resembled their immediate predecessors less and less closely since 1948. Second, the 1964 data provide clear geographical traces of alignment patterns more usually associated with the 1896–1932 or even the Civil War alignment systems than with the alignment patterns of contemporary American politics. Since they cast penetrating light into an unexplored corner of American voting behavior, these peculiarities of present-day elections deserve study in some detail.

I

It is desirable at the outset to specify the research focus of this study with some clarity. This focus is essentially geographical, involving an examination both of regional biases in the University of Michigan Survey Research Center's 1964 study and aggregate data analysis of relationships among state components of the national voting system and county components of certain state voting systems. Aggregate-data analysis, of course, has a number of limitations which have been thoroughly discussed in the literature.[3] In particular, the statewide correlations employed here are designed solely to make inferences concerning the interrelationships of aggregates at that level, and that level alone. It hardly needs saying that macroanalytic study cannot be successfully employed to make direct causal inferences concerning microanalytic units, for example, concerning the motivations of individual actors in the larger voting system. At the same time, if an irreducible X factor emerges from analysis at this level — a factor whose presence has not yet been adequately recognized by the mainstream of microanalytic research — it cannot but have implications for the future direction of this research, as well as for our knowledge of the social context in which individual voting decisions are made. Moreover, examination of electoral behavior in terms of geographical components need not be defended so far as the 1964 election is concerned. As we shall see, this election was more heavily influenced by sectional factors than any other in the past generation.

If one turns, then, to the statewide correlation arrays by paired elections, he might expect to find both a "normal" pattern of close relationship and a deviation from this norm for 1964. Table 1 reveals not only

Table 1. Correlations of contiguous pairs of
presidential elections by states, 1880–1884—1960–1964

Election pair	$r =$	$r^2 \times 100 =$
1880–1884	+0.88	77.44
1884–1888	+0.94	88.36
1888–1892	+0.81	65.61
1892–1896	+0.78	60.84
1896–1900	+0.84	70.56
1900–1904	+0.89	79.21
1904–1908	+0.94	88.36
1908–1912	+0.95	90.25
1912–1916	+0.91	82.81
1916–1920	+0.90	81.00
1920–1924	+0.98	96.04
1924–1928	+0.75	56.25
1928–1932	+0.78	60.84
1932–1936	+0.94	88.36
1936–1940	+0.90	81.00
1940–1944	+0.98	96.04
1944–1948	+0.96	92.16
1948–1952	+0.74	54.76
1952–1956	+0.60	36.00
1956–1960	+0.54	29.16
1960–1964	−0.11	1.21

a confirmation of this expectation, but something else besides.[4] It is clear enough that these correlations describe both a relative positioning of states along a continuum and the degree of congruence between that positioning in one election and its immediate successor. The extreme importance of the realignment of 1896 is not captured in the data presented, for example, since nationally it tended to reinforce a sectional alignment which was already partially in existence. Correlation analysis tends to reflect the influence of extreme values only too well, and the "Solid South's" lopsidedly Democratic percentages were in evidence as early as 1880. Thus it is hardly surprising that the lowest contiguous correlations yielded by the data before World War II were found in the 1924–1928 and 1928–1932 pairs. This reflected the partial disruption of the "normal" array which resulted, especially in the South, from Al Smith's candidacy in 1928.

Even with these limitations in mind, the pattern of postwar statewide alignments is strikingly deviant from the historical norm. In the first place there is clearly a downward progression of correlation in each pair of contiguous elections from the 1948–1952 pair down to the present, with each election resembling its predecessor less and less closely. Prior to 1948–1952 the assumption of congruence between two contiguous elections with which this study began was confirmed: in only three of seventeen pairs between 1880 and 1948 did r fall below +0.80, and all three of these pairs were above +0.70. There is much evidence from other sources to support the proposition that short-term influences in presidential voting alignments have been growing in relative importance at the expense of long-term continuities and "standing decisions." [5] The evidence here, though hardly amounting to a definitive confirmation of this hypothesis, is entirely consistent with it.

The second point for reflection which arises from Table 1 is the extraordinary result of pairing the 1960 and 1964 elections: the production of a r which is not only so low as to indicate a virtually random relationship between the statewide percentages in these two elections, but which is actually slightly *negative*. Were such low correlations to become the norm in the present and immediate future, we should be led to suspect that at this level presidential elections would be well on the way to becoming "happenings," discrete phenomena in which long-term continuities play a vanishing role and short-term influences become overwhelming. Nevertheless, it is a major thesis of this study that the system does not in fact operate at random, even when short-term influences are at a maximum. More precisely, it is possible to demonstrate that at least some extraordinarily massive short-term displacements are not random fluctuations, but invoke clear reflections of political alignments which had been widely thought to be dead and buried since the realignments of the 1930's.

The peculiarities of the campaign and election of 1964 need not be recounted in detail here. It is enough to note that the Goldwater campaign was manifestly archaic in substance and tactics, to the extent that discussion of its antique qualities tended to dominate contemporary writing on the subject. This campaign, moreover, broke many of the unwritten rules of modern-day American party politics, particularly those involving coalition-building aimed at winning elections.[6] Goldwater's supporters rose in revolt against the substantive policies of the post-1932 "moving consensus," and in doing so raised significant questions about the mobility of that consensus which were only partially answered by the outcome of the election. Particularly concentrated in the South and West, they constructed an explicitly sectional electoral strategy which was aimed at isolating the Northeast in general and the "Eastern establishment" in particular.[7] If they did not produce a critical realignment in the process, it was not for want of trying to do so.

As it was, the election of 1964 displayed many of the behavioral properties which have been associated with major realignments in the past.[8] More precisely, both the tone of the Goldwater campaign and the extraordinary and geographically concentrated voter shifts in November evoke striking impressions of similarity with such sectionally polarized elections as the McKinley-Bryan contest of 1896. This parallelism between 1896 and 1964 is especially marked if similarities in both the nomination and election patterns are viewed together. Of course, one never steps twice into the same river; what appears is thus not a precisely inverse correspondence but a visible though blurred similarity. It nevertheless seems accurate to say, first, that the shape of the 1964 election outcome more closely resembles earlier elections marked by a "colonial" revolt of South and West agianst a Northeastern metropole than it resembles any others; and, second, that the alignment era which was inaugurated by the epic struggle of 1896 produced more such elections than any other era before or since.

If such parallelism exists, it should be possible to measure it in quantitative terms, beginning with the nominating convention. In the period from 1896 to 1964 there have been five national party conventions which have been marked by exceptional internal tension: the Democratic conventions of 1896 and 1924, and the Republican conventions of 1912, 1952, and 1964. In each of them major factional disputes were central to the decisions made; all of them constituted significant turning points in the histories of the respective parties; and all of them except the 1912 Republican convention were marked by sharp sectional cleavages. A study of key votes on procedural questions and platform amendments produces the following regional profiles for each convention (see Table 2).[9] As is evident, the 1896 Democratic and 1964 Republican convention

Table 2. *Similarities and dissimilarities in regional bases*
of intraparty cleavage, 1896–1964

Region	1896 D Gold plank % yea	1912 R Rules % nay	1924 D Klan % yea	1952 R Brown am. % nay	1964 R Civil rights % yea
Northeast	90.5	50.3	86.3	82.8	87.0
Midwest	14.2	70.9	54.1	39.5	17.7
West	10.0	32.5	26.2	62.9	10.5
South	1.1	23.7	15.6	24.9	0.3
Total	32.6	47.2	50.0	54.6	31.3

voting profiles are virtually identical on the regional level. Indeed, the 1964 Republican pattern has more in common even with the 1924 Democratic convention vote on the Ku Klux Klan than with either of the two other Republican conventions. A correlation of state percentages yields similar results (see Table 3).

Table 3. *Correlations between key votes in*
five party conventions, by state, 1896–1964

	1896 D	1912 R	1924 D	1952 R	1964 R
1896 D	—	+.07	+.68	+.50	+.78
1912 R	+.07	—	+.09	+.15	−.02
1924 D	+.68	+.09	—	+.29	+.71
1952 R	+.50	+.15	+.29	—	+.51
1964 R	+.78	−.02	+.71	+.51	—

A cluster relationship seems to emerge from this set of coefficients: there are high correlations among 1896 D, 1924 D, and 1964 R, with the highest being that between 1896 D and 1964 R: 1952 R "explains" nearly 35% less of the 1964 R variance than does 1896 D. There is little or no correlation among the other elements in the matrix; in particular, the 1912 R cleavage seems quite unrelated to anything else.

A reasonable explanation of this set of relationships may be that the 1964 Republican convention involved, beneath differences in overt issues, many of the same latencies of regional antagonism which afflicted the Democratic party during the 1896–1932 alignment era. The functional parallels between the two conventions are indeed striking: the prior existence of "Eastern establishment" control of presidential nominations, in uneasy balance with a quite different regional center of the party's gravity in Congress; the development of interest and value antagonisms which provided the fuel for a successful effort to overthrow the Northeastern president-makers; the effort by the new masters of the convention to construct a coalition strategy which excluded the vote-rich Northeast; and the massive dislocations in voting behavior, particularly in the Northeast, which contributed heavily to a defeat for those who sought a new winning coalition. The gold standard and a civil-rights plank may have little enough in common on the overt level, but they may also share a partial common identity as stalking-horses for a major confrontation between regional power interests and political subcultures.

But the foregoing discussion merely describes some aspects of elite behavior. Assuming that symbolic appeals based on regional and other subcultural antagonisms are of continuing importance in elections, we should expect to find analogous, if less clearly etched, relationships in an analysis of mass voting behavior. The case of 1964 should thus point toward a quite different pattern of relationships among the state components in the national voting system than those assumed at the outset. Correlations on the state level between 1964 and each preceding presidential election back into the nineteenth century should be uniformly negative *and should show some signs of becoming higher as one moves backward over time.* These statewide comparisons, of course, suggest less dramatic differences between elections in the 1930's and their predecessors than do other, more refined modes of analysis, since relative positioning among states during the New Deal was shifted less significantly than within-state alignments. The increasing spans of time between 1964 and the election with which it is paired could also be expected to produce a flattening of the ascending negative curve. Even so, a pattern of the expected type seems to emerge (see Table 4).

Excluding the 1960–1964 pair, a moderately sloped regression line can be traced back to the 1896–1964 pair. On this line a −0.57 for the 1956–1964 pair would become approximately −0.73 for the 1896–1964 pair. There are reasons — associated with the immense short-term appeal of the Bryan campaign to the silvermining states — for a somewhat lower correlation between that election itself and 1964 than between 1900 or 1916 and 1964. Even so, it seems reasonably clear that the negative relationship between 1964 and the period of elections extending from 1896 through 1916 is significantly stronger than for any other comparable

Table 4. *Correlations of the election of 1964 with all earlier presidential elections, by state, 1880–1960*

Election pair 1964 and	$r =$	$r^2 \times 100 =$
1880	−0.60	36.00
1884	−0.54	29.16
1888	−0.67	44.89
1892	−0.64	40.96
1896	−0.69	47.61
1900	−0.76	57.76
1904	−0.64	40.96
1908	−0.71	50.41
1912	−0.71	50.41
1916	−0.75	56.25
1920	−0.67	44.89
1924	−0.63	39.69
1928	−0.55	30.25
1932	−0.72	51.84
1936	−0.72	51.84
1940	−0.67	44.89
1944	−0.64	40.96
1948	−0.61	38.44
1952	−0.39	15.21
1956	−0.64	40.96
1960	−0.11	1.21

period of time before or after. Assuming with E. E. Schattschneider, Key, and others that critical realignments bring a kind of alignment system of some durability into being, this tends to support the thesis that the events of 1964 activated a rough but visible mirror image of the alignment "system of 1896–1932" as a whole.[10]

A somewhat different type of analysis brings into sharper focus the peculiar relationship of 1964 with earlier elections which possessed similar geographically concentrated components. Two procedures have been followed in this analysis. In the first place, the eleven ex-Confederate states have been excluded, because they formed a separate subsystem which did not undergo realignment along national lines until the 1950's and because the extreme values which they generate in correlations significantly reduce the sharpness of comparisons involving 1964. Secondly, correlations were made between the percentage Republican of the two-party vote in the non-Southern states, 1880–1960, and the 1964 Z-score displacement by state.

The standard, or Z, score is a useful device for measuring the relative magnitude of deviation of a data point from an "expected" norm based on past observation. It is derived by dividing the standard deviation of a mean into the deviation from that mean registered by the data point under investigation. In this case the standard deviation of a 1932–1960 mean for each state is divided into the 1964 deviation from the 1932–1960 mean percentage Democratic of the two-party vote.[11] Each of the two given geographical areas may, for example, show a displacement of 12% toward the Democratic nominee between 1960 and 1964. But if one of these areas has shown a tight clustering of percentages around the mean in the 1932–1960 period, while the other has displayed considerable amplitude of partisan swing during that period, two quite different relative electoral movements will be reflected in the same absolute movement. In this instance the greater the positive or negative score, the greater the pro-Democratic or pro-Republican 1964 deviation from "normal," as defined by the 1932–1960 mean.[12] Measurement of partisan percentages against the 1964 Z score over the period 1880–1960 appears more precisely to identify elections in the past with which 1964 has the most in common (see Table 5).

Of the twenty-one election pairs in Table 5, only five realize correlations in excess of ±0.50. In descending order they are 1932, 1936, 1896, 1916, and 1900. It is notable that no election since 1936 produces a coefficient as high even as the rather mediocre correlation between 1908 and 1964 Z. Indeed, each of the high-scoring elections, with the exception of 1936, is to be found in the 1896–1932 alignment era, and each is prominently associated with a strong sectional component, arraying South and West against Northeast, in the aggregate vote.[13]

It may be possible to regard 1936, the most recent election which has a relatively high correlation with 1964, as a transitional phase between the old alignment and the stable phase of the New Deal alignment. There was undoubtedly a heavy and novel increment of class-related realignment in this election. Although working-class areas massively increased both their total vote and the Democratic share of it between 1932 and 1936, Democratic support tended to remain abnormally heavy among middle-class and white-collar elements in 1936. This maintenance of Democratic

Table 5. *Relationship between 1964 Z scores and*
percentage republican by state, non-southern states,
1880–1960[a]

Election pair 1964 Z and	$r =$	$r^2 \times 100 =$
1880	+0.17	2.89
1884	+0.16	2.56
1888	+0.21	4.41
1892	−0.33	10.89
1896	+0.74	54.76
1900	+0.59	34.81
1904	−0.21	4.41
1908	+0.48	23.04
1912	+0.38	14.44
1916	+0.69	47.61
1920	+0.19	3.61
1924	−0.22	4.84
1928	+0.09	0.81
1932	+0.84	70.56
1936	+0.77	59.29
1940	+0.29	8.41
1944	+0.01	0.00+
1948	+0.34	11.56
1952	−0.18	3.24
1956	+0.23	5.29
1960	−0.44	19.36

[a] The same general procedure which was outlined in Note 4 applies here also. For 1880–1888, N = 27; for 1892, N = 33; for 1896–1904, N = 34; for 1908, N = 35; for 1912–1960, N = 37. Because it is not possible to derive a 1932–1960 Z score for Alaska and Hawaii, they are omitted in the 1960–1964 Z pair. $r_{1964/1964\ Z} = -0.995$.

support among these groups — a support which was to be severely diminished in 1940 — was also paralleled by Democratic percentages in the West which far exceeded even the landslide margins of 1932. Even though the antics of the Liberty League and the fate of the *Literary Digest* poll might lead us to think otherwise, it nevertheless seems that there was a lower index of class voting in 1936 than in any subsequent elections except those of 1956 and 1960.[14] In any event the data indicate pretty clearly that, on balance, the 1964 election more closely resembled elections held during the era of the fourth party system (1896–1932) than those of the fifth (1934–196?).[15]

II

The word "sectionalism" may mean a variety of things. On the level of voting behavior, sectional influences may be defined as involving differentials in voting alignments along geographical lines, which are not to be confused with urbanization levels or other demographic or social variables which may also be skewed geographically. In extreme cases a sectional alignment may produce a sharp reduction or even obliteration of within-area voting cleavages, replacing them with a relatively homogeneous structure of voting behavior among most or all politically active social strata. The implication may be further drawn that this homogeneity arises from a clear voter consciousness of external threat to regional interests or cultural values, though no definitive showing of any such phenomenon can be made from the use of aggregate data alone.

The concept of sectionalism has also been employed systematically to describe an interrelated pattern of elite and nonelite behavior, legislation affecting the size and composition of the regional electorate, and so on, which is aimed at stabilizing and perpetuating a dominant regional interest, as in the case of the formerly "Solid South." In this broader systemic sense, sectional politics is a major variant of nonclass politics. Dominant political cleavages formed around persistent conflicts among regions of uneven socioeconomic development are, indeed, virtually incompatible by definition with a stable division of the electorate along lines of socio-economic status. So are such alternative variants of nonclass politics as the conflict between French-speaking and English-speaking Canadians, or that between Nationalist and Unionist in Ireland prior to that nation's independence. Such a politics is analogous to politics among nation-states which, even in the Communist world, effectively prevents the emergence of transnational "working-class solidarity." Sectional politics within a given political system tends to be reactionary, since it greatly facilitates control of politics by those who are already economically dominant.[16] It is hardly accidental that the most sectionally polarized alignment system in American political history, that of 1896–1932, was closely associated with a transcendant dominance by corporate business over public policy.[17] Nor is it accidental that the policy deadlock which has existed with few interruptions since 1938 owes much of its existence to the survival of one-partyism in the South into the contemporary period.

For the purposes of this study, however, such larger meanings of sectionalism may be noted and then laid aside. For our purposes it is necessary to demonstrate only that there was a heavy, regionally structured voter response, a response which, in reaction to the archaisms of the 1964 campaign, produced measurable echoes of archaic electoral alignments. Whether or not individual voters were motivated by regional self-defense, or whether or not permanent policy consequences come to be associated with the aftermath of 1964, the most salient question for the analyst of American voting behavior is this: why was it possible for such an atavism to occur at all as late as the mid-1960's?

The Survey Research Center's 1964 election study reveals the existence of this sectionalism in two ways. It captures the sharp differentiation between voting response in the Northeast and in the rest of the country (see Table 6).[18] Curiously, it also radically overreports the Democratic vote in the South, an anomaly to be discussed later. As is clear from Table 6, in the Northeast the 1964 election largely obliterated the traditional post–New Deal political stratification along class, education, and occupation lines, though — according to this sample — it did nothing of the sort in other regions of the country. This result was brought about by an extraordinarily heavy Democratic vote in the better-educated and higher-status elements of the Northeast's electorate, a swing which evidently brought up the Democratic percentage of the vote among such groups nearly to 1960 working-class levels.[19] Thus, the Northeast produced an index of class voting of only 4 in 1964, compared with 27 in the rest of the country and 18 in the United States as a whole.[20]

Further exploration by aggregate-data analysis perforce takes us below the gross levels of regions or states and thus, because of a plethora of available data, to a selective study of certain extreme deviations from the norm, primarily in the Northeastern states. There are a variety of measures which can be developed to study sectional voting alignments. In the case of the Northeast, they all seem to do the same thing, with variations in emphasis and implication. The first of such measures is the party defection ratio — in this case the Republican defection ratio — which was developed by Key in his study of the 1960 election.[21] Analysis of the 1960–1964 defection ratio by states and counties reveals the epicenter of anti-Goldwater reaction to be in eastern New England. Here, especially in Maine, Massachusetts, and Rhode Island, the movement

Table 6. Selected social characteristics and the 1964 vote:
the northeast as deviant region[a]

Social characteristic	Northeast (N)	Northeast % D	Northeast % R	Rest of U.S. (N)	Rest of U.S. % D	Rest of U.S. % R	Difference % D
Occupation							
Professional-managerial	(55)	62	38	(143)	52	48	+10
Clerical-sales	(36)	81	18	(100)	63	37	+18
Skilled workers	(29)	72	28	(66)	74	26	−2
Semi- and unskilled	(49)	76	24	(137)	87	13	−11
Retired	(25)	72	28	(79)	62	38	+10
Housewife, etc.	(105)	79	21	(228)	60	40	+19
Education							
College graduate	(43)	77	23	(99)	38	62	+39
Some college	(38)	66	34	(115)	56	44	+10
High school graduate	(126)	73	27	(244)	64	36	+9
Some high school	(45)	71	29	(161)	74	26	−3
Grade school, none	(56)	84	16	(178)	79	21	+5
Perceived social class							
Self-identified:							
Middle class	(88)	69	31	(198)	49	51	+20
Working class	(98)	82	18	(294)	77	23	+5
Not self-identified:							
Middle class	(54)	67	33	(143)	53	47	+14
Working class	(55)	80	20	(132)	79	21	+1
Rejection of classes	(8)	50	50	(19)	44	56	+6
All sample responses	(309)	74	26	(802)	65	35	+9

[a] Data computed from the 1964 election study of the Survey Research Center, University of Michigan; courtesy of the Inter-University Consortium for Political Research. The Northeast is here defined as the New England and Middle Atlantic census regions, plus Delaware, Maryland, the District of Columbia, and West Virginia.

was so great and widely spread as to be nearly uniform. Of the thirty-five counties in these three states, only seven showed Republican defection ratios of less than 40, and four had defection ratios in excess of 50 — among the highest for white jurisdictions in the nation.[22]

As one moves westward in this region, however, considerable internal variations begin to emerge. In New York State, for example, there is a very clear-cut internal differentiation between the New York City metropolitan area — especially in predominantly white parts of the city's four residential boroughs and the suburban counties — and upstate New York.

Thus, predominantly white assembly districts of the city showed a 1960–1964 defection ratio of 24.7; in the suburban counties it was 29.2; north of the Westchester county line it reached 41.2.[23] (The Negro assembly districts of the city, with a defection ratio of 74.6, were in a class by themselves, as were similar areas in other cities.) As measured by this yardstick, the upstate displacements were more or less uniformly massive, with urban centers showing nearly as substantial a Republican defection as the rural areas.

If one explores within-state county variances from a statewide mean over time, a similar pattern emerges.[24] It can be supposed *a priori* that the greater the within-state variance, the greater the relative weight of components of voting behavior which divide the electorate of a state internally. Conversely, the smaller the variance, the more likely it is that some nationwide political factor or factors suppressing these internal cleavages are at work. Such analysis, of course, does not tell us directly what the focus of these internal cleavages is and certainly does not imply that this focus remains the same over long periods of time. *Ceteris paribus*, however, a sudden drop in within-state variances would seem to point toward the emergence of a major sectional component in the collective voting decision. A comparison of four Northeastern states with three Mountain states for the period 1920–1964 vividly illustrates both temporal and regional differentiations of this sort.

Table 7. Sectionalism and within-state variances,
1920–1964 (selected states)

Year	Maine	N.J.	Pa.	Vt.	N.M.	Utah	Wyo.
1920	33.42	48.28	81.06	45.98	138.01	37.34	18.97
1924	17.79	56.30	115.10	48.85	173.75	46.84	23.05
1928	48.29	97.56	110.78	152.40	41.98	80.29	45.35
1932	31.40	54.63	81.44	85.09	121.15	74.79	22.75
1936	85.89	66.37	86.54	97.40	108.72	55.89	61.13
1940	81.55	72.94	101.48	81.55	84.25	58.87	76.94
1944	99.95	79.06	94.64	99.95	61.33	71.41	66.55
1948	111.55	87.62	103.63	102.00	104.51	73.27	54.01
1952	75.13	87.62	103.26	74.88	37.06	83.62	95.11
1956	63.45	76.05	73.46	69.93	30.28	65.36	74.68
1960	101.09	87.21	104.48	104.26	74.13	87.21	90.93
1964	39.77	30.57	60.44	25.55	62.46	80.82	90.71

Several features of Table 7 stand out with particular clarity. In the first place, five of the seven states displayed markedly lower county variances before 1928 than they have since. Secondly, both 1928 and — to a lesser degree — 1948 and 1960 emerge in most of these states as years of exceptional internal polarization, a finding which is also confirmed by other evidence. Finally, and most important, the 1964 variances show major differences among the four states of the Northeast and the three Mountain states. In New Jersey, Pennsylvania, and Vermont, indeed, the magnitude of the 1964 variance was the smallest on record for the period under consideration, and Maine's variance fell to the lowest level since 1932. In the three Mountain states, on the other hand, the differences between the 1960 and 1964 variances were insignificant. It seems clear that the 1964 configuration of issues and candidate images produced a virtually unprecedented compression of traditional within-state cleavages in the Northeast, and that no such effect was visible in the parts of the West examined here. A vast regional differential in the effect of the Goldwater candidacy on voting behavior almost certainly underlies these movements.

Under certain circumstances a partial liquidation of internal cleavages within given jurisdictions may be associated with differentials which evoke far older, often virtually forgotten cleavage patterns. In the study of this problem the Republican defection ratio has the limitation that it measures only the movement between two contiguous elections. Similarly,

Table 8. Sectionalism and the 1964 election:
Z scores by quartile and region[a]

Region	Z-score quartiles (USA: Z = +1.27)				
	1 (+2.35 to +4.36)	2 (+1.02 to +2.24)	3 (+0.03 to +0.99)	4 (−5.45 to −0.35)	Total (+4.36 to −5.45)
Northeast	11	1	—	—	12
Midwest	1	8	3	—	12
West	—	2	8	1	11
South	—	1	1	11	13
Total	12	12	12	12	48

[a] Alaska and Hawaii excluded. Regions: East-New England, Middle Atlantic, Delaware, Maryland, and West Virginia. Midwest-East and West North Central. West-Mountain and Pacific South—the eleven ex-Confederate states plus Kentucky and Oklahoma.

the measurement of within-state variances over time may prove illuminating in dealing with the relative importance of internal and exogenous factors in political cleavage, but it can hardly provide direct information of the sort that would be useful in studying the relevance of the 1964 displacement to pre-1932 alignments. For this purpose, some measure of deviation from "expected" two-party balance in a given area, based on its behavior in the recent past, is more revealing. The Z-score measure discussed above seems well suited to this task. As Tables 8 and 9 indicate, a Z-score calculation of the 1964 displacements in the national system reveals marked regional differentials which are not simply masks for such social variables as the extent of urbanization.[25]

III

Two states have been selected for detailed county-level analysis by this method: New York and Pennsylvania. The criteria for their selection include their northeastern location, the existence, historically, of large and well-documented differentials in original settlement patterns, and the presence of large numbers of counties which are not in metropolitan areas and are "off the beaten path," so far as recent population change is concerned. Other things being equal, we would expect that a county which has shown small variations from a mean will frequently be such an out-of-the-way area, probably rural or semirural and largely insulated in its partisan balance from short-term influences — the sort of community most likely to be dominated by an unusually stable "standing decision."[26] Finally, the hypothesis underlying this part of the study can be set forth

Table 9. Urbanism and the 1964 election:
Z scores and percentage urban (1960), by quartile

Urbanism quartiles (USA: 69.9%)	Z-score quartiles (USA: Z = +1.27)				Total (+4.36 to −5.45)
	1 (+2.35 to +4.36)	2 (+1.02 to +2.24)	3 (+0.03 to +0.99)	4 (−5.45 to −0.35)	
1 (73.7–88.6%)	5	2	2	3	12
2 (62.9–73.4%)	3	4	4	1	12
3 (52.3–62.4%)	1	5	2	4	12
4 (35.2–51.3%)	3	1	4	4	12
Total	12	12	12	12	48

briefly in propositional terms. If the Goldwater candidacy was structured around a nostalgic sectional appeal historically associated with Democratic rather than Republican campaigns, and if it succeeded in triggering old and deep-rooted cultural hostilities which were latent but not extinct, it should follow that the greatest pro-Democratic deviations from the norm should be associated precisely with the areas having the longest, most durable "standing decision" favoring the Republicans. In such circumstances, in other words, the Z scores should be highest in areas originally settled by New England Yankees, and proportionately lower in areas of different settlement but equally heavy 1932–1960 Republicanism.

Table 10. The 1964 election and the influence
of original settlement patterns: the case of
New York State

Type of county	Z scores, 1964					N	Mean Z by type of county
	0 to +1.99	+2.00 to +2.99	+3.00 to +3.99	+4.00 to +4.99	+5.00 and over		
New York City	4	1	—	—	—	(5)	1.36
New York suburban	—	—	4	—	—	(4)	3.47
Upstate metropolitan	—	1	5	4	—	(10)	3.71
Upstate non-metropolitan: "Yorker" and mixed (1845)	—	2	9	2	2	(15)	3.94
"Yankee" and Pa. (1845)	—	—	—	4	24	(28)	7.00
Total	4	4	18	10	26	(62)	2.71

As Table 10 indicates, just such a pattern emerges in New York, a state fortunately blessed with early census data necessary for the comparison.[27]

As is evident from this array, New York City showed a pro-Democratic displacement in 1964 which was by far the lowest in the state; indeed, it corresponded almost exactly to the national figure. The suburban, upstate metropolitan and nonmetropolitan, non-Yankee counties occupied roughly the same intermediate position, with means in all these categories falling below +4.00. The counties of original New England and Pennsylvania-New England settlement, on the other hand, showed an extraordinarily high and uniform 1964 Z-score displacement. Of the twenty-four counties in the nineteenth-century "Burned-over district," for example, fourteen had 1964 Z scores of over +6.00, compared with +1.27 for the country as a whole and +4.36 for the two most "Yankee" of the New England states, Maine and Vermont. Eight of the remaining thirty-eight counties in New York also had displacements of more than +6.00. Of these, all but one were known areas of transplanted New England settlement, and two of them — Madison and St. Lawrence — played unusually prominent roles in the social-reform politics of a century ago.[28] It thus seems reasonable to suppose, especially when the nonmetropolitan counties are compared, that the New York voting outcome in 1964 was heavily influenced by factors associated with local political subcultures which have not yet evaporated after more than a century.

The ethnocultural cleavages arising out of original settlement patterns in New York and their influences on the state's politics have been so prominent that they have given rise to a substantial literature.[29] Broadly speaking, the most significant original cleavage was between "Yankees" and "Yorkers," that is, between those of New England ancestry, who mostly settled in western New York, and descendants of the Dutch, who were concentrated in the Hudson and Mohawk valleys. As is well known, the Yankees in time developed an extreme social and political activism, which reached its culmination during the political realignments of the 1850's. The area west of a line drawn from Binghamton to Watertown, for example, became known throughout the country as the "Burned-over district" because of the endless succession of religious, social, and political reform movements which flourished there.[30] Politically, the areas of Yankee settlement were prominent in their support for Anti-Masonry, abolitionism, and eventually Republicanism. Other major groups, such as the Yorker Dutch and the Irish-German immigrants concentrated in the cities, not only had no such urge to reform but were profoundly antagonized by the Yankees who did.[31] It was in this period, more than a century ago, that the foundations were laid for a cleavage which was destined to rival and then supplant the primordial Yankee-Yorker antagonism: the cleavage between New York City and the upstate counties.

Thus the relative displacements of 1964 seem to have a visible relationship in parts of the Northeast to a still earlier alignment era than that of the "system of 1896," that is, to the era in which the Republican party itself was born out of these antagonisms and the larger rivalries between North and South. For purposes of analysis the 1856 election in the Middle Atlantic states seems a particularly useful point of departure. In this election old-line Whigs, for whom the slavery-containment issue was not salient and who were probably not predominantly of New England rural origin, voted in large numbers for a third party, the American, or Know-Nothing, party. The Democratic following established during the earlier second party system remained largely intact, except in some areas of the New England diaspora; it was, indeed, later to be augmented considerably by former Whigs who had voted for Fillmore in 1856. The original Republican groupings, which were evidently heavily concentrated in the New England diaspora, carried the state in 1856 with 46.3% of the total vote (see Table 11).

*Table 11. Relationships between 1856 and 1964:
the case of New York*

% R of three-party vote, 1856	County Z scores, 1964[a]				Total N
	0 to +2.99	+3.00 to +3.99	+4.00 to +5.99	+6.00 and over	
20.0–29.9	4	3	1	—	8
30.0–39.9	1	7	1	—	9
40.0–49.9	1	6	2	1	10
50.0–59.9	1	—	7	8	16
60.0 and over	—	1	3	13	17
Total	7	17	14	22	60

[a] Based on mean derived from the Democratic percentage of the two-party vote, 1932–1960.

As is evident from Table 11, there is considerable positive relationship between the original distribution of Republican support in New York and the relative magnitude of the pro-Democratic displacements which occurred in 1964. Although many far more contemporarily-grounded factors were doubtless at work in 1964, a significant subcultural differentiating factor also existed. A comparison of the 1860 referendum proposal to enfranchise Negroes — a major symbolic point of early political cleavage with contemporary overtones — with early percentages Republican and 1964 Z scores underlines the point. The r of county percentages in favor of the proposed enfranchisement and percentages Republican was +0.85 for 1856 and +0.90 for 1860.[32] A rank ordering of the 1856 Republican percentage of the three-party vote and 1964 Z scores by counties yields an r_s of +0.73; the corresponding r_s for the 1860 enfranchisement amendment and 1964 Z yields an almost identical result, +0.74.

It should not be inferred from this discussion that the 1856 election is regarded here as *uniquely* close in relationship to 1964 displacements in New York, any more than that 1896 is regarded as *uniquely* close in national voter response to the 1964 outcome. In all probability, the relationship is closer between 1964 Z and 1856 than between 1964 Z and any other election down to modern alignments in the 1930's. But it is also very likely that there is a stronger relationship between most or all elections in the 1928–1948 period and 1964 Z than between any earlier elections and that measure. Once again, the question arises of what is being measured here.

Leaving aside the possibility that some inflation of post-1932 relationships with 1964 may arise from autocorrelation, the 1940 result in Table 12 can be explained as the product of peculiar systematic factors

Table 12. Relationships between county Z scores, 1964, and Republican percentages of the vote in selected elections: the case of New York

Election pair 1964 Z and	$r =$	$r^2 \times 100 =$
1856	+0.73	53.29
1860	+0.72	51.84
1880	+0.60	36.00
1900	+0.46	21.16
1920	+0.58	33.87
1940	+0.86	73.96
1960	+0.69	47.61

which have been a conspicuous aspect of recent New York political life. In large part it is probably an artifact of the standing political antagonism between New York City and upstate New York. As a recent study of New York politics has pointed out, there has been a clear long-term tendency for massive increases in city Democratic majorities to be met by equally massive increases in upstate Republican majorities, thus preserving close statewide competition while modifying the bases of party support.[33] One consequence has been that post-1932 upstate New York has remained quite abnormally Republican, considering the high levels of urbanization found in many parts of this region.[34] It can be implied from this latter observation that the city-upstate polarization has tended to reinforce many original voting alignments and that class politics has probably been less salient in upstate New York than in most other parts of the North since the 1930's. If this explanation is correct, one would in fact anticipate that the net effect of the realignments of the 1920's and 1930's, as measured in terms of the 1964 Z score, would be to produce correspondences as high as or higher than those associated with the mid-nineteenth century. All things considered, the point remains that the electoral displacements of 1964 are remarkably closely associated in New York with intrastate political divisions which can be traced back to the first instance in which New England subculture became a solidary force in the state's politics. As Table 13 shows, this relationship also holds

Table 13. Urbanization, 1856 Republican support,
and 1964 Z-score displacements: the case of New York

| | 1856 % Republican of three-party vote | | | |
| | Below state mean | | Above state mean | |
% urban, 1960	Mean 1964 Z	N	Mean 1964 Z	N
100.0 (New York City)	1.52	4	—	—
80.0–99.9	3.62	4	3.62	2
50.0–79.9	3.43	4	5.10	9
40.0–49.9	3.40	3	5.79	11
30.0–39.9	4.37	2	8.09	9
0–29.9	3.68	6	7.25	6
Average of county means	3.27	23	6.30	37

up when such variables as levels of urbanization are held constant.

The same analysis produces quite similar, though somewhat less sharply defined, results when it is applied to Pennsylvania. An arraying of the Keystone State's counties by the magnitude of their 1964 Z-score displacements produces a sharp geographical cleavage within the state. The top quartile (range: +4.21 to +4.43) is overwhelmingly concentrated in the extreme northern and northwestern counties. The bottom quartile (range: +1.02 to +2.09) is, with the major exception of Allegheny County

(Pittsburgh), predominantly located in south-central Pennsylvania. The two middle quartiles are broadly distributed in the regions situated between these extremes, and in the Philadelphia metropolitan area.

Those familiar with the historical geography of Pennsylvania can easily recognize this as the most recent manifestation of a very old cleavage pattern within the state. The quartile of counties with the highest 1964 Z scores generally forms a compact area which has been closely identified with two major patterns of settlement and culture for more than a century: the New England-Yankee subculture and the Scots-Irish Presbyterians who settled west of the mountains. It was in this area that the strength of political antislaveryism was concentrated; for example, the congressional district represented by the author of the Wilmot Proviso was located here. Since the 1850's this region has remained a Republican bastion, except in the very few areas — such as Erie County — in which heavy industry has subsequently developed. Similarly, with the major exception of the area around Pittsburgh, the quartile of counties showing the greatest relative resistance to the anti-Republican swing of 1964 is largely coterminous with the Pennsylvania Dutch country.

The antagonism between these regions and the subcultures which have dominated them goes back in history about as far as similar divisions in New York. Wherever they settled, the Yankees tended to be strongly reformist and socially activist a century ago, particularly where such issues as free public education and slavery were concerned.[35] The Pennsylvania Germans, like their Dutch and Irish counterparts in New York, were well known for their insularity and their hostility to positive state action in such areas. Unfortunately, we do not possess early census data for this state, or such referenda as the New York proposals of 1846, 1860, and 1869 to grant full suffrage to Negroes. But the historical record leaves little doubt that these Germans a century ago were far more likely to be anti-Negro, on the whole, than anti-Southern or antislavery in their attitudes. The Democratic gubernatorial candidate of 1863 probably spoke for many of them when he said that if ever the country were to be divided, he wanted the line of division to run north of Pennsylvania. If one examines the county array in a mode similar to that employed in Table 10, but with nonmetropolitan counties dichotomized relative to their location above or below the state mean percentage Republican in 1856 (32.0% of the three-party vote), the following pattern emerges (see Table 14).

As is evident, there are marked differences between New York and

Table 14. The 1964 election and the influence of original
settlement patterns: the case of Pennsylvania

	Z scores, 1964					
Type of county	0 to +1.99	+2.00 to +2.99	+3.00 to +3.99	+4.00 and over	N	Mean Z by type of county
Philadelphia						
Metropolitan	—	3	—	2	(2)	3.21
Pittsburgh						
Metropolitan	1	1	2	—	(4)	2.83
Other metropolitan	3	5	2	3	(13)	2.78
Nonmetropolitan:						
Less than 32% R, 1856	6	10	4	2	(22)	2.63
More than 32% R, 1856	1	1	8	11	(21)	4.66
Total	11	20	16	18	(65)	3.61

Pennsylvania, which have the net effect of producing a more diffuse 1964 displacement in the latter state than in the former. In particular, there is far less evidence of sharp differences between major-metropolitan and outstate displacements in Pennsylvania than in New York. Several of the suburban Philadelphia counties, in fact, had higher 1964 Z scores than any upstate New York metropolitan area. Conversely, very few Pennsylvania counties had displacements of +6.00: four out of sixty-seven in this state, compared with twenty-two out of sixty-two in New York. Even so, the differential pattern of response in the nonmetropolitan counties tends to indicate a considerable similarity with that of like counties in New York. It seems considerably more than by chance that, of the thirty-one counties showing a Z score of less than +3.00 in 1964, twenty-two had given less than 30% of their vote to the first Republican presidential candidate, or that twelve of the eighteen counties with 1964 Z scores in excess of +4.00 gave 48% or more of their total vote to Fremont. The same general point is made — analogous but more diffuse displacement patterns — by the derivation of a rank-order correlation of +0.61 between 1856 % R and 1964 Z. It also emerges when current levels of urbanization are controlled (see Table 15).

Thus in Pennsylvania as in New York, counties with the oldest Republican "standing decisions" tended to be the most massive 1964 defectors

Table 15. *Urbanization, 1956 Republican support and*
1964 Z-score displacements: the case of Pennsylvania[a]

	1856 % Republican of three-party vote				
	Below state mean			Above state mean	
% urban, 1960	Mean 1964 Z	N		Mean 1964 Z	N
75.0–100.0	2.16	2		3.22	6
60.0–74.9	2.90	8		3.47	2
45.0–59.9	2.26	5		4.01	5
30.0–44.9	2.63	6		4.00	8
0–29.9	2.75	12		4.87	10
Average of county means	2.65	33		3.94	31

[a] Intervals in percentage urban differ somewhat from those in Table 13 in order to provide adequate numbers of counties in each category.

from the Republican candidate. In Pennsylvania as in New York, such counties tended to be historically associated with original settlement by people of New England culture.

It is also of interest to compare the rank-ordering of county percentages Republican with 1964 Z for the two states. Quite dissimilar patterns emerge (see Table 16). While the initial correspondence of 1856 and 1964 Z was lower in Pennsylvania than in New York, it remained higher within this state than for any subsequent election in this array, including post-1932 elections. The New York pattern, on the other hand, tends to display a markedly higher correspondence between 1964 Z and *all* preceding elections than is the case in Pennsylvania. Again, it seems reasonable to suppose that the most significant differentiating factor between the two states is the existence of city-upstate antagonism as an intervening and reinforcing variable in New York and its relative absence in Pennsylvania. They share in common a strong relationship between 1964 Z and the distribution of partisan preferences in the remote past.

IV

In their study of the 1948 campaign in Elmira, the authors of *Voting* mention the existence of a "Republican atmosphere" that contributes significantly to voting outcomes in this community.[36] Much work urgently needs to be done to develop this concept further and fully to put it into

Table 16. Spearman rank-order correlations of county
percentages of Republican and 1964 Z scores: a comparison of
Pennsylvania and New York

State	Election pair[a] 1964 Z and	$r_s =$
Pennsylvania		
	1856	+0.61
	1866[a]	+0.39
	1892	+0.35
	1908	+0.30
	1920	+0.49
	1928	+0.13
	1936	+0.43
	1940	+0.44
	1952	+0.16
	1960	−0.09
New York		
	1856	+0.73
	1860	+0.72
	1880	+0.61
	1900	+0.54
	1920	+0.57
	1928	+0.81
	1936	+0.85
	1940	+0.80
	1952	+0.62
	1960	+0.76

[a] The 1866 election was a gubernatorial election; all others are presidential.

operation. If such an atmosphere exists as a major determinant variable in voting, this of course does not presuppose absolute stability in the ethnocultural composition of a given community over time. But if the concept has any meaning — and the findings of this study suggest that it has a great deal — it would imply that the persistence of the cultural norms on which the atmosphere rests probably requires broad long-term continuities in local ethnocultural distributions. In any case, short-term population shifts ought not to be made so massive or heterogeneous as to destroy the capacity of the existing norm structure to socialize newcomers, whether migrants or the young of the community. Moreover, it would seem a logical inference from this argument, and one which this study tends to support, that there will be various *kinds* of "Republican atmospheres" in predominantly Republican areas, depending on the nuances of the local political subcultures involved.

The evidence developed here supports the view that the 1964 election was to a striking degree a conflict, laden with political symbolism, between regional political subcultures whose recurrent antagonisms form so much of the stuff of American political history. The symbolism developed by the Republican campaign was archaic: many of the themes of sectional and subcultural conflict on which the Goldwater campaign played had not been seen in explicit form in a national campaign for many decades. Moreover, there is good reason to believe, both on qualitative and quantitative grounds, that the internal convulsions within the Republican party in 1964 had more in common with those afflicting the pre-1932 Democrats than with those which have occurred in the course of the GOP's own historical development. It is worth recalling again that the alignment pattern in a typical county with a high and positive 1964 Z score had survived two national party realignments and several major crises in the larger society — such as the economic crises of 1893 and 1929, and both World Wars — with very little change, and that in a Republican direction.

At least two preliminary conclusions arise from this information. First, the data suggest both the existence, and occasionally the extreme salience, of durable community political norms which have their historical origins in the values of the original settlers and their descendants. Secondly, the evidence clearly indicates that mass political alignments may fluctuate very widely in response to electoral stimuli, but that they do not fluctuate at random. Put another way, it appears that at any given time there is a dominant or overt cleavage or set of cleavages, but that there are also latent or suppressed cleavages which may endure for decades without losing their capacity to influence voting outcomes. Such cleavages can suddenly be brought into clear view long after they were thought to have become extinct or only of antiquarian interest, and with little regard to intervening, even longstanding, partisan balances in the communities in question.

Whether this phenomenon of multiple latent voting cleavages has always been a feature of American political life, or has come into view only during the past generation or so, is an open question to which no definitive answer can be given at our current level of knowledge. It does seem clear that there has been a series of sharp, if not radical, changes in the salience of major factors involved in political coalition-building since World War II. As *The American Voter* demonstrates, for example, status polarization was quite sharp in 1948, but severely declined in 1952 and 1956.[37] In 1960, in turn, the activation of religious-group antagonisms was of great importance to the outcome. Among other things, it reactivated a Catholic group-involvement frame of reference which was quite unexpected in terms of survey work done during the 1950's. As Philip Converse points out:

We note immediately that in 1958 the gradients of party preference as a function of both involvement measures were entirely degenerate: either there was no relationship at all or a non-monotonic progression which summed to a weak positive relationship. On the basis of 1956 data we had once surmised that such seedy patterns as were present at that time in the Catholic instance must reflect the late stages of a decline in group political relevance . . . (t)he events of 1960 dramatically resuscitated the correlation between involvement terms and at least momentary partisan choice.[38]

In 1964, as both survey and aggregate data abundantly demonstrate, powerful regional or sectional frames of reference produced a similarly dramatic, unexpected result.

In all probability the phenomenon which Converse describes applies far more generally than has commonly been supposed. If the argument to this point has validity, there appears to be virtually no time limit between a point in political history marked by any given "correlation between involvement terms and . . . partisan choice," and a subsequent election whose specific stimuli reactivate that correlation positively or negatively. This, perhaps, may be argued to assume too close an assimilation between the findings of aggregate analysis and survey research. In point of fact, however, it is not easy to see how the community displacements examined above — and reflected, for that matter, in the 1964 SRC sample — can be adequately conceptualized or even tentatively explained without reference to activated group-related involvements among large parts of the community electorate. Part of the problem rests with attempting *any* temporal analysis which takes us back before the beginning of systematic survey analysis. We cannot even be *absolutely* sure, for example, that the Catholic group relevance described by Converse for 1960 was present at all in the 1928 election.[39] A second part of the problem involves the paucity of survey-research literature dealing with community "political atmospheres" and their influences in presidential elections, and a corresponding shortage of interview questions designed to trap regional or subregional attitudes derived from local political subcultures.

What still remains to be explained persuasively is the mechanism which produced such massive displacements as those which have been identified here. In the absence of any direct cross-sectional isolation of that mechanism or measurement of its force, we are left only with probabilist inferences which may or may not be verified by subsequent, more intensive analysis. Among these is the strong likelihood that American voting behavior in the present era is cross-cut with a far richer mixture of overt and latent cleavages, cleavages of "ancient" and "modern" vintage, than has hitherto been supposed. This behavior appears to have a major and still largely unexplored dimension which, for want of a better term, may be called "political geology." [40]

V

Major implications, both for the understanding and for the substantive dynamics of American voting behavior, arise from such a hypothesis. Though some of them are clearly speculative, they may prove useful as points of departure for further work in this area — if only to stimulate the asking of different questions than those raised here, and the giving of more satisfactory answers.

1. *The Study of Voting Behavior.* It follows from the argument thus far that any theory of American voting behavior with explanatory power extending beyond an election or a decade must be firmly grounded in comparative analysis across both space and time. Moreover, a more comprehensively satisfactory behavioral theory of voting in the United States will probably have to be constructed out of empirical research as a set of interrelated, conditional problem statements: if condition A exists, behavior pattern X will emerge; if condition B, pattern Y, and so on. The extraordinary variety in political stimuli and resultant mass voting behavior over the past twenty years suggests rather forcefully that the tentative model of nineteenth-century voting behavior developed by Lee Benson is probably still highly relevant for the study of such behavior in the last half of the twentieth century. [41] That is, in the absence of any permanent, systematically organized conflict within the society over the nature of the political regime or over the legitimacy of the capitalist

economic system and the structure of social rewards and status derived from it, an extremely broad range of political conflicts on other dimensions can exist. Of these, ethnocultural and sectional conflicts, emerging from the clash of subcultures with sharply differing values and reference symbols, have historically been the most important. Such conflicts, as the 1964 experience reveals, are still quite capable of moving into at least temporary ascendancy.

Much contemporary research on American voting behavior begins from tacitly uniform assumptions about the American voter. Yet it now seems that any such assumptions are problematic at best. It is very likely that at any level of analysis generalizations about voting behavior which are based on a limited span of observations in any dimension — across time, geographically, or by type of election situation — may prove to be partly or wholly invalid under circumstances other than those in which the generalizations were made. Researchers might well also study the possibility that current cross-sectional methods, including questionnaire construction, were developed without adequate reference to the kinds of deviant situations discussed here. This would hardly be either surprising or blameworthy, but it might lead to a poor fit between the sample and reality in the exceptional situation. Thus, in the 1964 Survey Research Center study, 67.5% of its panel said after the election that they had voted for Johnson. The discrepancy between this and the true figure for the electorate, 61.3%, is greater than the allowable margin of error for samples of this size.

Aage R. Clausen of the Center has recently reported a validation study which was made to identify the sources of error.[42] Clausen concludes that the most reasonable explanation for the overreporting was that the interview situation itself stimulated marginal nonvoters in the sample to vote.[43] But there is reason to believe that this explanation does not entirely account for the discrepancy. In particular, it takes no account at all of the fact that there was a marked geographic differential in the overreporting of the Democratic vote. To take the extreme regional case, the overreporting of the Democratic vote in the South was 11.5%, nearly twice the national average. Moreover, though there was nearly perfect correspondence between survey and aggregate outcomes in the Southern metropolitan areas, the overreporting of the Johnson vote was over 20% in the nonmetropolitan areas of this section.[44] Thus, so far as Clausen's hypothesis is concerned, it requires still to be explained why the interview stimulus should have had such different gross effects within the South or between the South and the rest of the country.

Moreover, another possible source of error, not mentioned in the validation study report, may be the geographical incompleteness of the probability-sample grid itself, *under the special circumstances of the 1964 election.* Necessarily, the most economical probability sample will be constructed on the tacit assumption that no extreme, geographically concentrated discrepancies will develop in voter response to short-term campaign stimuli, a perfectly reasonable assumption in light of 1936–1960

Table 17. *Regional differentials in overreporting the Democratic vote: 1964 SRC study*

Region[a]	% D of two-party vote (aggregate)	% D of two-party vote (SRC)	Pro-D overreporting	N
Northeast	68.4	74 (74.1)	6 (5.7)	(309)
Midwest	61.4	66 (65.6)	4 (4.2)	(358)
West	59.6	65 (65.2)	6 (5.6)	(181)
South	52.5[b]	64 (63.9)	11.5 (11.4)	(263)
Total	61.5[b]	67.5	6 (6.0)	(1111)

[a] The regions are the same as in Note 24, except that Alaska and Hawaii are included in the aggregate totals for the West. Exclusion of them from the aggregate Western vote would yield a Democratic percentage of 59.2 and a regional overreporting of 6.0.

[b] These percentages assume that the vote for Alabama unpledged Democratic electors is credited to Johnson; the Clausen report evidently does also. Excluding these votes, the correct national percentage is 61.3, and in the South 51.8.

experience. In 1964, however, such discrepancies suddenly appeared as major elements in voting behavior, and there is reason to believe that they were not picked up accurately within the existing grid. In particular, there were notable differentiations in Southern voting patterns between the Deep Southern states which Goldwater carried (plus some adjacent areas in other states such as Florida) and the rest of the Southern region. A detailed study of the grid in this region reveals, first, that a disproportionate portion of the sample was drawn in metropolitan areas or counties immediately adjacent to them, and, second, that the Deep South subregion was heavily underrepresented in the total regional sample. As to the latter, the Deep South contributed 25.6% of the total Southern vote, but only 10% of the sample.

There is no reason to believe — as there probably is with Clausen's hypothesis — that any long-term error factors of significance are necessarily associated with the geographical basis of this national sample. But it is clear that they were present in 1964 because of the heavy geographical partitioning involved in the election outcome, and probable that they would recur if a similar election were to occur. Had the Deep South been proportionately represented, for example, the response error in the Southern region might well have been cut in half.

None of the foregoing discussion should be understood as in any way disparaging the great contribution of survey research to our knowledge of American voting behavior. It does suggest that many complexities and difficulties still exist which preclude any early claim that the study of this behavior has achieved the status of an exact science, whatever the method of study may be. In any event, it would be most desirable now to take up the lead suggested by Peter H. Rossi nearly a decade ago and redirect our resources toward much more thorough examination of the influence of local subcultural variables on nationwide election outcomes.[45] It might even be possible to develop a series of intensive local surveys, with overall coordination at Michigan or elsewhere, which could parallel the nationwide studies and provide invaluable comparative frames of reference in the study of the same event.

The importance of aggregate data in further work on the American electorate need not be stressed here. Aggregate data, of course, gives us an indispensable, "hard" set of universe boundaries against which the accuracy of all probability samples can be checked. More than that, however, all past aggregate data may be at least potentially relevant for the study of current voting behavior, granted the peculiar properties of the American voting system. While this may appear to place an enormous burden on scholarship, the recent construction of computerized aggregate-data archives should help to overcome it and result in a proliferation in the near future of long-needed longitudinal studies of electoral phenomena.

2. *Continuity and Change in American Voting Behavior.* What are the substantive implications of this study? There are two lines of speculation which seem of particular relevance in light of the analysis attempted here. In the first place, it seems very likely that the intensity of the movements described above is associated with a quite exceptional penetration into the mass electorate of some form of political consciousness specifically related to the issues and candidates. Of course, there is no way to

ascertain directly from aggregate materials what the nature of that consciousness is, but it is possible to construct a reasonable hypothesis involving it. Assuming that the massive deviations from the norm in 1964
were more than randomly related to the relative awareness of candidates
and issues — especially among the older-stock, Protestant electorate in
the Northeast — it follows that major short-term differentials in candidate and issue perceptions probably exist among mass electorates. In
other words, it is probably useful to think of political consciousness or
awareness in any given electorate in terms of its specific context.[46]

The degree of conscious self- or group-defense in the voting act is
probably directly dependent upon the larger structure of partisan politics at any given time. If most Americans, most of the time, have tended
to vote in accordance with a "standing decision," such behavior would
inevitably appear to the observer to be traditionalist, ritualistic, and
probably indicative of a very low level of voter attention to the issues,
candidates, or campaign styles of any specific election. The ritualized or
routinized defense of group solidarity or family tradition reflects the
peripheral role which politics and elections play in the lives of most
Americans most of the time. It also reflects the nonideological, low-
pressure political styles which normally dominate major-party organizations and election campaigns in the United States.

But there are at least two kinds of cases in which this norm does not
apply. One involves the discrete and insular minority, such as the American Negro, which operates in the political arena under extreme conditions of adverse social pressure. In a multiparty system Negroes would
probably have constructed a *Verzuiling* type of party some time ago;
under such conditions their voting patterns would have tended to display
the kind of extreme long-term stability associated with nationality or
confessional parties in Europe. Lacking that option, this group is quite
capable of moving with astonishing speed and uniformity from one of
the major parties to the other, depending on the perceived existence and
partisan locus of racist campaigning by one of the major-party candidates.
Thus, for example, Negro wards in Baltimore showed an enormous pro-
Republican displacement between the presidential election of 1964 and
the gubernatorial election of 1966. The Democratic percentage of the
two-party vote in these wards fell from 92.6% to 13.4% in the space of
two years, producing a defection ratio of 85.5 compared with a ratio of
20.0 for the city's white wards. There is little question that the specific
contexts of each of these elections — particularly the issue of race rela-

tions which surfaced in both — were decisive in producing such an extra-ordinary Negro swing between the parties.[47]

Movements such as these virtually presuppose a high order of issue consciousness among the group's members when the interests and values of the group itself appear at stake and a very close relating of that consciousness and the voting act. It is particularly suggestive that such clear traces of perceived self- and group-related interest are to be found among a stratum of the population universally conceded to be among the most socially deprived in the nation. But group consciousness and its linkage to political behavior is not inexorably linked to superior education or affluence. It is a function of the structure of politics itself and ultimately of the social context in which members of the group are formed. If that larger context is one of massive deprivation and constraint, and if the usual influence of cross-pressuring and overlapping memberships is weak or nonexistent, the group will have a far different set of political characteristics from the American norm and its members will have an exceptionally well-developed sense of political consciousness whenever group-related issues appear, as they do so frequently for Negroes.

Rather similar contextual dynamics may well underlie the large electoral movements associated with eras of critical realignment. Certainly there are fundamental differences in voting behavior between such transitional periods and the much longer, more "typical" stable phases of electoral alignments. It is not argued here that 1964 was a realigning election in the classic sense, such as the elections of the 1850's, the 1890's, and the 1930's. The election did, however — as we have seen in detail — produce massive deviations from "standing decisions" in many parts of the country, and it was otherwise associated with much the same kind of complex value and policy polarization which has been conspicuous in such elections. The areas of maximum displacement from the norm in 1964, as in earlier elections marked by similarly massive electoral shifts, were in all probability areas which were marked by an abnormally high level of public consciousness about issues, related in some way to the defense of threatened local values against external attack.

This would make sense in terms of a pluralistic contextual theory of political consciousness in the electorate. As Donald E. Stokes suggests, critical realignments are probably associated with a tendency for "position issues," those involving apparently clear alternative policy choices, to be much more visible to the mass electorate than usual. Conversely, "valence issues," about which there are often no "sides," may be the more usual currency of American politics.[48] It is not surprising that when fundamental policy dissensus comes to the surface and is united with value dissensus among well-defined political subcultures, the result is political conflict which has an abnormal tendency to appear as "total" or zero-sum in character. The point is worth making here that such conflicts are just as integral a part of the evolutionary dynamics of American electoral politics as are the more usual, lower-pressure party contests. A working empirical theory of American voting behavior must include both and recognize that there are major differences between them. It is quite possible that a critical election — or one with many characteristics similar to such an election, such as 1964 — may involve the electorate at large in somewhat the same kinds of contextual dynamics for the short term which affect the contemporary Negro electorate on a more or less permanent basis.

The second set of speculative implications arising from this study involves the broader patterns of political development in the United States. The 1964 Republican campaign, with its many archaisms, seems to fit with difficulty into the hypothesis of American electoral development to which the late V. O. Key, Jr., gave the name "dualism in a moving consensus." [49] The operational word in this phrase is the adjective "moving." It involves the proposition that issues which were once highly controversial receive some kind of resolution through the policy process over time, and that the resolution is confirmed and reconfirmed by successive elections won by the dominant coalition responsible for it. Eventually, after the opposition has come to accept this resolution — and especially after it has administered programs once associated with the heart of the controversy — the whole question becomes a matter of historical interest. New ranges of controversy develop elsewhere in this evolving policy continuum.

This view would thus seem to imply some form of stability and sequential development in electoral coalitions themselves. At the very least, throwbacks to earlier coalition alignments, granted the growing nationalization of American politics, ought to be as far removed from the politically possible as a major-party campaign against the substance of domestic programs which have been in operation for more than thirty years. Yet just such a throwback did occur in 1964, and at both levels. This is not to say, of course, that there was no consensus emergent from the election concerning the broad issues associated with welfare-state policies. The lopsided election outcome involved a reaffirmation of it, in fact. But can it be said that the case for movement or progression has been as solidly made?

It seems much more likely that the phenomena which have been studied here represent not movement but a curious timelessness. They constitute one more range of data which suggest a remarkably static party system, one which lacks the patterns of sequential evolution or development which are to be found in the life cycles of other Western democratic systems.[50] It would seem, among other things, that the contemporary American party system has found as yet no single organizing dimension for its cleavages which can definitely retire earlier cleavages to the history texts. In particular, it seems very likely that the realignments of the 1930's permitted the entry of class-based alignments into the mainstream of American voting behavior, but only to the extent of permitting them to compete with other and often older alignments.

We can so easily discover measurable parallels between discrete elections so far apart in time because American political history shows so few evidences of cumulative development. Such a history, and such a party system, could be expected to exist in a polity which has had a monolithic Lockean-liberal value consensus, but which has been preoccupied from its foundation with problems involving the national integration of diverse and often antagonistic subcultures. Although it would be grossly misleading to assume that only a kind of stasis exists in American electoral politics, or to ignore the clear evidences of nationalization of political alignments in recent decades, cases such as 1964 suggest that we are still far from a completion of the national-integration phase of political development. Until such time as this phase is completed, the rich and historically textured diversity of campaign stimuli and voter response which has been described here will continue, in all probability, to be a major factor in the study and practice of American electoral politics.

8. WORKING-CLASS SOCIAL MOBILITY
IN INDUSTRIAL AMERICA

Stephan Thernstrom

Few clichés are more venerable than that which holds that the more fluid the composition of the working class of a given society and the greater the opportunity to climb from lower to higher rungs of the class ladder, the less the likelihood of sharply class-conscious collective working-class protest. Marx, of course, assumed this in his well-known remark about mid-nineteenth-century America, where, "though classes, indeed, already exist, they have not yet become fixed, but continually change and interchange their elements in a constant state of flux," and American public figures from the Age of Jackson to the Age of Johnson have devoted much rhetoric to the same alleged phenomenon, though disagreeing with Marx, I need hardly say, about both its permanence and its desirability.[1]

It is the fate of clichés, however, to escape serious critical scrutiny. So at least in this instance. It is impossible to write about a social group — the working class, the bourgeoisie, or whatever — without making assumptions about the extent to which its composition is stable or in flux, without making assumptions about patterns of social recruitment and social mobility. And yet few students of working-class history have made systematic — in this case, I believe, systematic is synonymous with quantitative — attempts to measure the social mobility of ordinary working people in the past. Thus we have an excellent and generally well-documented survey of the American laboring man in the 1920's baldly asserting, without supporting evidence, that "the worker was seldom afforded the opportunity to rise in the social scale. He lacked the qualifications for the professions and the capital for business." [2] More surprising and amusing is a major historical study of the American labor force by one of the "new" economic historians, who prefaces some ingenious new

statistical estimates of unemployment rates in nineteenth-century de-
pressions with the sound remark that the traditional historian's tendency
to rely upon the impressions of contemporary observers yields a better
measure of variations in the prose styles of those observers than of variations in actual unemployment; he then blithely proceeds to explain
America's rapid economic development as the consequence of the country's exceptionally fluid social system, with nary a hard fact to support the
claim that American society was less rigidly stratified than any other.[3]
The need for careful empirical examination of propositions such as these
should be self-evident.

This paper reports on some of the recent work which is beginning to
provide something more than an impressionistic outline of working-class
social mobility patterns in the United States in the past century or so,
drawing heavily on my own work on Boston in the period 1880–1963.
Research of this kind, I believe, can take us one small step toward a better
understanding of the vast question of the relationship between social
mobility and class solidarity, and the slightly less vast related question of
the sources of American exceptionalism. Studies of American materials
alone, of course, can take us but a limited distance, for these questions
demand comparisons between nations. The absence of an American labor
party cannot be explained in terms of the uniquely high level of mobility
opportunities open to the American worker without demonstrating that
the composition of the working class in the United States has been
highly volatile not in some absolute sense, but volatile relative to other
societies in which a strong labor or socialist party has emerged.

As yet there has been very little historical research on social mobility
in other societies, though there has been a good deal of contemporary
work by sociologists, so that for the present we must settle for the un-
satisfactory tactic of evaluating the American findings largely in isolation.
It should be noted, however, that the two major efforts at comparative
analysis of national differences in mobility rates and patterns since World
War II, those by Lipset and Bendix and S. M. Miller, pose a powerful
challenge to the assumption that American society has been uniquely
open and that its relatively classless politics may be attributed to that
circumstance. Lipset and Bendix argue that "widespread social mobility
has been a concomitant of industrialization and a basic characteristic of
modern industrial society, and though Miller is somewhat more impressed
with differences between nations, his analysis too has a basically revision-
ist thrust.[4] There are a good many technical objections which might be

raised against these studies — most important, that their measure of mobility, the rate of intergeneration movement between blue-collar and white-collar occupations, is much too narrow, that major differences between national social structures cannot be captured in so crude a sieve. And there is the obvious objection that occurs to the historian: that whatever similarities there may be between mobility rates in various industrialized countries since World War II, it is by no means evident that we may safely extrapolate these findings backward to the time, probably somewhere in the nineteenth century, at which the political role of the working class was initially defined. The as-yet unpublished research of William H. Sewell, Jr. on the working class of nineteenth-century Marseille, coupled with my own work on Boston, suggests that such extrapolation may be quite unfounded. The two of us are presently collaborating on a paper which will argue that the sons of Marseille workers escaped into nonmanual occupations with far less frequency than was the case in Boston.

Nevertheless, we must be prepared for the possibility that further mobility research, which should some day permit elaborate and systematic comparative historical analysis, will yield the conclusion that variations in objective mobility opportunities, between nations or over time within a nation, do not in themselves explain very much, that mobility data are meaningless except within a context of well-defined attitudes and expectations about the class system, and that these attitudes and expectations may be most unstable and susceptible to change. Thus, as I have argued elsewhere, the current complaints of American Negroes about their constricted opportunities are the result not of any real deterioration of the position of blacks, but rather of the fact that blacks today are no longer comparing their achievements with those of blacks yesterday, but with those of previous white immigrants and indeed with a romanticized stereotype of the immigrant experience, a stereotype drawn more from the experience of the Jews than that of the Irish or Italians.[5] Similarly, in a fascinating recent paper on social mobility in France on the eve of the explosion of 1789, Philip Dawson and Gilbert Shapiro have shown paradoxically that in those areas where the institutional structure of the ancient regime "made it possible for a bourgeois to improve his social position in a most significant way — by becoming legally a noble — . . . disapproval of the existing system, particularly the details of class and status, was most vigorously manifested. And conversely, where the bourgeois was denied the right to improve his social position in this way

. . . demands for change in general and for reform of the system of rewards for achievement in particular were neither powerful nor widespread." [6] This too should remind us that there is no simple mechanical relationship among social mobility, class solidarity, and political radicalism that holds for all classes, societies, and historical epochs, and that the austerely objective facts uncovered by empirical social research influence the course of history only as they are mediated through the consciousness of obstinately subjective human beings. Though in the body of this paper I largely confine myself to some conveniently measurable aspects of the historical experience of the American working class, I would agree with Edward Thompson that the development of the working class "is a fact of political and cultural, as much as of economic, history." [7] The political and cultural dimensions get short shrift in what follows, not because I think them unimportant but because space is limited and I think it appropriate to concentrate on the least well-known aspects of American working-class history.

I

The first phenomenon which demands attention — geographical mobility, or population turnover — is not normally considered an aspect of social mobility, but I suggest that movement through space, movement into and out of communities, may retard the development of class consciousness in a manner somewhat analogous to movement into a higher social stratum. In his suggestive paper on interindustry differences in the propensity of workers to strike, Clark Kerr proposes that varying degrees of social integration or isolation of the labor force account for the tendency of workers in certain industries to be exceptionally strike-prone and in others to be exceptionally quiescent.[8] In some industrial environments — most notoriously the logging camp, the mining town, the ship, the docks — laboring men form what Kerr calls "an isolated mass." One element making for isolation in these cases is the absence of a complex occupational hierarchy — the absence of a labor aristocracy, really — and minimal opportunities for upward social mobility. This is the venerable assumption mentioned at the outset of this paper, and I will present some data pertaining to it at a later point. But Kerr also alludes to the related variable which is of immediate concern when he remarks that men in the "isolated mass" not only "have the same grievances, but they have them at the same time, at the same place, and against the same people." Conversely, it is well known that certain occupations are inordinately resistant to efforts at trade union organization because they have spectacularly high rates of job turnover. When only 5 percent of the men working at a particular job in a given city at the start of a year are still employed there twelve months later (as is the case in the United States today with short-order cooks and menial hospital employees, for instance), how do you build a stable disciplined organization? An adequate model of the conditions which promote working-class solidarity must presume not only relative permanence of membership in the class — that is, low levels of upward occupational mobility — but also some continuity of class membership *in one setting*, so that workers come to know one another and to develop bonds of solidarity and common opposition to the class above them. This might require a stable labor force in a given place of work; data on labor turnover at the plant level are important if this be the case. But I will give "continuity of class membership in one setting" a looser definition and use it to mean considerable stability of the working class at least within a given city, which would seem to be a minimal necessity if mere complaints are to be translated effectively into class grievances and to inspire collective protest.

Such is the model suggested by Kerr, but he regrettably did nothing to *test* his assumptions about rates of labor turnover, or for that matter rates of occupational mobility, in relatively strike-prone and relatively strike-free industries. Kerr's article provides a persuasive theoretical rationale for systematic scrutiny of labor turnover and occupational mobility; we will have to look elsewhere for solid evidence bearing on these two subjects.

As to the first — geographical mobility — it has long been assumed that the American population has been exceptionally volatile, that Americans have been a uniquely restless, wandering breed. Not until 1940, however, did the Census Bureau include a census question asking where respondents had lived five years previously. Before 1935, population mobility from place to place can be studied in only two ways. One can examine the Census Bureau's tabulations of state of birth data and discover in any census year what fraction of the American population was living in a state other than their state of birth, a useful but exceedingly crude index of internal migration patterns.[9] The other method is what I and a few others have begun to do — to take manuscript census schedules or some other lists of a city's inhabitants at two points in time, and to compute rates of persistence and turnover for the intervening period. This is slow, tedious, and expensive, but it gives a far more accurate sense of the degree to which past Americans — and in particular, working-class Americans — have characteristically remained long within the boundaries of a unit more meaningful than an entire state.

All of the work which has been done — and it is admittedly exceedingly fragmentary — tends to support the stereotype of American rootlessness and to suggest that an "isolated mass" whose members have grievances "at the same time, at the same place, and against the same people" has been a rare species in the United States. The first study of this kind was James C. Malin's classic article "The Turn-over of the Farm Population in Kansas," written thirty-three years ago and little noticed.[10] Both Malin's article and the later inquiry which stimulated much of the current American interest in quantitative social history — Merle Curti's 1959 book on a Wisconsin frontier county in the 1850–1880 period — seemed for a time to be of doubtful relevance to the larger question, since the staggeringly fluid and shifting population they described was on the booming agricultural frontier.[11] It was entirely possible that Americans were more settled in more settled regions of the country, perhaps especially within the cities. And there was the further possibility that figures registering high turnover rates for the population as a whole concealed large deviations from the mean by particular groups — that, for example, there was a majority of ambitious, rising men incessantly on the move, but a substantial minority of low-skilled laborers trapped in urban ghettos.

Both of these possibilities may now be dismissed. Blake McKelvey's examination of Rochester, New York, in the middle of the nineteenth century, my Newburyport inquiry for the same period, and Doherty's research in progress on Northampton, Massachusetts, suggest that the urban population was highly volatile, with half or more of the adult population disappearing from the community in the course of only a decade.[12] Nor is it the case that men on the bottom were immobilized by their poverty, an isolated mass, unlike their restless superiors. To the contrary. In Newburyport and Northampton the working class was more volatile than the middle class, with the least skilled and least well-paid workers most volatile of all. Ray Ginger's analysis of the turnover of textile workers in Holyoke, Massachusetts, in the 1850's points to the same conclusion.[13]

When I began my Boston study, however, I was still a little uneasy about how far this argument could be pressed. Newburyport, after all, was a way station in the orbit of a major metropolis — many of the Irish laborers there had landed in Canada and were in fact slowly working their way down the coast to Boston. Rochester was similarly a stepping stone to the West. Thus these cities might have an unusually large transient population, and there was the more general consideration that relatively small cities might well differ from big cities in this respect. It seemed reasonable to assume that the laborers who drifted out of Newburyport so quickly after their arrival must eventually have settled down somewhere else and that a great metropolis would have offered a more inviting haven than a small community, where anonymity was impossible and institutions of social control pervasive, as contrasted with the classic big-city lower-class ghetto, in which the down-and-out might huddle together in an enduring, protective "culture of poverty." In a major metropolis like Boston, if anywhere in the United States, one might expect to find a stable lower-class population, an isolated mass, a permanent proletariat.

This expectation proved false. If Boston was at all typical, and I believe that it was, in no American city has there been a large lower-class element with continuity of membership. More or less continuously lower-class *areas* can be identified, but *the same individuals do not live in them very long.* As in Newburyport and other small nineteenth-century cities which have been studied, the chance that a worker appearing in a Boston census would be in the community to be counted at the next one a decade later was roughly fifty-fifty throughout the period from 1880 to the present. It is possible that these men in motion typically went to find better jobs, if not fame and fortune, elsewhere. American folklore has always held that migration and upward social mobility go hand in hand, but the point has never been demonstrated with historical evidence; given the sources, it is virtually impossible to explore the issue before the age of modern survey research. In any event it is clear that the bottom layer of the social order of the American city in the past century has included large numbers of permanent transients, unable to sink roots and to form organizations. So rapid was the turnover at this level that the seemingly innocuous residency requirements for voting — typically requiring a year's residence prior to the election — must have disenfranchised a sizable fraction of the working-class population. If the population turnover for Boston is computed on an annual rather than a decennial basis, as I have been able to do using the city directories for the period 1837–1921, it can be determined that roughly a quarter of the population at any one date had not been living in the community 365 days before! This figure is for the entire population, not simply the working class, and the volatility of the working class, especially the unskilled and semiskilled portion of the working class, was even greater. A great many workers, therefore, were legally barred from political participation because they were birds of passage; a great many more, though they remained in Boston long enough to meet the legal residency requirement, were doubtless sufficiently transient in psychology to be politically and socially inert.

These findings are very suggestive, even in the absence of comparable information about working-class-population turnover rates in other societies. The absolute figures themselves are so dramatic as to give considerable credence to the interpretation I put upon them. But it is, of course, important to know if the American experience is at all special in this respect, or if we are instead confronted with a phenomenon common to all industrial societies — or indeed all societies. We know pathetically little about this aspect of demographic history. There are some recently published fragments which raise questions about the assumption of American uniqueness — the remarkable volatility disclosed by the Laslett and Wrigley studies of two seventeenth-century English villages and Laurence Wylie's demonstration that the population of the seemingly placid, sleepy rural commune of Rousillon today is strikingly unstable.[14] Some fascinating research in progress on late nineteenth-century France, however, squares nicely with the argument advanced here. Joan Scott's study of the glassblowers of Carmaux and Albi links the sharp rise in labor militancy that occurred in the 1890's to the sudden settling down of formerly itinerant artisans.[15] With the French glassblowers as well as Eric Hobsbawm's "tramping artisans" and the sheep shearers of Australia and the United States, of course, a high degree of solidarity and craft identification was possible even in the itinerant phase; the distinction between labor turnover of this type and what I have been describing in the American city should be obvious. But that the disappearance of the itinerant pattern should heighten solidarity and militancy as it did in Carmaux and Albi helps to confirm the general hypothesis I have drawn from Clark Kerr's paper. Clearly it will take a good deal of European work comparable to that now going on in the United States to further clarify the relationship between physical mobility and class identification, but pending that I think there is a prima facie case for the view that remarkable volatility of the American working class, past and present, has been an important influence retarding the development and expression of distinctive class loyalties.

II

Let me now turn to the question of occupational mobility. Sometimes it is mistakenly taken to be the only dimension of social mobility worthy of close study, but that it is an important one goes without saying.

Enormous gaps exist in our knowledge about occupational mobility patterns in nineteenth and early twentieth-century America. A good deal is known about patterns of recruitment into the national business and political elite, but this tells us very little indeed about the range of opportunity at the lower and middle levels.[16] There is Curti's study of Trempeauleau County in the 1850–1880 period, but it would obviously be perilous to generalize from the Wisconsin frontier to the urban frontier. There is my work on the unskilled laborers of Newburyport in the same years. But my attempt at the end of that book to argue that Newburyport was America in microcosm was more open to questions than I realized at the time. I had found little movement from working-class to middle-class occupations in my samples, though there was considerable upgrading within the manual category; the major achievement of the typical laborer in the community was to become a homeowner. At least four questions about the generalizability of this finding remained open:

1) Was it possible that the social structure of the large cities of this era was notably different — either more or less fluid?

2) Was Newburyport atypical even for small cities, in that its rate of population growth and economic expansion in the years I treated was unusually low?

3) I examined the career patterns of unskilled workmen and their children. Might not a study of the skilled craftsmen have yielded much greater evidence of interclass mobility?

4) A large majority of the unskilled laborers in Newburyport were recently arrived Irish immigrants. To what extent would mobility patterns have differed in a community in which the working class was less heavily immigrant, or immigrant but not Irish?

It was in hopes of clearing up some of these uncertainties that some years ago I began work on a large-scale statistical study of the career patterns of some 6,500 ordinary residents of Boston in the years 1880–1963. The analysis is not yet complete, but the main outlines of the argument are fairly clear.

It does appear either that Newburyport was an unusually sluggish place for aspiring laborers, or that small cities in general offer fewer opportunities; rates of movement from blue-collar to white-collar posts, both in the course of a career and between generations, were much higher in Boston throughout the entire period. If an individual's first job was in a blue-collar calling, the odds were that at the end of his career he would still be in the working class. But a substantial minority of men climbed to a middle-class post, usually in small business or in minor clerical and sales positions, and remained there — 25 to 30 percent in the five cohorts I traced. There were, in addition, others who began in the blue-collar world, worked for a period in a nonmanual position, and fell back into a manual job later in life. Very little of this upward mobility involved penetration into the upper reaches of the middle class, to be sure; these men did not become professionals, corporation managers, or the heads of large business operations. But certainly here was evidence which challenged the socialist critic's assumption that the dream of individual mobility was illusory and that collective advance was the only realistic hope for the worker.

Even more impressive was the opportunity to escape the class into which one was born — the class of one's father. Fully 40 percent of the working-class sons in Boston held middle-class jobs of some kind by the end of their own careers. The comparable figure for mid-nineteenth-century Marseille, William H. Sewell, Jr., has found, was a mere 11 percent. And if there was any rationality in the system by which the 40 percent who climbed were selected from the entire pool of working-class sons, they must have included much of the leadership potential which would have accrued to the working-class cause in a more rigidly stratified society.

Both types of mobility — career and intergenerational — occurred at a relatively constant rate over this entire eighty-year period. There were some minor temporal fluctuations, with the Great Depression of the 1930's showing diminished opportunities, as we would expect, but the overall similarity of the figures is very striking. To lament the creeping arteriosclerosis of the class system has been a popular American pastime for many a year, but the facts do not sustain this diagnosis.[17] The economy, the political structure, and a good many other aspects of Boston changed dramatically over this long span of time, but whatever governs the rate of circulation between occupations seems to have been highly resistant to change.

It is also noteworthy, and not a little surprising, that the sons of the least advantaged members of the working class — the sons of the unskilled and semiskilled — fared just as well in the competition for middle-class jobs as did the children of the labor aristocracy. That my Newburyport study dealt only with unskilled laboring families was therefore not as limiting as I had feared. The average rate of penetration into the middle-class world by the sons of unskilled and semiskilled workmen in Boston was actually a little above the 40 percent figure for the entire working class, with the figure for the children of skilled craftsmen a little below 40 percent. Similarly with respect to intragenerational, or career mobility, the 25 to 30 percent rate of ascent into the middle class for men who began their careers in a working-class job held for all grades of manual jobs — the lowest as well as the highest.

This is striking in light of the observation of Eric Hobsbawm and Royden Harrison that in nineteenth-century Britain perhaps the greatest break in the class hierarchy was between the labor aristocrat and the less skilled men below him. "The boundaries of the labor aristocracy were fluid on one side of its territory," the upper side, where it "merged with" the lower middle class, but "they were precise on the other." This is in part, though only in part, a judgment about mobility opportunities; the English labor aristocrat's "prospects of future advancement and those of his children" were allegedly much better than the prospects of ordinary workingmen.[18] That does not seem to have been the case in Boston. Now it is possible that Hobsbawm and Harrison are mistaken in their claim; the most judicious observers can go astray when they attempt to gauge mobility rates on the basis of qualitative rather than quantitative evidence. It should also be noted that we are not talking about precisely the same group; my working-class elite is simply all men in recognized skilled trades, whereas Hobsbawm and Harrison have in mind a much more select group, at most the top 15 percent of wage earners. For a variety of reasons I was unable to isolate a small element within the skilled category that would be exactly comparable to what they mean by "the labor aristocracy." Nevertheless, it is quite possible that we are dealing here with a genuine historical difference between the social structures of the two societies, with the imperceptible blending of the British labor aristocracy into the lower middle class taking in the United States the form of a blending of the entire urban working class into the lower middle class. Sewell's work in Marseille suggests that there was indeed a labor aristocracy there; the sons of skilled craftsmen rose into middle-class callings at three times the rate of sons of unskilled workers.

The work of Hobsbawm and Harrison is also helpful in suggesting the desirability of examining occupational advance within the working class, as well as from the working class to the middle class. The mobility of a common laborer's son into the skilled category as I have defined it was less of an achievement than the presumably rare entry of a laborer's son into the labor aristocracy of nineteenth-century Britain, but it was surely a clear-cut advance with respect to wages, vulnerability to unemployment, and so forth. If we consider the total movement of sons of unskilled or semiskilled workmen into skilled or white-collar occupations in Boston, we find that somewhat more than 60 percent of the sons of the semiskilled and slightly less than 60 percent of the sons of the unskilled were upwardly mobile. (The comparable figure for the sons of skilled craftsmen — the percentage who reached either skilled or nonmanual occupations — was 75 percent.) If this is at all valid as a measure of opportunity for working-class children — if entry into a skilled trade is a significant accomplishment, as I think it was — a distinct minority of the sons of Boston workers had grounds for doubting that the United States was the land of opportunity, where classes "have not yet become fixed, but continually change and interchange their elements in a constant state of flux."

I should hasten to say that these figures are, in one significant way, inflated. They sum up the mobility experiences not of all of the hundreds of thousands of workingmen who lived in Boston at some time in the 1800–1963 period, but rather of those who settled down in the community long enough to have careers which might be measured. I have already stressed the remarkable volatility of the American population, and here I should point out that this fact must be taken into account in interpreting findings based on the study of people who were sufficiently settled to remain under the investigator's microscope long enough to be examined. This would pose no great difficulty if it could be assumed that disappearance from the universe of the study was more or less random, but the problem is that migration and occupational mobility were intimately and intricately related, that those men most likely to leave the community and to go uncounted probably had different occupational mobility prospects than those who remained. Different types of people left the city for a host of different reasons, and I wouldn't dare attempt to generalize about them all. But I would suggest that though much of the movement of men with skills or capital was in response to new opportunities elsewhere, much of the movement of relatively unskilled and uneducated working-class people was of a very different kind — it was helpless drifting rather than rational pursuit of more favorable circumstances elsewhere. I strongly suspect, therefore, that if it were possible for me to track down all of the laboring men who appeared in one of my Boston samples but migrated elsewhere — most likely several elsewheres — and worked the rest of their lives outside of Boston, the net effect of including them would be to depress somewhat the mobility rates I have reported. Some of these working-class migrants were doubtless highly successful elsewhere, but my guess is that most were not and that indeed their departure from Boston was a symptom of failure and an omen of future failure.

This is speculative — necessarily speculative, I fear, in that there is no way of systematically tracing migrants from an American community in the past. But it does appear from my data that the American city — perhaps the European city too, but it remains to be seen — is a kind of Darwinian jungle into which vast numbers of low-status migrants pour. Most of them do not flourish, most of them do not stay very long; a process of selection, of unnatural selection if you like, takes place. Those who do manage to make a go of it economically are not as likely to depart physically, which is why any collection of individuals who simply survive ten years to be counted in the next census have an average occupational rank higher than a sample of newcomers in the intervening decade.

Perhaps it is this Darwinian process which explains why my estimates of working-class mobility in Boston are somewhat higher than those which come from American sociological studies conducted in the past thirty years or so.[19] Some of these studies are based on interviews of nationally representative samples; some of them deal with particular cities. But none were affected by this selective process, for they depended on interviews or records which made it possible to compare the occupations of fathers and sons even when they lived in different communities. Migrants were not lost to the study, as was the case in Boston, and that presumably served to moderately depress working-class occupational mobility rates accordingly.

These studies, I suppose, might be said to give a more accurate portrait of the American class structure, in that they did not exclude the drifting men who passed through Boston so quickly as to escape my scrutiny. I have two rejoinders to that. One is simply to plead necessity. The drifters can be included if the researcher is willing to confine himself to the very recent past, which is all that can be dealt with through survey research techniques; they can be included when the investigator is fortunate enough to find historical records which provide the necessary information, such as the population registers of some Northern European countries, the French military registration records (never tapped for this purpose, so far as I know), or the marriage license applications of a state like Indiana, which give the occupation of the groom and of the father of the groom. But for most of the American past such helpful records do not exist, and it seems to me foolishly perfectionist to take this as a reason for abandoning systematic study altogether. Systematic analysis of the experiences of part of the population — the relatively settled part — seems clearly preferable to the sheer guesswork that has been rampant up until now.

A second and more important line of defense is that my Boston figures, and any others based on the tracing of individuals within particular cities, may be more realistic, in a certain sense, than the findings of more inclusive studies which do not lose the floating element of the working-class population — more realistic, that is, if we are interested in the political and social consequences of the stratification system. I suggested earlier that the permanent transients of the American scene were unable to make their presence felt. Some were technically disenfranchised much of the time; most were psychologically disenfranchised, so that however sharp their grievances, however much the national mythology that this was the land of opportunity was contradicted by their own experience, it made little difference. These men may have been America's permanent proletariat — we don't know enough to be sure how many of them, and how many of their children, were trapped in this pattern — but in any case they were a disorganized, pulverized proletariat. It is justifiable, therefore, not to count them because they did not count, though today we would certainly want to count them in drawing up a moral balance sheet on the performance of the American social system. If the Boston data on working-class occupational mobility is any guide, most American workers in the past eighty years who were in a position to make themselves heard had good reason to think that they were edging their way up the social scale, that there was no impassable gulf which separated the exploited masses from the privileged class which lived on the fruits of their labor. Many workers did not make it in Boston, but they did not remain on the scene long enough to make their weight felt and were tossed helplessly about from city to city, alienated but invisible and impotent.

III

The work I have done since the publication of my Newburyport study has convinced me that I was a little too quick to generalize from that case to American society as a whole, and yet I have been speaking here as if Boston can safely be assumed to be the United States in microcosm. I would concede that a good many more studies of this sort need to be conducted in American communities of various types before one can speak too confidently about these matters. Some of this work is already underway. For the first half of the nineteenth century there is Stuart Blumin's study of Philadelphia, Peter Knights's investigation of Boston, and Robert Doherty's comparative analysis of a number of small Massachusetts communities. For the latter part of the century there is the work of Herbert Gutman and his students on Paterson, New Jersey, Buffalo, and other cities; Richard Sennett on Chicago; Howard Gitelman on Waltham, Massachusetts; and Clyde Griffen on Poughkeepsie, New York.[20] These studies may well challenge the propositions set forth here. But my hunch is that the rest of industrial America will prove to resemble Boston more than Newburyport. The results of the sociological studies conducted in the past generation certainly suggest that conclusion, if appropriate adjustments are made for the fact that they included the transient types who were lost in the Boston case.

It is possible that relatively small cities like Paterson, Poughkeepsie, and South Bend will follow the Newburyport pattern of very restricted occupational mobility, but I am inclined to think that the unusual sluggishness of the Newburyport economy in these years limited opportunities more than in equally small but fast-growing cities.

Another characteristic which might possibly have made Newburyport somewhat distinctive was that its laborers were mostly Irish Catholic immigrants. The possibility that incoming groups with differing traditions have very different mobility patterns clearly deserves further investigation. My Boston findings seem to indicate that the Irish and other Catholic groups are indeed somewhat deviant from the general immigrant pattern, but not quite in the way I had anticipated. Contrary to Max

Weber and his latter-day followers like Gerhard Lenski, Boston working-class Catholics climbed into middle-class jobs and had sons who reached the middle class just as frequently as did Protestant workingmen.[21] Catholics, however, were highly distinctive in their inability to *remain* in the middle class. Catholics holding middle-class posts, and their sons, fell back down into the working class much more frequently than their Protestant counterparts did. This may say something about Catholic, particularly Irish Catholic, working-class culture; it may, however, reflect circumstances peculiar to Boston or perhaps to the large cities of the Northeast — the combination of a heavily Catholic, largely Irish, working class, and a local economy dominated by militantly Protestant Yankees. Obviously it will require studies in other types of communities to resolve this issue.

The final question on which I wish to comment briefly involves another discrepancy between the Newburyport and Boston studies. Perhaps the most striking finding of the former inquiry was that despite wage levels hovering close to what middle-class observers thought bare subsistence, recurring unemployment, and slight opportunities for occupational advance, the laborers of Newburyport (especially the Irish) were remarkably successful in accumulating substantial property holdings, largely in the form of small homes and plots of land. I argued that such property mobility — movement not into the middle class but from the floating lower class into the stable working class — was of great significance in minimizing discontent and tying these men into the prevailing order.

Herbert Gutman has quite properly taken me to task for my somewhat vulgar assumption that homeownership is an inherently conservatizing influence, and I am happy to retreat from my exposed position and concede that it all depends — upon the social setting, the expectations of the group in question, and perhaps other things as well.[22] What I would insist upon is only that possession of property is an important determinant of a man's social position and social allegiances, and that students of working-class history have been insufficiently diligent about investigating this aspect of their subject. Royden Harrison notes that at one point in *Order and Progress* (1875) Frederic Harrison wrote that "there is no greater break in our class hierarchy than that between the lowest of the propertied classes and the highest of the non-propertied classes" and at another place that "throughout all English society there is no break more marked than that which in cities divided the skilled from the unskilled workmen" without detecting the inconsistency.[23]

One appreciates Frederic Harrison's confusion, for it is a neat question whether occupational rank or property position is the more powerful influence. Not enough thought has been given to this question, partly because we have too readily assumed that the latter can safely be inferred from the former — that few workmen, except for the highly skilled, were able to save significant amounts. Doubtless this has been true of many societies, and it may well explain Frederic Harrison's seeming inconsistency; the distinction between the unskilled and the nonpropertied may have been a distinction without a difference in the England of the 1870's. It was, however, an important distinction in the United States, if the Newburyport experience is any guide. The Newburyport evidence suggests that a substantial fraction of the American working class, including many unskilled and semiskilled workers, stood on the propertied rather than the nonpropertied side of the break in the class hierarchy.

I had hoped to be able to illuminate this matter further with my Boston materials, but that hope was disappointed. The only records available for the period since 1880 disclose real-property but not personal-property holdings, and it happens that Boston was a city with very few single-family dwellings; the $1,000 which purchased a small dwelling in Newburyport had to be increased several-fold to buy a triple-decker tenement. The very inadequate measure I have of working-class property holdings — a measure of real estate holdings only — thus drastically underestimates total wealth of the group. At the last date at which the sources include information about personal as well as real property, 1870, real estate owners were only 41 percent of the total group of Boston workers holding some property. I therefore can say with confidence that the true incidence of property ownership in the Boston working class since 1870 was much higher than the real estate tax records suggest, but since I don't know which individuals in my samples had large savings accounts and which didn't, I cannot analyze the characteristics of the propertied as opposed to the unpropertied worker. For a variety of reasons I was unable to fill this gap by consulting the savings bank depositor's records that I found so helpful in Newburyport.

Future investigators who are fortunate enough to have more adequate sources of information about personal savings, however, will still face difficult problems of interpretation, for it is evident that American working-class attitudes toward saving, investment, and consumption have shifted dramatically in this century. Whether today's automobiles and appliances, often purchased on the installment plan, are in any way equivalent to the nineteenth-century home — which is not to imply that working-class homeownership is a vanishing phenomenon, quite the contrary — is a knotty question I can't attempt to answer here, except to suggest that it seems important that becoming a homeowner in nineteenth-century Newburyport required prolonged disciplined behavior long before the goal could be attained, whereas today even the poor have become accustomed to flying now and paying later. This makes them highly vulnerable to economic vicissitudes, because many have made long-term financial commitments based on the most optimistic assumptions about future income and few have developed the remarkable penny-pinching facility of the laborers of Newburyport. They have more possessions, certainly, but perhaps less security comes with the possessions.

Systematic knowledge about working-class social mobility in industrial America, in sum, is scanty and spotty, but what little there is does seem to square with the age-old belief that social classes in the United States "continually change and interchange their elements in a constant state of flux." High rates of occupational and property mobility and selective patterns of urban migration which weeded out the unsuccessful and constantly reshuffled them together produced a social context in which a unified "isolated mass" of dispossessed, disaffected workmen could not develop. It would be valuable to be more certain that these generalizations do indeed apply throughout industrial America in the past century. It would be interesting to see if deviations from what I take to be the national pattern could help explain these instances in which groups of American workmen acted in a more militantly class-conscious manner than has generally been the case; studies of population turnover and social mobility in such settings as mining towns organized by the Western Federation of Miners and the I.W.W. could be very revealing. It would also be helpful to discover whether these forms of working-class mobility were equally available in societies in which class solidarity was a more conspicuous fact of national life — Britain, France, Germany, and so forth. The answers to these questions are by no means obvious. I am certain only that they are worth asking and exploring if the social history of the common people is to advance beyond mere impressionism.

APPENDIXES
NOTES ON CONTRIBUTORS
NOTES
INDEX

APPENDIX A
READING LISTS AND EXAMINATIONS,
1951–1952, 1968–1969

FALL TERM READING LIST

Students are requested to buy:

1. G. M. Trevelyan, *A Shortened History of England* (Longmans, Green)
2. John Milton, *Aereopagitica* (Everyman, or any other cheap edition)
3. John Locke, *Treatise of Government* (Appleton-Century-Crofts)
4. Selections from Max Weber's *Theory of Social and Economic Organization* (multilithed; obtainable as announced in lecture)

Note: Lamont has only a few copies of the *Shortened History* and bookstores will not have it in quantity until November. If you cannot get the *Shortened History,* do the alternative reading in the unabridged edition, of which many copies are available in Lamont and Radcliffe Library.

For background and for references to books for further reading, consult:

1. Crane Brinton, *Ideas and Men*
2. G. H. Sabine, *A History of Political Theory*
3. J. W. Thompson, *History of the Middle Ages, 300–1500*
4. W. Y. Elliott and Neil MacDonald, *Western Political Heritage*
5. K. Feiling, *A History of England*

Also keep in mind the usefulness of:

1. *The Encyclopedia Britannica*
2. Hastings, *Encyclopedia of Religion and Ethics*
3. *The Catholic Encyclopedia*
4. *The Encyclopedia of the Social Sciences*

5. *The Cambridge Medieval History* and *The Cambridge Modern History*
6. W. R. Shepherd, *Historical Atlas*

Books in which reading has been assigned are on reserve in Lamont and the Radcliffe Library, where you will also find the reading indicated on the list as mimeographed. Also as shown on the list, certain documents, etc., have been reproduced and will be distributed to members of the class at section-meetings.

Topic I: THE CULTURE OF EARLY ANGLO-SAXON SOCIETY

(1) Week of Sept. 24

> *Required:* Ruth Benedict, *Patterns of Culture*, especially Chs. I–III.
> *Optional:* Ralph Linton, *The Study of Man*, Chs. I–VI; Clyde Kluckhohn and Wm. Kelly, *The Concept of Culture*.

(2) Weeks of Oct. 1 and Oct. 8

> *Required:* W. E. Lunt, *History of England*, Chs. II–IV;
> Tacitus, *Germania*, especially Chs. 1–26;
> F. B. Gummere, *The Oldest English Epic* (Beowulf); You may omit lines 1065–1160; 1900–2200; 2220–2310;
> Bede, *The Ecclesiastical History of England*, Book I, Chs. 1–16, 23, 24; Book II, Chs. 1–16, 20; Book III, Chs. 1–6, 14–18, 21, 22, 24; Book IV, Chs. 1, 2, 5, 17; Book V, Chs. 23, 24;
> The Laws of Aethelberht and The Laws of Ine; the Decree Concerning Hot Iron and Water; to be distributed.
> *Optional:* F. B. Gummere, *The Founders of England*;
> D. E. Martin-Clark, *Culture in Early Anglo-Saxon England*;
> K. S. Latourette, *History of the Expansion of Christianity*;
> Emile Durkheim, *The Elementary Forms of the Religious Life*, especially Ch. VII and Conclusion;
> Pollock and Maitland, *History of English Law*, Book I, Ch. I, "Anglo-Saxon Law";
> Jolliffe, *Constitutional History of Medieval England*, Ch. I, sec. i; Ch. II, sec. i;
> Carl Stephenson, "The Problem of the Common Man in Early Medieval Europe," *American Historical Review*, April, 1946;
> Walter Bagehot, *Physics and Politics*.

Appendix A

Topic II: THE SOCIAL AND POLITICAL STRUCTURE OF MEDIEVAL ENGLAND

(1) Week of Oct. 15

Required: W. E. Lunt, *History of England*, Chs. V–XI.

(2) Week of Oct. 22

Required: Linton, *The Study of Man*, Chs. VII, VIII;
G. C. Homans, *English Villagers of the 13th Century*, Chs. III–VI, XVI, XVII, XX–XXII.
Optional: J. T. Dunlop et al., *Toward a Common Language for the Area of Social Science*;
Homans, *English Villagers*, remaining chapters;
W. J. Ashley, *Introduction to English Economic History and Theory*, Vol. I;
H. S. Bennett, *Life on the English Manor*;
Austin Lane Poole, *Obligations of Society in the 12th and 13th Centuries*.

(3) Required:

C. H. McIlwain, *Growth of Political Thought in the West*, pp. 201–233.
John of Salisbury, *Policraticus* (In Dickinson, *Statesman's Book*), Book IV, Chs. I–IV, VII, X, XI; Book V, Chs. I–III, V; Book VI, Ch. XX; Book VIII, Chs. XVIII, XX.

(4) Week of Nov. 11: *The Struggle between Henry II and Thomas Becket*

W. R. W. Stephens, *The English Church from the Norman Conquest to the Accession of Edward I*, pp. 156–186 (mimeographed).
David Knowles, *The Episcopal Colleagues of Archbishop Thomas Becket*, pp. 142–154 (mimeographed).
Selections from Contemporary Writers (mimeographed).

Topic III: THE PURITAN REVOLUTION

1. Weeks of Nov. 18 and 25 and Dec. 2: *The Role of Ideas in History*

(1) K. Marx and F. Engels, *The German Ideology*, pp. 1–78 (mimeographed)
K. Marx, *Capital*, Ch. 24, "Primary Accumulation" (in some editions titled "Primitive Accumulation" and subdivided into chapters with titles beginning "The Secret of Primitive Accumulation" and ending "Historical Tendency of Capitalist Development.")

243

(2) Max Weber, *The Protestant Ethic and the Spirit of Capitalism*, pp. 35–183 (mimeographed).

2. Weeks of Dec. 9 to Jan. 15 (incl.): *Interpretations of the Puritan Revolution*

(1) Trevelyan, *Shortened History*, Book III and Book IV (except Ch. VI)
(2) I. Deane-Jones, *The English Revolution*, pp. 1–133 (mimeographed)
(3) Morton, *A People's History of England*, pp. 134–260 (mimeographed)
(4) Selections from the Putney Debates (to be distributed)
John Milton, *Aereopagitica*
John Locke, *Treatise of Government*, Chs. 1–9, and 19.

SPRING TERM READING LIST

REQUIRED READING

Students are requested to buy:

1. Thomas Hobbes, *Leviathan* (Everyman)
2. J. J. Rousseau, *Social Contract* (Everyman)
3. Walter Bagehot, *The English Constitution* (preferably World's Classics edition)
4. John Stuart Mill, *Utilitarianism*, Liberty & Rep. Govt. (Everyman)
5. F. Nietzsche, *The Genealogy of Morals* (Modern Library Giant)
6. Crane Brinton, *A Decade of Revolution* (Text ed., Harper & Bros.)

Topic V: THE FRENCH REVOLUTION (Feb. 4–March 17)

1. Theory (2 weeks)

Hobbes, *Leviathan*, Introduction & chs. 13–18, 21, 24, 26, 29, 30.
Rousseau, *Social Contract*, Bks. I & II; Bk. IV, chs. I, II, VII, VIII

2. History (4 weeks)

Hayes and Cole, *History of Europe since 1500*, chs. 34, 39–42.
Brinton, *A Decade of Revolution*
Selections from two of the following, as assigned in section meetings:

Thomas Carlyle (1795–1881), *The French Revolution*
H. A. Taine (1828–1893), *The Ancient Regime; The French Revol'n*
F. A. Aulard (1849–1923), *The French Revolution*
A. Mathiez (1874–1932), *The French Revolution*

Appendix A

Topic VI: BRITISH REFORMS IN THE 19TH CENTURY
March 18–April 21)

1. History (2 weeks)

Adam Smith, *The Wealth of Nations*, Introduction by Max Lerner;
Introduction & Plan of Work; Bk. I, chs. I & II; Bk. IV, chs. I & II
Selections from one of the following as assigned in section meetings:

E. Halévy, *History of England in 1815*
G. M. Trevelyan, *British History in the 19th Century*
G. D. H. Cole, *Short History of the British Working Class Movement*
Cole and Postgate, *The British People, 1746–1946*

2. Theory (2 weeks)

Walter Bagehot, *The English Constitution*, esp. chs. 1, 2, 5, 8.
J. S. Mill, *On Liberty.*

Topic VII: THE FALL OF THE WEIMAR REPUBLIC
(April 22–May 26)

1. Theory (1 week)

Nietzsche, *The Genealogy of Morals*

2. History (4 weeks)

Hayes and Cole, *History of Europe since 1500*, chs. 48–55.
Selections from two of the following, as assigned in section meetings;

Karl Loewenstein, "Government and Politics in Germany," in *Governments of Continental Europe*, ed. by J. T. Shotwell
Franz Neumann, *Behemoth*
Erich Fromm, *Escape from Freedom*
F. Meinecke, *The German Catastrophe*
Konrad Heiden, *Der Fuehrer*

1951–52
HARVARD UNIVERSITY
SOCIAL SCIENCES 2
(*Three hours*)

Write on FOUR of the following, including at least one starred (*) question.
Avoid overlapping in your answers.

1. "Weber's theory of authority is merely a scheme of classification. It does not help us understand why certain events occurred and certain institutions arose." Discuss, referring to specific historical examples.

2. "In spite of his reforms, Henry II was through and through a feudal monarch. . . . In spite of later misinterpretations, Magna Carta was a thoroughly feudal document."

3. "Agrarian capitalism could not develop within the framework of the medieval manor."

4. "Although James I's theory of the Divine Right of Kings was practically out-dated, it did serve to illuminate the crux of the issues which were only resolved by the Civil War."

5. "The economic structure of society always forms the real basis, from which, in the last analysis, is to be explained the whole superstructure of legal and political institutions, as well as of the religious, philosophical and other conceptions of each historical period." (Engels)

   Discuss, referring to English history in the 16th and 17th centuries.

*6. "In his struggle with Henry, Beckett was not an innovator, but was 'standing upon the ancient ways.'"

*7. According to Weber, although Lutheranism and Calvinism were alike individualistic and predestinarian, Lutheranism favored economic traditionalism, while Calvinism favored economic rationalism. In other words, not every form of the Protestant ethic promoted the spirit of capitalism. How does Weber account for this difference? What do you think of his explanation of the difference?

Mid-Year. February, 1952.

1951–52
HARVARD UNIVERSITY
SOCIAL SCIENCES 2

Write on FOUR of the following, including at least one of the starred (*) questions.

1. "If you will compare the old with the new conditions of life, you must grant that, on balance, the English working classes benefited very considerably from the Industrial Revolution."

2. "By a gradual transition towards democracy, seldom hastening and never turning back, political rights were extended to all without a catastrophe. This great manoeuvre was safely accomplished because all classes and all parties showed upon the whole sound political sense and good humor." (Trevelyan)

3. "It was purely by chance that the Nazi success came in Germany. The rise to power of such a group might have taken place just as easily in any other Western, industrial, rational-legal society." Weigh the evidence for and against this statement.

4. "Nietzsche was an early symptom of the decay of Western society that later produced Nazism."
(Do not write on this question if you have written on question 3.)

*5. "Hobbes was a liberal, but no democrat; Rousseau was a democrat, but no liberal."

*6. "Brinton's evidence does not, as he thinks, disprove the Marxist theory of revolution as applied to France 1789–99."

Final. May, 1952.

SOCIAL SCIENCES 2   FALL TERM 1968–69

READING LIST

The work of the Fall Term consists of three essays, one for each topic, and the mid-year examination. Section Men will make specific assignments and suggest additional reading for these essays.

Students should own the following books, available at the Harvard Coop, or elsewhere as announced:

1. BUNYAN, John, *The Pilgrim's Progress*
   Paperback: New American Library: Signet Classics CD221
2. *Documents for Class Use* (Assize of Clarendon, Writs in Glanville, Magna Carta, and the Constitutions of Clarendon). Pamphlet: University Printing Office. On sale in the General Education Office, 1737 Cambridge St., Rm. 602.
3. HILL, Christopher, *The Century of Revolution 1603–1714*
   Paperback: W. W. Norton: N365
4. MARX & ENGELS: *Basic Writings on Politics and Philosophy*, Edited by Lewis S. Feuer. Paperback: Doubleday: Anchor Books A185

5. MARX & ENGELS: *Communist Manifesto*
   Edited by Samuel H. Beer. Paperback: Appleton-Century Crofts: Crofts Classics
6. *Social Contract: Essays by Locke, Hume, and Rousseau,* Edited by Ernest Barker. Paperback: Oxford: Galaxy Books GB68
7. TIERNEY, Brian, *The Crisis of Church and State 1050–1300*
   Paperback: Prentice-Hall: Spectrum Books S102
8. WEBER, Max, Selection from *The Theory of Social and Economic Organization,* Translated by A. Henderson and T. Parsons
   Pamphlet: University Printing Office. On sale in the General Education Office: 1737 Cambridge St., Rm. 602.
9. WALZER, Michael, *The Revolution of the Saints.* Paperback: Atheneum

Everything on the following list is on "closed reserve" in Lamont and Hilles Libraries. The dates suggested here will vary during the semester; lectures and section discussions should be your guides.

Topic I: TRADITIONALISM AND THE MEDIEVAL POLITY

1. Week of September 23: *The Sociology of Authority*

   WEBER, Max, *The Theory of Social and Economic Organization,* pp. 324–392. This selection (No. 8 above) is bound separately as a pamphlet.

2. Weeks of Sept. 30, Oct. 7 and 14: *Feudal Monarchy in England*

   HOMANS, George, *English Villagers of the Thirteenth Century,* chaps. 3–6, 16, 17, 20–22.
   POOLE, Austin Lane, *From Domesday Book to Magna Carta 1087–1216,* Chaps. I–III, V, X–XIV.
   JOLLIFFE, J. E. A., *The Constitutional History of Medieval England,* pp. 139–263.
   JOHN OF SALISBURY, *The Statesman's Book* (from the *Policraticus*), Translated by John Dickinson, Introduction: chs. I–II, V. Text: IV: 1, 2, 4, 11; VI: 18; VIII: 17 (pp. 335–336), 18, 20.
   English Historical Documents 1042–1189 (Vol. II of series) Edited by David C. Douglas and George W. Greenaway. Nos. 1 (years 1135–1140), 43, 10a, 21, 12 (pp. 322–24, 331–33, 335–38).
   Documents for Class Use (Pamphlet), Assize of Clarendon, etc.

Topic II: DYNAMICS OF MEDIEVAL DEVELOPMENT

1. Week of Oct. 21: *The Sociology of Religion*

   WEBER, Max, *From Max Weber: Essays in Sociology,* Edited by H. Gerth and C. W. Mills, "The Social Psychology of World Religions," pp. 267–301

Appendix A

WEBER, Max, *The Sociology of Religion*, Edited by Talcott Parsons, chs. VIII, IX, and XIII.

2. Weeks of Oct. 28 and Nov. 4: *Theories of Spiritual and Temporal Power*

TIERNEY, Brian, *The Crisis of Church and State 1050–1300*, pp. 1–95, 127–138.

BROOKE, Z. N., *Lay Investiture and its Relation to the Conflict of Empire and Papacy* (Mimeographed)

TELLENBACH, Gerd, *Church, State, and Christian Society in the time of the Investiture Contest*, chs. 1 (sections 1, 3), and 2.

LOVEJOY, Arthur O., *The Great Chain of Being, A Study of the History of an Idea*, pp. 24–77.

JOHN OF SALISBURY, *The Statesman's Book*, Introduction: ch. IV
Text: IV: 3 (pp. 9–10); V: 1, 2, 5; VI: 20, 21, 24; VII: 17, 18, 19; VIII: 17 (p. 339), 23 (pp. 398–399, 405–410).

3. Week of Nov. 11: *The Gregorian Revolution in England*

POOLE, A. L., *From Domesday Book to Magna Carta*, chs. VI–VII.

KNOWLES, David, *The Episcopal Colleagues of Archbishop Thomas Becket*, ch. V.

KNOWLES, David, *Archbishop Thomas Becket; a Character Study.*
English Historical Documents, Nos. 79, 113, 121, 122, 124, 129, 133, 134, 136, 138, 149, 152, 156.
Documents for Class Use, Constitutions of Clarendon

Topic III: RELIGIOUS REVOLT AND POLITICAL MODERNIZATION

1. Weeks of Nov. 18 and 25: *Analytical Perspectives*

MARX & ENGELS: *Basic Writings on Politics and Philosophy*, Edited by Lewis S. Feuer, pp. 1–67, 82–111.

MARX, Karl, *Capital*, Modern Library Edition, pp. 784–837 (chs. 26–32). In some editions this is ch. 24, entitled, "Primary Accumulation."

BEER, Samuel H., Introduction to MARX & ENGELS, *Communist Manifesto*, pp. VII–XXIX, Crofts Classics.

WEBER, Max, *The Protestant Ethic and the Spirit of Capitalism*, Translated by Talcott Parsons, pp. 35–c. 62, 79–128, 144–183.

2. Weeks of Dec. 2, 9, 16: *The Puritan Revolution*

HILL, Christopher, *The Century of Revolution 1603–1714*, chs. 1–11.

TAWNEY, R. H., "The Rise of the Gentry 1558–1640" in *Economic History Review*, Vol. II. Mimeographed separately.

Appendix A

HEXTER, J. H., "Storm Over the Gentry," in HEXTER, *Reappraisals in History*

BUNYAN, John, *The Pilgrim's Progress*, Portions of the First Part: in Signet edition, pp. 17–30, 66–110, 131–148.

WALZER, Michael, *The Revolution of the Saints*, chs. I, II, IV, V (pp. 148–171), and IX.

LOCKE, John, *An Essay Concerning . . . Civil Government*, chs. 1–9, 19. Available in *Social Contract: Essays by Locke, Hume and Rousseau*.

SOCIAL SCIENCES 2   SPRING TERM 1968–69

READING LIST

Students are asked to buy the following books, which are available at the Harvard Coop or, in the one case, at the General Education Office.

1. BRIGGS, Asa, *The Making of Modern England*
   Paperback: Harper Torchbooks 1203
   (Hardcover title: *The Age of Improvement*)
2. BURKE, Edmund, *Reflections on the Revolution in France*
   Paperback: Bobbs-Merrill: The Library of Liberal Arts 46
3. COBBAN, Alfred, *A History of Modern France*, vol. I: 1715–1799
   Paperback: Pelican A403
4. HOBBES, Thomas, *Leviathan* (Parts I and II)
   Paperback: Bobbs-Merrill: The Library of Liberal Arts 69
5. MILL, John Stuart, *On Liberty*
   Paperback: Appleton-Century-Crofts: Crofts Classic
6. NIETZSCHE, Friedrich, *The Birth of Tragedy and the Genealogy of Morals* Paperback: Doubleday: Anchor Books A-81
7. de TOCQUEVILLE, Alexis, *The Old Regime and the French Revolution*
   Paperback: Anchor Books A-60
8. *Social Sciences 2 Selections* (Alfred Cobban, *The Myth of the French Revolution* and related excerpts)
   Pamphlet: University Printing Office

Everything on the following list is on "closed reserve" in Lamont and Hilles Libraries. The dates suggested here will vary during the semester; lectures and sections should be your guides

Topic IV: IDEOLOGY AND REVOLUTION

Weeks of February 2 & 9:

HOBBES, Thomas, *Leviathan*, esp. Intro., chs. 11, 13–15, 17–21, 26, 29–30, and Review and Concl.

ROUSSEAU, Jean-Jacques, *The Social Contract,* esp. Book I; Book II; Book III, chs. 1–4, 12–18; and Book IV, chs. 1–2, 7–8 (in the Galaxy paperback edition used for Locke's *Second Treatise* in the Fall Term)
BLACK, C. E., *The Dynamics of Modernization,* chapter I

Weeks of February 16 & 23:

COBBAN, Alfred, A *History of Modern France,* vol. I, Entire.
de TOCQUEVILLE, Alexis, *The Old Regime and the French Revolution,* Foreword, pp. 1–211.
Social Sciences 2 Selections (Alfred Cobban, *The Myth of the French Revolution* and related excerpts by Cobban and Lefebvre)
TILLY, Charles, *The Vendée,* chaps. 1, 2, 4, 9, 13.

Topic V: MODERNIZATION WITHOUT REVOLUTION

Week of March 2:

BURKE, Edmund, *Reflections on the Revolution in France,* esp. 3–4, 35–60, 66–73, 77–91, 95–115, 126–129, 138–144, 169–200, 247–266, and 286–291 (Page citations to the Library of Liberal Arts paperback edition)
PALMER, R. R., *History of the Modern World,* ch. XI (to p. 430; p. 458 to end)
RICHTER, Melvin, *The Politics of Conscience,* chs. I (sec. 2) and X (sec. 2) (On the Halévy Thesis)

Weeks of March 9, 16 & 23:

BRIGGS, Asa, *The Making of Modern England* (Hardcover title, *The Age of Improvement*), chs. I, II (secs. 2–3), III (sec. 5), IV–VI, VIII (secs. 1–3, through p. 416), and IX (sec. 3)
DICEY, A. V., *Lectures on the Relations between Law and Opinion in England during the 19th Century,* Lectures 4, 6, 9, 12 (pt. 1)
BEER, Samuel H., *British Politics in the Collectivist Age,* Intro., chs. I–II.
ECKSTEIN, Harry, "On the Etiology of Internal War" in *History and Theory,* vol. IV, no. 2 (1965), 133–163. Xeroxed separately.
MILL, John Stuart, *On Liberty,* chs. 1–2, 4

Topic VI: THE CRISIS OF MODERNITY

Week of April 6:

NIETZSCHE, Friedrich, *The Genealogy of Morals*

Weeks of April 13, 20, & 27:

PALMER, R. R., *History of the Modern World,* secs. 48, 58, 64, 84, 88, 90, 98, and 104

PINSON, Koppel S., *Modern Germany: Its History and Civilization*, chs. 15–21 (First or Second Edition)

BULLOCK, Alan, *Hitler: A Study in Tyranny*, chs. 1–4, 7
Reichstag, Election Statistics, 1919–1933, Mimeographed. To be distributed.

PARSONS, Talcott, "Certain Primary Sources and Patterns of Aggression in the Social Structure of the Western World" and "Democracy and Social Structure in Pre-Nazi Germany." Mimeographed. (These two essays also appear in Parsons, *Essays in Sociological Theory*)

VIERECK, Peter, *Metapolitics: From the Romantics to Hitler* (Capricorn paperback subtitle: *The Roots of the Nazi Mind*), Prefatory Note (or, in paperback, "New Survey," secs. 3–4, and chs. 1–2, 5–7, 11–13)

ERIKSON, Erik H. "The Legend of Hitler's Childhood" in *Childhood and Society*, ch. 9

ECKSTEIN, Harry, *A Theory of Stable Democracy*

Reading Period Extra: Nazi Films
Wednesday, May 7 at 7 p.m., Lowell Lecture Hall

FINAL EXAMINATION (*May 21*)

1968–69
HARVARD UNIVERSITY
SOCIAL SCIENCES 2

Choose ONE of the following questions and write an essay for the full length of the examination. Think carefully before making a choice, and take time to outline your ideas before you begin to write.

1. *Compare* the justifications for rebellion which can be derived from the belief systems of English feudalism, Gregorian Christianity, Puritanism, Lockean liberalism.

2. "Radical intellectuals, whatever their pretensions, have played a role in political change only to the extent that their teachings have contributed to the strengthening of social discipline or to the imposition of new modes of control." Discuss this proposition with reference to medieval and 17th century England.

3. "A 'situational analysis,' stressing the logic of events and the forces working 'behind the backs of individuals,' is far more useful in accounting for historical change than an 'intentional analysis' which limits itself to the motives and ideas of individual men." Discuss with reference to Marx and Weber, using examples from the historical material we have studied.

4. We have paid attention in this course to the influence of various institutions, and their beginnings, on political developments: kings, barons, administrators, and bishops; Church, bureaucracy, and congregation. Discuss the influence of institutional rationalization on the 12th century English monarchy and on the Puritan Revolution.

5. Write a discussion between Weber and Marx on the role of ideas and the "materialistic" analysis of society. What would each have said about John of Salisbury, Becket, Gregory VII, John Bunyan, and John Locke?

6. "Just as our opinion of an individual is not based on what he thinks of himself," Marx wrote, "so can we not judge such a period of transformation by its own consciousness; on the contrary, this consciousness must rather be explained from the contradictions of material life, from the existing conflict between the social forces of production and the relations of production." What was Weber's response to this point of view? Using examples from both the medieval and early modern periods we have studied, what contributions have Marx and Weber made to your understanding of the possible relations between human consciousness and social change?

Mid-year Examination, January 22, 1969.

HARVARD UNIVERSITY
SOCIAL SCIENCES 2
FINAL EXAMINATION

Choose ONE of the following questions and write an essay for the full length of the examination. Think carefully before making a choice, and take time to outline your ideas before you begin to write.

1. "The function of radical intellectuals is, as Nietzsche suggests, essentially life-conserving. They appear at times of intolerable anxiety and resentment among non-privileged classes. They do not create these emotions but construct myths to explain and redirect them. Aggression is thus focused outward, and life is saved: revolution and war are, after all, moderate when the alternative is self-annihilation."

Does this theory correctly describe the roles of the Puritan ministers, the 18th century *philosophes*, and the proto-Nazi and Nazi ideologues? Explain why or why not. If you find some other theory more useful in describing these roles, show how it differs from the above before going on to apply it to the three cases.

2. "Some people have criticized Weber's typology of authority for being static. Actually the concept of rationalization which is implied by his no-

tion of rational-legal authority throws a great deal of light upon revolutionary change."

Discuss with relation to the following: the Puritan Revolution, the French Revolution, and the Nazi revolution.

3. "Fundamental political change is possible only as a result of a fundamental change in the mode of production; political change does not last if it passes beyond, or contradicts, the economic basis. The final political consequences of the French Revolution were, accordingly, less radical than the English reforms of the 1830s. Similarly, Germany reverted to authoritarianism in 1933 because democracy was not appropriate to monopoly capitalism." Discuss.

4. "All the revolutions and political changes we have studied were undertaken in the name of liberty but ended in the imposition of repression on some new basis. The burden of order has been shifted, not lightened. It is an illusion to think that liberal society was a genuine emancipation." Do you agree?

5. Edmund Burke believed that radical ideas could destroy the web of attitudes and prejudices on which society is based; that radical intellectuals could be held accountable for social upheaval. With reference to the revolutionary changes we have studied, evaluate Burke's estimate of the power and consequences of ideas.

6. "As the rationalization of Western institutions has proceeded despite interruptions, political theorists have, paradoxically, become more sensitive to the non-rational aspects of society and public morality."

If this is an accurate estimate of a broad tendency, how do you explain it? In particular, does Weber's concept of rationalization help to account for this trend? Refer in your answer to specific theorists and specific social contexts.

Final Examination, May 21, 1969.

APPENDIX B
TEACHING STAFF,
SOCIAL SCIENCES 2 (1946–1970)

Adler, Charles C., Jr.
Allison, Graham T., Jr.
Baer, George W.
Bain, Henry McR.
Ban, Michael M.
Bathory, Peter D.
Beer, Samuel H.
Bernstein, John A.
Birnbaum, Norman
Boericke, W. T. S.
Brady, Jeremiah D.
Bujarski, George T.
Burnham, Walter D.
Chambers, William N.
Clark, Martin
Conway, John J.
Daniell, Jere R., II
Davis, Thomas J., III
Diamond, Norman W.
Ellenburg, Stephen
Epstein, Klaus W.
Fink, Richard M.
Greenbaum, Richard
Hagedorn, Homer J.
Henretta, James A.
Herbst, Juergen F. H.

Hoffman, John M.
Holland, Maurice J., Jr.
Horowitz, Gad
Jaher, Frederic C.
James, Sydney V., Jr.
Jay, Martin E.
Karl, Barry D.
Kerr, Clarence W.
Kissinger, Henry A.
Kolden, Rolf J.
LaGrand, John J.
Lowenthal, David
MacMaster, Robert E.
McCloskey, Robert G.
Macridis, Roy C.
Mead, Lawrence M., III
Nadel, George H.
Nash, Arnold E. K.
Olmsted, Michael S.
Orlov, Ann
Pauker, Guy J.
Pollack, Norman
Reisman, Karl M. L.
Resnick, Daniel P.
Richter, Melvin
Robinson, Glenn A.

Rosenberg, Isabel W. R.
Rothman, Stanley
Russell, Richard H.
Schlesinger, James R.
Sennett, Richard
Sletten, Charles A.
Smith, Francis D.
Sorum, Paul C.
Stamatopulos, Stephen
Stern, Sheldon M.
Struve, Guy M.
Tanzer, Michael D.
Thernstrom, Stephan A.
Thomas, David B.
Thomas, Stephen R.
Tilly, Charles H.
Tjoa, Hock G.
Ulam, Adam B.
Walzer, Michael L.
Wendon, John
Werlin, Robert J.
Werner, Louis K.
Woods, Elsworth
Wright, Christopher
Wurgaft, Lewis D.

NOTES ON CONTRIBUTORS

Samuel H. Beer, Professor of Government, Harvard University, is the author of the *City of Reason; Treasury Controls: Coordination of Financial and Economic Policy in Great Britain*; coeditor and author of *Patterns of Government: The Major Political Systems of Europe*; and *British Politics in the Collectivist Age*, which was awarded the Woodrow Wilson Foundation Award of the American Political Science Association in 1965. He has given Social Sciences 2 since 1946, except for those years when he has been on leave. He is currently at work on problems of centralization and decentralization, some aspects of which are treated in his 1969 Messenger Lectures at Cornell University on "The Power of the Center."

Walter Dean Burnham, Associate Professor of Political Science, Washington University, St. Louis, is the author of *Presidential Ballots, 1836–1892* and coauthor and coeditor with William Nisbet Chambers of *The American Party Systems: Stages of Political Development*. He has received a National Science Foundation grant for the years 1968–1970 to study quantitative aspects of party coalitions over the past century.

Klaus Epstein was Professor of History and Chairman, Department of History, Brown University, and the author of *Matthias Erzberger and the Dilemma of German Democracy* and the *Genesis of German Conservatism*, the second volume of which was nearly complete at the time of his death in 1967.

Sydney V. James, Professor of History, University of Iowa, is the author of *A People Among Peoples: Quaker Benevolence in Eighteenth-Century America*. He is at work on a study of changing configurations of institutions in colonial Rhode Island.

Notes on Contributors

Melvin Richter, Professor of Political Science, City University of New York, Hunter College, is the author of *The Politics of Conscience: T. H. Green and his Age,* which was awarded the Triennial Prize of the Conference on British Studies in 1966. He is at work on a study of Montesquieu, Tocqueville, Élie Halévy, and Raymond Aron as well as anthologies of Montesquieu and Tocqueville as political theorists.

Stephan Thernstrom, Professor of History, University of California, Los Angeles, is the author of *Poverty and Progress: Social Mobility in a Nineteenth Century City,* and *Poverty, planning, and Politics in the New Boston: The Origins of ABCD.* He is writing a monograph on social mobility in Boston, 1880–1963, and a broader volume on the social history of modern Boston.

Charles Tilly, Professor of Sociology and History, University of Michigan, is the author of *The Vendée.* A Fellow at the Center for Advanced Study in Behavioral Sciences, 1968–1969, he is engaged in studies of relationships between large-scale structural changes in society (especially urbanization and industrialization) and changes in the character of collective violence and protest, with France since the Revolution receiving the main emphasis.

Michael Walzer, Professor of Government, Harvard University, is the author of *The Revolution of the Saints* and has edited with Philip Green, *The Political Imagination in Literature.* He is also the author of *Obligations: Essays on Disobedience, War, and Citizenship.*

NOTES

Notes to Introduction

1. *General Education in a Free Society*. Report of the Harvard Committee (Cambridge, 1945).
2. *Ibid.*, p. 213.
3. Daniel Bell, *The Reforming of General Education* (New York, 1966), p. 51. In this passage I have paraphrased Professor Bell except for the citations indicated as taken directly from him.
4. *General Education*, p. viii.
5. *Ibid.*
6. Professor Beer has proposed this explanation in a memorandum on the background and history of Social Sciences 2.
7. *General Education*, p. viii.
8. *Ibid.*, p. ix.
9. *From Max Weber: Essays in Sociology*, tr. and ed. by H. H. Gerth and C. Wright Mills (New York, 1946); Max Weber, *The Theory of Social and Economic Organization*, tr. A. M. Henderson and Talcott Parsons (New York, 1947).
10. Talcott Parsons, *The Structure of Social Action* (New York, 1937).
11. Norman Birnbaum, "Conflicting Interpretations of the Rise of Capitalism: Marx and Weber," *British Journal of Sociology*, 4 (1953), 125–141.
12. Samuel H. Beer, *British Politics in the Collectivist Age* (New York, 1965), pp. 10–11.
13. Michael Walzer, *The Revolution of the Saints: A Study in the Origins of Radical Politics* (Cambridge, 1965).
14. Michael Walzer, "Puritanism as a Revolutionary Ideology," *History and Theory*, III (1967), 77.
15. *Ibid.*, p. 76.
16. Montesquieu, *The Spirit of the Laws*, XIX, 5.

17. Charles Tilly, *The Vendée* (Cambridge, 1964).

18. William Nisbet Chambers, *Political Parties in a New Nation: The American Experience, 1776–1809* (New York, 1963).

19. Others attending were Norman Birnbaum, Harry Eckstein, Klaus Epstein, and George Nadel. Several excerpts from manuscripts or papers especially written for the occasion were published by *History and Theory*, III (1963), pp. 1–120.

20. ". . . The Comparative Method is not a comparative method in the sense in which the term would be coined today. Everyday usage, as well as the analogy of well-established designations such as Comparative Religion, Comparative Law, etc., bring to mind something like a study of essential analogies, an investigation of entire structures for essential similarities and differences. They suggest an approach which presumably can be applied to any or all languages, and, when so applied, should yield a taxonomy. Of course there is such a branch of linguistics, but we call it typology. The label 'comparative linguistics (comparative philology)' is preempted by a different kind of pursuit. As Friedrich Schlegel (1772–1829), the German Romantic poet, writer, and Oriental scholar, said in 1808: 'That decisive factor which will clear up everything is the inner structure of languages, or comparative grammar, which will give us altogether new insights into the genealogy of languages, in a manner similar to that in which comparative anatomy has shed light on higher natural history.' And later Franz Bopp (1791–1867) speaks of a 'comparative dissection of languages,' of 'linguistic anatomy,' and the like. Ever since then, the term 'comparative' in technical linguistic use has referred, not to comparison at large, comparison for comparison's sake (i.e., typological comparison), but to a process whereby original features can be separated from recent ones, and where the aim of classification is subordinated to the aim of reconstruction. Thus, genealogical reconstruction, arrived at by the Comparative Method, may well be at variance with typological classification." Henry M. Hoenigswald, "On the History of the Comparative Method," *Anthropological Linguistics*, V (1963), 1–2.

21. E. A. Freeman, *Comparative Politics* (Oxford, 1873).

22. J. W. Burrow, *Evolution and Society* (Cambridge, 1966), pp. 12–13.

23. "The Parallel of Deism and Classicism," in A. O. Lovejoy, *Essays in the History of Ideas* (Baltimore, 1948), pp. 78–98.

24. Quite apart from the tradition of German *Historismus* but startlingly close to the position taken by Wilhelm Dilthey, Ernst Troeltsch, and their nearest English equivalent, R. G. Collingwood, is E. E. Evans-Pritchard, *The Comparative Method in Social Anthropology*, L. T. Hobhouse Memorial Trust Lecture, No. 33 (London, 1963).

25. *Economy and Society*, ed. Guenther Roth and Claus Wittich, 3 vols. (New York, 1968), I, xxix–xxxiv.

26. *Ibid.*, xxxi.

27. *Ibid.*, xxxii.

28. *The American Party Systems: Stages of Political Development*, ed. William Nisbet Chambers and Walter Dean Burnham (New York, 1967).

29. Klaus Epstein, *Matthias Erzberger and the Dilemma of German Democracy* (Princeton, 1959).

30. Klaus Epstein, *The Genesis of German Conservatism* (Princeton, 1966).

31. Tilly, *The Vendée*, p. 342.

32. Walter Dean Burnham, personal communication to Professor Beer.

33. Stephan Thernstrom, *Poverty and Progress: Social Mobility in a Nineteenth Century City* (Cambridge, 1964).

34. Stephan Thernstrom, "Notes on the Historical Study of Social Mobility," *Comparative Studies in Society and History*, X (1968), 162.

35. *Ibid.*, pp. 162–163.

36. *Ibid.*, p. 170.

37. *Ibid.*, p. 172.

38. Some examples of this interest are Melvin Richter, "Tocqueville's Contribution to the Theory of Revolution," in *Nomos VIII: Revolution*, ed. C. J. Friedrich (New York, 1966): "Montesquieu" and "Elie Halévy," in *International Encyclopedia of the Social Sciences* (New York, 1968); "Comparative Political Analysis in Montesquieu and Tocqueville," *Comparative Politics* I (1969), pp. 129–160.

39. Sydney James, *A People Among Peoples: Quaker Benevolence in the Eighteenth Century* (Cambridge, 1963); Melvin Richter, *The Politics of Conscience: T. H. Green and his Age* (Cambridge, 1964); Norman Birnbaum, "The Zwinglian Reformation in Zurich," *Past and Present* (April 1959), pp. 27–47; and in Werner J. Cahnman and Alvin Boskoff, eds., *Sociology and History* (New York and London, 1964), and Norman Birnbaum, "The Sociological Analysis of Ideologies, 1940–60," in *Current Sociology*, IX, no. 2 (1960); Michael Walzer, *The Revolution of the Saints*.

Notes to Chapter 1.

1. Karl Popper, *The Poverty of Historicism* (London, 1957), p. 122. See also Popper, *The Logic of Scientific Discovery* (New York, 1961), pp. 59–60.

2. Carl G. Hempel, "The Function of General Laws in History," *Journal of Philosophy*, XXXIX (1942), 35.

3. Willard Van Quine briefly pointed out this difficulty in 1948 in a review of Hans Reichenbach's *Elements of Symbolic Logic* in *The Journal of Philosophy* at p. 165. Nelson Goodman discusses it in great detail in *Fact, Fiction and Forecast* (Cambridge, Mass., 1955), see esp. pp. 77–78.

4. Carl G. Hempel, *Aspects of Scientific Explanation* (New York, 1965), pp. 264–270. This discussion comes in an essay originally published in 1948. Popper takes up the question of the characteristics of universal statements in his *Logic*, esp. sections 14 and 15. The whole controversy is examined by R. S. Walters in Vol. IV of the *Encyclopedia of Philosophy* (New York, 1967) under the entry "Laws of Science and Law-like Statements," pp. 40–44.

5. Hempel, *Scientific Explanation*, p. 270.

6. Samuel H. Beer and Adam B. Ulam (eds.), *Patterns of Government: The Major Political Systems of Europe* (rev. ed.; New York, 1962).

7. See, e.g., *ibid.*, pp. 14–15.

8. Angus Campbell et al., *The American Voter* (New York, 1960), p. 521.

9. *Ibid.*, pp. 9–10.

10. William O. Aydelotte, "Notes on the Problem of Historical Generalization," in Louis Gottschalk (ed.), *Generalization in the Writing of History* (Chicago, 1963), p. 148.

11. Marc Bloch, *Feudal Society*, trans. L. A. Manyon (Chicago, 1961), p. 447.

12. Ernest Nagel, *The Structure of Science: Problems in the Logic of Scientific Explanation* (New York, 1961), pp. 544–545.

13. Wittgenstein, *Lectures and Conversations* (Berkeley, 1966), Part I.

14. A. R. Louch in *Explanation and Human Action* (Blackwell, Oxford; 1967), argues that since human action is to be explained in terms of the goal of particular actions and not by reference to general theories, the hopes of behavioral scientists for a general theory of human action is misconceived.

15. Samuel H. Beer, *British Politics in the Collectivist Age* (New York, 1965), *passim*.

16. Max Weber, *The Theory of Social and Economic Organization*, trans. Henderson and Parsons (New York, 1947), p. 91.

17. William Dray, *Laws and Explanation in History* (London, 1957), p. 122.

18. *Ibid.*

19. Richard C. Snyder, "Game Theory and the Analysis of Political Behavior," in Nelson W. Polsby et al., *Politics and Social Life* (Boston, 1963), p. 132.

20. Weber, *Social and Economic Organization*, p. 96.

21. *Ibid.*, p. 92.

22. It is certainly not my intention to try to analyze this enormously complex process of artistic creation. An example, however, may help bring out the similarity as well as the difference when we compare the use of the imagination by artists and social scientists. In his notebooks Henry James describes in great detail how he conceived and wrote *The Spoils of Poynton*. He has a twofold concern. Primarily, of course, he has his dramatic and aesthetic purposes — purposes presumably absent from a social science inquiry. We see these develop as he becomes more and more interested in Fleda's "heroism," which ultimately comes to dominate this "drama of renunciation."

There is, however, also another "control" (— the term is Monroe Beardsley's, cf. "On the Creation of Art," *Journal of Aesthetics and Art Criticism*, Vol. 23 (Spring 1965) — on the process of composition. This is the need to make the narrative behaviorally convincing; in short, the problem of its "truth-value." Continually we see James making adjustments of character and action in order to meet this criterion. One brief example: for dramatic purposes he must have Mrs. Gereth voluntarily return the "spoils" to Poynton. This action, however, requires a convincing motivation. At first he explains her action as flowing simply from her desire that Fleda, so much like her in appreciation, possess these beautiful things. On reflection he sees that this is not a "sufficient motive" and so draws out another motive, namely, her desire to impel Fleda to win Owen away from Mona.

We see this concern for behavioral credibility in various general reflections of James. He wants the action to be "natural." He is concerned that the whole story be "closely and admirably *mouvementé*." "It must be," he wrote, "in a word, a close little march of cause and effect." (p. 251) F. O. Matthiessen and Kenneth Murdock (eds.) *The Notebooks of Henry James* (New York, 1947) esp. 136, 198, 201, 214, 247, 251, 252. Also see James's Preface to *The Spoils of Poynton, Collected Works.* (New York, 1908).

23. *British Politics in the Collectivist Age,* esp. chaps. iii and xii.

24. While unintended by the norms and in this sense not legitimized by them, it nevertheless does not violate them. For instance, it is legitimate under these norms for a producer group to refuse its advice to a government department. It cannot simply refuse outright, but only if, for instance, it feels that it is being unfairly treated, or that its reasonable advice is being wantonly disregarded. Although such a refusal is legitimate, in fact the government is put in an impossible position because of the virtual monopoly of experience which the group may possess. As a result, the government gives in, or rather anticipating this possibility, is a good deal more considerate of group opinion than the term "advice" would suggest. Thus, without any violation of norms, advising has become bargaining and a new pattern of behavior has emerged.

25. Sir Charles Lyell, *Principles of Geology* (New York, 1887) vol. I, p. 318. Cf. pp. 314–20 and vol. I, chap. v, "Prejudices Which Have Retarded The Progress of Geology," pp. 88–109.

26. In a powerful attack on the attempt to treat history as a science, Isaiah Berlin writes: "All seemed ready, particularly in the nineteenth century, for the formulation of this new, powerful, and illuminating discipline . . . All was ready, but practically nothing came forth. No general laws were formulated — nor even moderately reliable maxims — from which historians could deduce (together with knowledge of the initial conditions) either what would happen next, or what had happened in the past." "History and Theory: The Concept of Scientific Theory," *History and Theory,* I, 1 (1960), 6–7.

27. Marc Bloch, *The Historian's Craft,* trans. P. Putnam (New York, 1967), p. 14.

28. In a letter to the author from which I have also taken the quotations in this paragraph. See also his article in this volume.

29. Charles Tilly, *The Vendée* (Cambridge, Mass., 1964), p. 342.

30. Refer to this essay, p. 44r9.

31. For an example of the importance of the time dimension in the study of American voting behavior, see Walter Dean Burnham, "The Changing Shape of the American Political Universe," *American Political Science Review,* Vol. 59, 1 (March 1965), 7–28. By extending his concern historically, he

reveals some remarkable and massive changes in the "relative size and characteristics in the American voting universe."

32. William N. Chambers and Walter Dean Burnham, *The American Party Systems* (New York, 1967). By taking a long historical perspective, Chambers is able to show how American parties have shifted from being an independent to a dependent variable in the political system.

33. S. M. Lipset, "History and Sociology — An Introductory Statement," in R. Hofstadter and S. M. Lipset (eds.), *Turner and the Sociology of the Frontier: The Sociology of American History* (New York, 1968).

34. Robert A. Dahl, "The Behavioral Approach in Political Science," in Nelson W. Polsby, et al., *Politics and Social Life* (Boston, 1963), pp. 15–25.

35. The work of Robert F. Bales on small groups greatly helped with the development of Parsonian theory. See Talcott Parsons, et al., *Working Papers in the Theory of Action* (Glencoe, 1953), pp. 10–11.

36. I am using the term "historicism" in the sense made familiar by Karl Popper in his *Poverty of Historicism*.

37. *Ibid.*, p. 108.

38. Quoted in Talcott Parsons et al., *Theories of Society: Foundations of Modern Sociological Theory* (New York, 1961), pp. 1275–1276.

39. Popper, *Poverty of Historicism*, p. x.

40. Since conditions of both sorts will almost always be present in some degree, our formulation will be more quantitative. As Harry Eckstein suggests in his discussion of a paradigm for the analysis of internal war, we will attempt to "weigh" the positive and negative conditions. "On the Etiology of Internal War," *History and Theory*, Vol. IV, no. 2.

41. J. S. Mill, *Logic*, III, v, par. 3.

42. John Dewey, *Logic: The Theory of Inquiry* (New York, 1938), p. 320.

43. Nagel, *The Structure of Science*, p. 468.

44. See Dankwart A. Rustow, *A World of Nations: Problems of Political Modernization* (Washington, D.C., 1967).

45. Refer to pp. 48–57, this essay.

46. Beer, *British Politics*, p. 78.

47. Quoted by Alasdair MacIntyre in "Sociology and the Novel," *Times Literary Supplement*, no. 3, 413 (July 27, 1967), 657.

48. Popper, *The Poverty of Historicism*, p. x.

49. Refer to p. 52, this essay.

50. MacIntyre, in the *Supplement*.

Notes to Chapter 2.

1. Alexis de Tocqueville, *De la Démocratie en Amérique, Oeuvres complètes. Edition définitive publiée sous la direction de J. P. Mayer*, 2 vols. (Paris: 1951), Vol. I. Hereafter cited as Tocqueville, *Oeuvres* (M) I, i. All translations are my own.

2. *Ibid.*, p. 4; John Stuart Mill, "Bentham," in *Essays on Politics and Culture*, Gertrude Himmelfarb, ed. (New York, 1962), p. 123.

3. George Wilson Pierson, *Tocqueville and Beaumont in America* (New York, 1938).

4. *Ibid.*, p. 768.

5. *Oeuvres complètes d'Alexis de Tocqueville*, Gustave de Beaumont, ed. (9 volumes; Paris: 1864–1866), letter from Tocqueville to Louis de Kergolay, November 10, 1836, I, 338. Hereafter cited as *Oeuvres* (B).

6. Himmelfarb, *Essays*, p. 232.

7. Seymour Drescher, *Tocqueville and England* (Cambridge, Mass., 1964); Melvin Richter, "Tocqueville on Algeria," *Review of Politics* XXV (1963), 362–398.

8. Pierson, *Tocqueville and Beaumont*, pp. 758–760, 769.

9. *Ibid.*, p. 769.

10. Hans Baron, *The Crisis of the Early Italian Renaissance* (rev. ed.; Princeton, 1966).

11. Cf. R. R. Palmer, *The Age of the Democratic Revolution*, 2 vols., (Princeton, 1959, 1965) I, chaps. ii–iv; Franklin L. Ford, *Robe and Sword* (New York, 1965); Louis Althusser, *Montesquieu: la politique et l'histoire* (Paris, 1959).

12. *Oeuvres complètes de Montesquieu*, ed. Roger Caillois, 2 vols. (Paris, 1949), II, 1137.

13. Cf. Melvin Richter, "Charles-Louis de Secondat, Baron de Montesquieu (1689–1755)," *International Encyclopedia of the Social Sciences* (New York, 1968).

14. "Essai sur les Causes qui peuvent affecter les esprits et les caractères," in *Oeuvres*, ed. Caillois, II, 39–68.

15. *Ibid.*, 39, 49.

16. *Ibid.*, 1103.

17. *Ibid.*, 39–68.

18. *Ibid.*, 61.

19. *Ibid.*, 57.

20. Montesquieu gives different lists in different places, Cf. *Ibid.*, 58; *De l'Esprit des lois*, XIX.

21. John Plamenatz, *Man and Society*, 2 vols. (New York, 1963), II, 263.

22. Montesquieu, *De l'Esprit des lois*, XIX, chap. xvi.

23. *Ibid.*, XIX, chap. xxii.

24. *Ibid.*, XIX, chap. xvii.

25. *Ibid.*, II, III.

26. *Ibid.*, II, chap. iv.

27. *Ibid.*, V, chap. vi.

28. *Ibid.*, II, chap. iv.

29. *Ibid.*, "Avertissement de l'auteur" (explanatory note).

30. *Ibid.*, XI, chap. vi; XIX, chap. xxvii.

31. Montesquieu, *Considérations sur les causes de la grandeur des Romains et de leur décadence*, chap. ix.

32. Montesquieu, *De l'Esprit des Lois*, III, chap. x.

33. I wish to acknowledge the kind permission of Professor G. W. Pierson to consult the Tocqueville Collection in the Yale University Library. I have conflated here *Cahier Alphabétique* A and *Cahier Alphabétique* B IIe. I have chosen topics derivative from Montesquieu, but have not referred to all the topics in the two lists. Tocqueville by no means included all of Montesquieu's categories of causes.

34. Tocqueville, *Oeuvres* (B), I, 378. Letter to Louis de Kergolay, October 18, 1847. This translation is taken from *Memoir, Letters and Remains of Alexis de Tocqueville*, trans. by the translator of *Napoleon's Correspondence with King Joseph*, 2 vols. (Boston, 1862), I, 342.

35. Tocqueville, *Oeuvres* (M), I, i, 322–323.

36. Cf. Melvin Richter, "Tocqueville's Contributions to the Theory of Revolution," in *Nomos VIII: Revolution*, ed. C. J. Friedrich (New York, 1966), 79–82.

37. Tocqueville, *Oeuvres* (M), I, i, 300.

38. *Ibid.*, 306.

39. *Ibid.*, 312.

40. *Ibid.*, 301–315.

41. J. G. A. Pocock, "Machiavelli, Harrington, and English Political Ideologies in the Eighteenth Century," *William and Mary Quarterly*, 3rd ser., XXII (1965), 549–583; " 'The Onely Politician': Machiavelli, Harrington and Felix Raab," *Historical Studies: Australia and New Zealand*, XII, 46 (1966), 265–293; "The Strategies of Institutionalized Time," unpublished lecture, 1966, pp. 1–21; "Civic humanism and its role in Anglo-American Thought," *Il Pensiero Politico*, I (1968), pp. 172–189. The best treatment of the place of citizenship in Tocqueville's thought is Doris S. Goldstein's, "Alexis de Tocqueville's Concept of Citizenship," *Proceedings of the American Philosophical Society*, 108, no. 1 (February, 1964), 39–53.

42. Pocock, "Civic humanism and its role in Anglo-American Thought," p. 179.

43. *Ibid.*, p. 178.

44. Pocock, "Machiavelli, Harrington, and English Political Ideologies in the Eighteenth Century," p. 565.

45. Gaetano Mosca, *The Ruling Class* (New York, 1939); Vilfredo Pareto, *The Mind and Society*, 4 vols. (New York, 1935); M. Ostrogorski, *Democracy and the Organization of Political Parties*, 2 vols. (New York, 1964); Robert Michels, *Political Parties* (Glencoe, 1949).

46. Joseph A. Schumpeter, *Capitalism, Socialism, and Democracy* (New York, 1942); Giovanni Sartori, *Democratic Theory* (New York, 1965); Robert Dahl, *Who Governs* (New Haven, 1961).

47. Pocock, "Civic humanism," p. 188.

48. *Ibid.*, p. 189.

49. Tocqueville, "Sur la Démocratie en Amerique," (*Fragments inédits*), introduction by J. P. Mayer, *La Nouvelle Revue Française* (1959), 7.

50. *Ibid.*

51. Tocqueville, *Oeuvres* (M), I, ii, 109–112.
52. Tocqueville, "Sur la Démocratie . . . ," p. 8.
53. *Ibid.*, p. 10.

Notes to Chapter 3.

1. See Robert Michels, "Conservatism," *Encyclopedia of the Soical Sciences*, Vol. IV (1931), for the uselessness of a general definition like "the tendency to maintain the *status quo*," and consequent plea for a "philosophical use and meaning" which "implies a particular *Weltanschauung.*" Michels fails to develop the intermediate, specifically historical definition used by me.

2. A. Morton Auerbach, *The Conservative Illusion* (New York, 1959), passim, especially pp. 7ff. A definition which stresses the universal psychological roots of conservatism — love of the familiar and fear of the unknown — is no more useful than Auerbach's universal ideology for the understanding of specific post-1770 European conservatism.

3. Russell Kirk is a prime offender in this respect. See, for example, his *The Conservative Mind: from Burke to Santayana* (Chicago, 1953).

4. Guido de Ruggiero, *History of European Liberalism*. English translation by R. G. Collingwood (Oxford, 1927).

5. Though it must not be forgotten, of course, that liberalism knows national variations. For Germany, see the important book by Leonard Krieger, *The German Idea of Freedom* (Boston, 1957).

6. Though *status quo* conservatism also appeals to certain sections of the lower class with whom "the cake of custom" (Bagehot) is still unbroken and deference to social superiors unimpaired.

7. The triple typology here used does not make provision for the "revolutionary conservative," a type that has played such an important role in twentieth-century German history (i.e., men like Moeller van den Bruck, Ernst Jünger, and Oswald Spengler). The omission is deliberate and inevitable, for it reflects the fact that the challenges confronting conservatism in the twentieth century are fundamentally different from those of the eighteenth. The conservatism dealt with here was a defensive movement which sought to preserve the ancien régime characterized by the principles and practice of social hierarchy, political authoritarianism, and Christian culture. It fought modernity from an entrenched position of social, political, and ecclesiastical power — even the reactionary usually belongs to a class which has been only partly dispossessed. Where he has been totally dispossessed — and when his vision of the good society has little objective resemblance to an earlier condition of society — the line of distinction between the reactionary and the revolutionary conservative becomes fluid.

The revolutionary conservatives during the Weimar Republic were an offensive group dedicated to the overthrow — not the conservation — of the German political, social, and cultural status quo. That status quo was determined by the triumph, however temporary, of the "modern forces" of egalitarianism, democracy, and secularism in 1918 — a belated triumph which had been preceded by more than a hundred years of unusually tenacious and successful conservative defense of the survivals of the ancien régime (the beginnings of which are covered here). Many pre-1918 conservative defenders of monarchy, Junker domination, and the "Christian state" became reactionaries after 1918. They hankered after the good old days of imperial Germany, remaining true to their pre-1918 substantive convictions on society and politics; from being status quo conservatives they became reactionaries pari passu with the alteration of the German status quo.

The revolutionary conservatives were not conservative in any of the three senses of our typology. They hated the status quo; they were not reactionaries and in fact dissociated themselves from the reactionary *Deutschnationale Volkspartei*, realizing that the pre-1918 world was irretrievably gone; and they were not reform conservatives because they wished to destroy the Weimar state rather than adapt it to new deeds through a creative synthesis of the new and the old. They shared the radical desire for a total reconstruction of society in accordance with theoretical blueprints, while differing, of course, in their substantive goals and the use of a vocabulary studded with conservative phrases (used, however, with connotations divorced from their traditional meanings). Their radicalism of intent alone suffices to put them outside the conservative fold; their paradoxical role as revolutionary conservatives, a contradictio in adjecto, was only possible in a society where conservatives could no longer act defensively from a position of established economic, political, or ecclesiastical power. It may be added that their positive goals were hopelessly fuzzy and never had any chance of realization since revolutionary conservatism could not possibly become a mass movement or compete with Nazi demagoguery on equal terms. Its historic impact was completely destructive because revolutionary conservatism helped to tear down the Weimar state for the ultimate benefit of Nazism. On the phenomenon of the conservative revolutionary during the history of the Weimar Republic — one of the most thoroughly explored topics of recent German history — see the following studies, all strong on the ideological and comparatively weak on the sociological side: Armin Mohler, *Die konservative Revolution in Deutschland* (Stuttgart, 1950); Klemens von Klemperer, *Germany's New Conservatism* (Princeton, 1957); Firtz Stern, *The Politics of Cultural Despair* (Berkeley, 1960); Otto Ernst Schüddekopf, *Linke Leute von Rechts* (Stuttgart, 1960); Kurt Sontheimer, *Anti-demokratisches Denken in der Weimarer Republik* (Munich, 1962); H. J. Schwierskott, *Moeller van den Bruck und der revolutionäre Nationalismus der Weimarer Republik* (Göttingen, 1962); and Hans Peter Schwarz, *Der konservative Anarchist. Politik und Zeitkritik Ernst Jüngers* (Freiburg, 1962).

8. *The Works of the Right Honorable Edmund Burke* (Boston, 1865), III, 241–242.

Notes to Chapter 4.

1. Burke is the classic example, though he probably thought it worse to kill aristocrats than men from other social classes; he identified revolutionary terror with liberal deterrence. "At the end of every vista, you see nothing but the gallows" (see Note 14): that was his description of Lockean *and* Jacobin society. More often, of course, repressive revolutionary regimes are simply identified with the repressive ancien régimes that they succeed, e.g., by the many writers who see no difference between Bolshevik and Czarist tyranny.

2. M. Merleau-Ponty, *Humanisme et Terreur* (Paris, 1947); Herbert Marcuse, "Repressive Tolerance" in Robert Paul Wolff, Barrington Moore, and Herbert Marcuse, A *Critique of Pure Tolerance* (Boston, 1965).

3. The Huguenots and their Protestant supporters in England and America produced an extraordinary atrocity literature during the eighteenth and early nineteenth centuries, but today the horrors are almost forgotten — so many have come since. Still, Max Beloff in his *Age of Absolutism* (New York, 1954) misses a chance to say something important about the early modern state when he confines his remarks on the destruction of the Huguenots to two sentences: ". . . in the course of the century [the Huguenot political position] had been whittled away to the point where Louis XIV could safely dispense with the Edict. The great majority of the people had been won back to the Catholic fold; and the tradition of dissent was substantially driven underground" (p. 58). Some peculiar rule seems at work among historians, whereby the outrages perpetrated by established governments are examined through the diminishing end of the scholarly microscope, those of revolutionary governments through the magnifying end.

4. In 1500 there were eight capital crimes; in 1688, nearly fifty; in 1800, over two hundred. Most of the increase has to do with crimes against property. See Leon Radzinowicz, *History of English Criminal Law* (London, 1948), Vol. I.

5. Lawrence Stone, *The Crisis of the Aristocracy 1558–1641* (Oxford, 1965), chap. v. Stone rightly emphasizes the importance of means other than simple repression in reducing violence, above all, the provision of alternative channels: litigation, court intrigue, political struggle.

6. John Milton, *Areopagitica* (1644); Milton is writing about the church and arguing against the use of force to achieve unity.

7. St. Just, "Fragments sur les institutions républicaines," troisième fragment, in *L'Esprit de la Révolution* (Paris, 1963).

8. Sigmund Freud, *Civilization and Its Discontents*, chap. iii. Freud is, of course, aware that not all revolts contribute to this "end result."

9. R. D. Laing and D. G. Cooper, *Reason and Violence: A Decade of Sartre's Philosophy 1950–1960* (London, 1964), p. 137.

10. John Milton, *Second Defense of the People of England* (1654).

11. Jean-Jacques Rousseau, *Emile*, Book I; Rousseau is discussing the

crucial importance of medicine in the modern world, but his remark has, and is intended to have, wider relevance.

12. B. Kidd, *Documents Illustrative of the Continental Reformation* (Oxford, 1911), p. 595.

13. ". . . control will really become universal, general, national, and there will be no way of getting away from it, there will be 'nowhere to go.' " Lenin, *State and Revolution* (New York, 1932), p. 84.

14. Edmund Burke, *Reflections on the French Revolution* (Everyman's edition, London, 1953), p. 75.

15. The phrase is from the diary of the Puritan minister Richard Rogers: "Twelve of us met to the stirring up of ourselves and others, four or five hours, with much moving of our affections." And again: "The sixth of this month we fasted betwixt ourselves . . . to the stirring up of ourselves to greater godliness." Rogers and Ward, *Two Elizabethan Diaries*, ed. M. M. Knappen (Chicago, 1933), pp. 69ff.

16. Richard Baxter, *Reliquiae Baxterianae* (London, 1696), p. 97. Baxter is discussing the 1650's.

17. Cf. St. Just: "You must punish not only traitors, but the indifferent, you must punish all who are inactive in the republic, all who do nothing for it." Quoted in Milovan Djilas, *The New Class* (New York, 1957), p. 147.

18. Alexis de Tocqueville, *Democracy in America*, ed. J. P. Mayer and Max Lerner (New York, 1966), appendix vi.

19. "It was anxiety which drove liberal man to unrelenting activity . . ." Sheldon Wolin, *Politics and Vision* (Boston, 1960), p. 324.

20. Michael Walzer, *The Revolution of the Saints* (Cambridge, Mass., 1965). I have drawn extensively on materials used here in order to make explicit an argument that is only implicit in the book.

21. Baxter, *Reliquiae Baxterianae*, p. 87.

22. Jean-Jacques Rousseau, *Politics and the Arts: Letter to D'Alembert on the Theater*, ed. Allan Bloom (Glencoe, Ill., 1960), p. 106.

23. Quoted in Crane Brinton, *The Jacobins* (New York, 1950), pp. 207–208.

24. For these and other quotations, see Walzer, *The Revolution of the Saints*, pp. 190–193.

25. *Letters of Lady Brilliana Harley* (London, 1854), pp. 8, 69, 101, 178, 180.

26. But Lenin is almost certainly too optimistic when he writes: ". . . *very soon* . . . observing the simple, fundamental rules of every-day social life in common will have become a habit." (emphasis added), *State and Revolution*, p. 85.

27. Richard Rogers, in *Two Elizabethan Diaries*, p. 67; *Diary of Lady Margaret Hoby, 1599–1605* (London, 1930), p. 97; William Scott, *Essay of Drapery* (London, 1635), p. 101.

28. On Methodism, see Élie Halévy, *England in 1815* (New York, 1961), pp. 410ff.

Notes to Chapter 5.

1. The National Science Foundation (Grant GS-580) and the Canada Council supported the work reported in this paper. I want to thank Muhammad Fiaz, Lynn Hollen Lees, Abdul Qaiyum Lodhi, and Ted Margadant for help in the analyses this paper draws on. Louise Tilly and Ian Weinberg gave me valuable advice and criticism. All translations are mine.

2. Philippe Vigier, *La Seconde République dans la région alpine* (Paris, 1963), I, 10; cf. André Armengaud, *Les Populations de l'Est-Aquitain au début de l'époque contemporaine* (The Hague, 1961), pp. 466–467.

3. E.g., Herbert Blumer, "Early Industrialization and the Laboring Class," *Sociological Quarterly*, I (January 1960), 5–14; S. N. Eisenstadt, *Modernization: Protest and Change* (Englewood Cliffs, 1966); Clark Kerr et al., *Industrialism and Industrial Man* (Cambridge, 1960); S. M. Lipset, *Political Man* (New York, 1960); Mancur Olson, Jr., "Rapid Economic Growth as a Destabilizing Force," *Journal of Economic History*, XXIII (December 1963), 529–562; Ronald Ridker, "Discontent and Economic Growth," *Economic Development and Cultural Change*, X, (October 1962), 1–15.

4. Crane Brinton, *The Anatomy of Revolution* (New York, 1938).

5. Neil Smelser, *Theory of Collective Behavior* (New York, 1963).

6. Chalmers Johnson, *Revolutionary Change* (Boston, 1966); Barrington Moore, Jr., *Social Origins of Dictatorship and Democracy*, (Boston, 1966).

7. E.g., Arthur S. Banks and Robert B. Textor, *A Cross-Polity Survey* (Cambridge, 1963); Ivo K. Feierabend and Rosalind L. Feierabend, "Aggressive Behaviors within Polities, 1948–1962: A Cross-National Study," *Journal of Conflict Resolution*, X, (September 1966), 249–271; Ted Gurr and Charles Ruttenberg, *The Conditions of Civil Violence: First Tests of a Causal Model* (Princeton, 1967); Bruce M. Russett and others, *World Handbook of Social and Economic Indicators* (New Haven, 1964).

8. This set of ideas on national development is similar in logic to Norton Long's treatment of urban politics, from which I have drawn some inspiration. See, for example, his "The Local Community as an Ecology of Games," *American Journal of Sociology*, LXIV (1958), 251–261. For a general review of this literature see Henry D. Bienen, *Violence and Social Change* (Chicago, 1968).

9. Precisely because these forms of collective violence belong to the traditional landscape of preindustrial France, historians rarely give them any attention except when they occur in conjunction with a major political upheaval. See, for example, H. Diné, "Emeutes et paniques de 1848 en Poitou et en Charentes," *Actes du 89e Congrès National des Sociétés Savantes*, Lyon, 1964 (Paris, 1965), 949–962; S. Posener, "La Révolution de Juillet dans le Gard," *Mercure de France*, CCXXI (1930), 621–626. In very backward areas like Corsica, ancient forms of violence like the communal feud were so prevalent that they frequently burst out under circumstances which would have pro-

duced a more modern form of disturbance elsewhere. A report from the government's solicitor in Bastia, describing an affair of April 1848, which just missed becoming violent, captures something of the tone: "Les scènes de désordre qui en 1830 ensanglantèrent la ville de Sartène ont failli se renouveler à l'occasion des élections pour l'assemblée constituante. Au moment où les habitants des communes de Cirolaggio, Grotta et Bilia arrivaient en armes pour prendre part au vote, on a fair courir le bruit qu'ils avaient l'intention d'attaquer les citoyens de Sartène. Tout la population de la ville a couru aussitôt aux armes et une barricade a même été elevée dans une petite ruelle prenant son issue sur la place de Porta. Une collision paroissait imminente, d'autant plus que les habitants des trois communes precitées etaient exaspérées d'une réception a laquelle ils étaient bien loin de s'attendre, puisque leurs intentions étaient pures, et qu'ils vendient dans le seul but de voter librement. Déjà la voix des autorités n'était plus écoutée, le sang allait couler, lorsque tout à coup le curé à la tête de son clergé et portant dans sa main l'imâge du Christ, se présenta au milieu de toutes ces irritations. Aussitôt chacun se prosterne devant l'image sacrée, les esprits se calment et les élections un instant interrompues continuent et se terminent dans la plus parfaite harmonie." Archives Nationales BB [30] 333. Other similar events which actually passed the point of ignition made Corsica very likely the bloodiest department of France during the turbulent elections of April 1848. See Archives Nationales BB[30] 360 on 1848–1849 and the "rapport sur le banditisme dans la Corse" of April 1852 in BB[18] 1473. But its violence was of a much more primitive variety than that of Seine or Rhône. Perhaps the widespread rural fires of 1829 and 1830 fit into the same primitive category. However, because of their concentration in the textile areas of Normandy and Anjou and their apparent attraction to the barns and houses of the local rich, I suspect that when more closely investigated they will turn out to have a good deal in common with grain riots, tax protests, and forest disorders. Detailed reports on the fires are in Archives Nationales CC 550. See Frederick Artz, "La crise des incendies en 1830 et les compagnies d'assurances," *Revue d'histoire moderne,* IV (1929), 96–105; Paul Gonnet, "Esquisse de la crise économique en France de 1827 à 1832," *Revue d'histoire économique et sociale,* XXXIII (1955), 249–292; Evelyn Ackerman, "Incendiarism in France during the Year 1830," (unpublished paper, Harvard University, 1967).

    10. Report in *Le Constitutionnel,* 11 June 1832.

    11. Paul Piolin, *L'Eglise du Mans durant la Révolution* (Le Mans, 1868), II, 192–201; M. Vovelle, "From Beggary to Brigandage: The Wanderers in the Beauce during the French Revolution," in Jeffry Kaplow, ed., *New Perspectives on the French Revolution* (New York, 1965), 287–304; Richard Cobb, "Politique et subsistances en l'an III. L'exemple du Havre," *Annales de Normandie,* V, (May 1955), 135–159; Cobb, "Une émeute de la faim dans la banlieue rouennaise," *Annales de Normandie,* VI (May 1956), 151–157; V. Duchemin and H. Triger, "Les premiers troubles de la Révolution dans la Mayenne," *Revue historique et archéologique du Maine,* (1887), 21–22, 42–86, 274–310; F. Mourlot, *La fin de l'ancien regime dans la généralité de*

Caen (1787–1790) (Paris, 1913), pp. 309–316; P. Nicolle, *Histoire de Vire pendant la Révolution* (1789–1800), (Vire, 1923), pp. 42–43, 109; Robert Triger, *L'année 1789 au Mans et dans le Haut-Maine* (Mamers, 1889), pp. 217–218; Daniel Colasseau, *Histoire de Baugé* (Baugé, 1960), II, 27–28; Georges Lefebvre, *La Grande Peur de 1789* (Paris, 1932).

12. Reports in Archives Nationales BB[18] 1378; *Le Droit*, 20–21 January 1840; *Le Constitutionnel*, 19–20 September 1839; *Le Moniteur universel*, 19 September 1839.

13. Extensive reports in Archives Nationales BB[18] 1375–1383; Archives Historiques de l'Armée, E[5] 152–154. See also Alexandre Chabert, *Essai sur les mouvements des prix et des revenus en France de 1798 à 1820* (Paris, 1945), pp. 398–421, which includes maps of grain production, prices, and the troubles of 1816–1817; likewise Maurice Lévy-Leboyer, *Les Banques européennes et l'industrialisation internationale dans la première moitié du XIXe siècle* (Paris, 1964), pp. 529–535, which includes a map of subsistence troubles in the West from 1838 to 1840; cf. Rémi Gossez's map and Paul Bois's discussion in Ernest Labrousse, ed., *Aspects de la crise et de la dépression de l'économie française au milieu du XIXe siècle* (La Roche-sur-Yon, 1956); Bibliothèque de la Révolution de 1848, Vol. XIX. I have also used an interesting unpublished paper by Barbara Herman, "Some Reflections on the Grain Riots in France: 1839–1840," (Harvard University, 1967).

14. See sources cited in note 9, Gonnet, "Esquisse de la crise economique," and Archives Nationales BB[30] 432, summaries of subsistence troubles, 1853–1854.

15. On the question of food supply, see J. C. Toutain, *Le produit de l'agriculture française de 1700 à 1958*, II. La Croissance. (Paris, 1961). Cahiers de l'Institut de Science Economique Appliquée, supp. no. 115. See also André Armengaud, "La Question du blé dans la Haute Garonne au milieu du XIXe siècle," Société d'Histoire de la Révolution de 1848, *Etudes*, XVI, (1954), 109–123.

16. Jean Meuvret, "Comment les Français du XVIIe siècle voyaient l'impôt," *XVIIe siècle*, IV (1955), 59–82.

17. A convenient compilation of the controversy appears in Trevor Aston, ed., *Crisis in Europe, 1560–1660* (London, 1965).

18. Boris Porchnev, *Les Soulèvements populaires en France de 1623 à 1648* (Paris, 1963). Roland Mousnier, "Recherches sur les soulèvements populaires en France avant la Fronde," *Revue d'histoire moderne et contemporaine*, V (1958), 81–113, and his article in Aston, *Crisis in Europe*; Robert Mandrou, *Classes et luttes de classes en France au début du XVIIe siècle* (Messina, 1965).

19. Archives Nationales BB[18] 1186.

20. Archives Nationales BB[18] 1187.

21. *Ibid.*

22. *Le Constitutionnel*, 20 July 1833; quoting *Mémorial bordelais*.

23. Gabriel Ardant, *Théorie sociologique de l'impôt* (Paris, 1965), p. 816. Elsewhere, Ardant says: "Another type of revolt is marked by its negative

character. Those who rise want to keep the state from entering into their domain and modifying their customs, their way of life — or making them pay taxes. Thus it is an act of refusal. The rebels — at least at first — do not want to take power. They want to expel the state. To this type belong the purest fiscal rebellions." (p. 744).

24. Félix Ponteil, "Le Ministre des Finances Georges Humann et les émeutes antifiscales en 1841," *Revue historique,* CLXXIX (January–June 1937), 324.

25. *Ibid.,* p. 351.

26. Rémi Gossez, "La résistance à l'impôt: les quarante-cinq centimes," Société d'Histoire de la Révolution de 1848, *Etudes,* XV (1953), 90.

27. Gossez gives an adequate summary of the Malabat affair, but these quotations are drawn directly from Archives Nationales BB[18] 1462.

28. Gossez, "La résistance à l'impôt," p. 96.

29. Frank E. Manuel, "The Luddite Movement in France," *Journal of Modern History,* X (June 1938), 180–211; Manuel, "L'introduction des machines en France et les ouvriers: la grève des tisserands de Lodève en 1845," *Revue d'histoire moderne,* n.s. 18 (June–August 1935), 209–225; 19 (September–October 1935), 352–372; Octave Festy, *Le mouvement ouvrier au début de la Monarchie de Juillet (1830–1834)* (Paris, 1908); André Dubuc, "Les émeutes de Rouen et d'Elbeuf (27, 28, et 29 avril 1848)," *Etudes d'histoire moderne et contemporaine,* II (1948), 243–275. The whole question of machine-breaking in France badly needs another look comparable in depth and sympathy to E. P. Thompson's *Making of the English Working Class.* The revolt against military conscription (except for the recurrent riots which grew from the attempts of the police to seize deserters) was already on its way out early in the nineteenth century, perhaps because the Revolution itself so firmly established the universal liability of young men to conscription.

30. Rémi Gossez, "Diversité des antagonismes sociaux vers le milieu du XIXe siècle," *Revue économique,* (May 1956), 439–457; David Pinkney, "The Crowd in the French Revolution of 1830," *American Historical Review,* LXX (October 1964), 1–17; George Rudé, *The Crowd in History* (New York, 1964); Robert Bezucha, "The 'Republican' Insurrection of 1834 in Lyon," unpublished paper presented to the American Historical Association, Toronto, December 1967.

31. Reports in Archives Nationales BB[18] 1187, 1189; *Journal des Debâts,* 18 October 1830; *Le Moniteur universel,* 29 December 1830; *Gazette des Tribunaux,* 16 August, 17, 18, 19 October and 26 December 1830.

32. Charles Schmidt, *Les Journées de juin 1848* (Paris, 1926), p. 40. The best review of the participation of workshops members in the June days is in Donald McKay, *The National Workshops* (Cambridge, 1933). The publication of the long-awaited thesis of Rémi Gossez should bring this neglected question up to date. See the preliminary statements in his *Les Ouvriers de Paris* (Paris, 1967).

33. Archives Nationales, C 929.

34. The following statements are based on statistical analysis of an alpha-

betic register describing over 11,000 of the persons arrested for participation in the June days (Archives Nationales F⁷ 2586). I have examined the June Days and other events of the period 1845 to 1855 in far greater detail, and with considerable quantitative documentation, in "How Protest Modernized in France, 1845 to 1855," a paper presented to the Conference on the Use of Quantitative Data in Political, Economic and Social History, University of Chicago (June 1969), to be published in revised form in a volume edited by Robert Fogel.

35. Charles Pouthas, *Démocraties et capitalisme* (Paris, 1961), p. 180.

36. General reports in Archives Nationales BB³⁰ 395–397, 402; Archives Historiques de la Guerre G⁸ 189–190; Joseph Décembre and E. Alonnier, *Histoire des conseils de guerre de 1852* (Paris, 1868); Eugène Ténot, *La Province en décembre 1851* (Paris, 1868); Claude Lévy, "Notes sur les fondements sociaux de l'insurrection de décembre 1851 en province," *Information historique*, XVI (no. 10, 1954), 142–145; J. Dagnan, *Le coup d'état et la répression dans le Gers (décembre 1851–décembre 1852)*, (Auch, 1929); Leo Loubère, "The Emergence of the Extreme Left in Lower Languedoc, 1848–1851; Social and Economic Factors in Politics," *American Historical Review*, LXXIII (April 1968), 1019–1051; Vigier, *La Seconde Republique*. Ted Margadant, whose forthcoming doctoral dissertation will change a number of commonly held ideas about the insurrection of 1851, has shown me the errors in the picture of the rebellion presented in earlier drafts of this paper; the insurrection had many more "modern" features than even I had thought. The revision actually strengthens the hypothesis of an extremely rapid shift of politics (and hence of collective violence) to the national scale at mid-century.

37. For the incidents mentioned here, see the sources cited in note 36, plus *Le Moniteur universel*, 9–21 December 1851; *Le Constitutionnel*, 8–27 December 1851; *Année historique*, 1851; Georges Duveau, *La vie ouvrière sous le Second Empire* (Paris, 1846), p. 86; "Atrocités commises à Clamency en 1851," *L'Intermédiaire*, XXXXVI, (1902), 179–181; Eugene Tenot, *Paris en décembre 1851* (Paris, 1868).

38. The quantitative statements are based on statistical analysis of Archives Nationales BB³⁰ 424, "Insurrection de décembre 1851, Statistique." There is, of course, the perpetual danger that those arrested are a distorted sample of the participants in the insurrection. I am inclined to think that the statistics give a reasonable picture of the men who were most heavily involved, although variations in repressive strategies from one department to another make them a risky source of information on regional variations.

39. Karl Marx, *The Civil Wars in France* (New York, 1935), p. 39.

40. Friedrich Engels, introduction to Karl Marx, *The Class Struggles in France*, (New York, 1935), pp. 21–25; William Langer, "The Pattern of Urban Revolution in 1848," in Evelyn Acomb and Marvin L. Brown, Jr., eds., *French Society and Culture since the Old Regime* (New York, 1966).

41. Albert Soboul, "La question paysanne en 1848," *La Pensée*, n.s. 18 (May–June 1948), 55–66; 19 (July–August 1948), 25–37; 20 (September–October 1948), 48–56; cf. Soboul, "La communauté rurale (XVIIIe et XIXe

siècles): Problèms de base," *Revue de synthese*, LXXVIII (July–September 1957), 283–307.

42. Rude, *The Crowd*, p. 177.

43. See, for example, Ardant, *Théorie sociologique*, pp. 756ff.

Notes to Chapter 6.

1. Research for this paper was made possible by grants from the Social Science Research Council, the American Philosophical Society, the American Council of Learned Societies, the Center for the Study of the History of Liberty in America, and the Old Gold Foundation of the University of Iowa.

Dates in the text are given in Old Style, except that the new year is reckoned from January 1; dates in the notes are Old Style as they appear in the documentation.

2. Max Weber, *The Theory of Social and Economic Organization*, tr. A. M. Henderson and T. Parsons (New York, 1947), p. 328.

3. R. R. Palmer, *The Age of the Democratic Revolution: A Political History of Europe and America, 1760–1800*, vol. I (Princeton, N.J., 1959), pp. 48–50, 194–197, 201, 216–227, 235.

4. *Ibid.*, 268.

5. *Ibid.*, 232.

6. Louis Hartz, *The Liberal Tradition in America* (New York, 1955), p. 72 and *passim*.

7. Bernard Bailyn, *The Ideological Origins of the American Revolution* (Cambridge, Mass., 1967), pp. 34–54.

8. Hartz, *Liberal Tradition*, 3n–4n.

9. Émile Lousse, *La Société d'ancien régime: organisation et représentation corporatives* (Louvain, 1943), has been used for this and succeeding paragraphs.

10. Franz Neumann (ed.), *The Spirit of the Laws by Baron de Montesquieu*, tr. Thomas Nugent (New York, 1949), Book II, chap. iv (Vol. I, pp. 15–16), provides an illustration of this situation as understood by a political analyst who lived with it. Montesquieu considered privileged corporative bodies to be valuable "intermediate channels" through which monarchical power flowed. "Abolish the privileges of the lords, the clergy and cities in a monarchy," he wrote, "and you will soon have a popular state, or else a despotic government."

11. Howard M. Chapin, *Documentary History of Rhode Island*, Vol. I (Providence, R.I., 1916), pp. 32, 36–39, 70–73, 95–96, 145–147, and *Early Records of the Town of Providence*, Vol. XV (Providence, R.I., 1899), pp. 219–220, provide convenient examples of early ideas about institutions. The attitudes toward land rights, however, must be deduced from the first deeds and the absence of public recording of deeds until land rights were regarded as the foundation of towns (c. 1661).

12. John R. Bartlett (ed.), *Records of the Colony of Rhode Island in New England,* Vol. I (Providence, R.I., 1856), pp. 143–146; Vol. II (Providence, R.I., 1857), pp. 3–21.

13. E.g., [Providence] *Early Records,* VI (Providence, R.I., 1894), pp. 28–29; Rhode Island Colony Records (MS, Rhode Island State Archives, Providence), Vol. I, pt. 2, p. 206; Vol. II, p. 100.

14. Chapin, *Documentary History,* I, 252–254, 269–271.

15. E.g., Newport sought a new grant of authority in 1705 as though it had never had one. Bartlett, *Records,* III (Providence, R.I., 1858), 525–526.

16. Bartlett, *Records,* II, 589. This grant was to East Greenwich in 1677.

17. On land and voting rights see, e.g., [Providence] *Early Records* III (Providence, R.I., 1893), 50, for distinction between purchasers and non-purchasers at town meeting (1663); *Early Records,* III, 20, for early subdivision of Grand Purchase (1661/62); *Early Records,* III, 53–54, for distinction between full and quarter rights; *Early Records,* XIV (Providence, R.I., 1899), 68–69, 121–122, for sale of parts of rights; *Early Records,* VIII (Providence, R.I., 1895), 177–178, for separation of purchasers' organization from town meeting and election of officers (1691); *Early Records* XI (Providence, R.I., 1896), 38, for assessment by purchasers and use of treasurer distinct from the town's (1697/8); *Early Records* XXI (Providence, R.I., 1915), 10–11, for adjudication of claims (1710/11); *Early Records,* IX (Providence, R.I., 1895), 3–4, for purchasers choosing route of highway (1713/14). Only adult males voted in purchaser's meetings, if the procedure was like that of other purchasers' organizations; women, children, and estates were represented by adult males to exercise voting rights.

18. [Providence] *Early Records,* II (Providence, R.I., 1893), 112 (15 May 1658, the town meeting "Ordered yt all those that jnioy land in ye jurisdiction of this Towne are freemen") and in general, *Early Records,* III, 18, 19, 90–91; IV (Providence, R.I., 1893), 70; V (Providence, R.I., 1894), 283–286, 297–309.

19. [Providence] *Early Records,* XV, 216. Cf. Revelations 18:2.

20. The "Articles of Agreement" of the Conanicut purchasers, together with records of decisions of their Trustees (to January 1659/60) and other notations exist in what is either an original form or a copy made for one of the purchasers (in Elisha R. Potter Papers, Rhode Island Historical Society); the "Articles of Agreement" and basic Indian deeds may be consulted most conveniently in the typewritten copy in Jamestown Land Evidences (MS, town clerk's office, Jamestown, R.I.), Vol. I, 5–9. Charles M. Andrews made a distinction (in respect to English understanding) between joint-stock companies with charters and "associations," which were the same except that they did not have charters or the legal standing which charters conferred. (*Colonial Period of American History,* Vol. I [New Haven, Conn., 1935], 41–42.) No such distinction entered law, terminology, or behavior in Rhode Island.

21. Francis Brinley, "A Breife Accot of ye Purchasing & Settling of ye Island Quononaquut . . ." and list of purchasers' papers (MS, Newport Historical Society, Box 117, folder 1).

22. Rhode Island Colony Records, Vol. II, 69; Jamestown Land Evidences, I (typewritten pages), 5.

23. Number 12 of "Articles of Agreement," Elisha R. Potter Papers; Brinley "Breife Accot."

24. E.g., East Greenwich Town Council records (MS, town clerk's office, East Greenwich, R.I.), Vol. I, 38 (minutes of a town meeting); Clarence S. Brigham (ed.), *Early Records of the Town of Portsmouth* (Providence, R.I., 1901), 128, 140, 217; [Providence] *Early Records* VIII, 36.

25. E.g., articles of agreement concerning Mumford's mill in Elisha R. Potter Papers.

26. C. Edwin Barrows (ed.), "The Diary of John Comer," in Rhode Island Historical Society *Collections*, VIII (Providence, R.I., 1893), 60–62.

27. Rhode Island Historical Society *Collections*, X (Providence, R.I., 1902), *passim*.

28. Bartlett, *Records*, III, 139–147.

29. *Ibid.*, 127–134, 147–149.

30. *Ibid.*, 292–300, 459–463, 575–576; Proceedings of the General Assembly (MS, Rhode Island State Archives), Vol. V, 137–138, 167.

31. Bartlett, *Records*, III, 326–331, 376–377, 396–397, 558; IV (Providence, R.I., 1859), 257; Proceedings of the General Assembly, V, 251, 366.

32. E.g., Bartlett, *Records*, III, 288–290, 326–331, 351–353, 508–510; Proceedings of the General Assembly, VI, 83.

33. Proceedings of the General Assembly, V, 78, 135, 171–172, 211.

34. Bartlett, *Records*, III, 369–371, 385–400, 575–576; Proceedings of the General Assembly, V, 176, 212.

35. Proceedings of the General Assembly, V, 243, 299, 326–327, 335, 338, 339, 358–359; VI, 43, 421–422; VII, 140–143; Bartlett, *Records*, IV, 221.

36. Proceedings of the General Assembly, VI, 153.

37. *Ibid.*, 154–155.

38. Bartlett, *Records*, IV, 234, 257; *Acts and Laws of his Majesties Colony of Rhode-Island, and Providence-Plantations in America* (Boston, 1719), notably pp. 13–15, 22–23, 35–36.

39. Proceedings of the General Assembly, VI, 43; Isaac Backus, *Church History of New-England. Vol. II* . . . (Boston, 1784), 48; George C. Mason (ed.), *Annals of Trinity Church, Newport, Rhode Island* (Newport, R.I., 1890), 27; Bartlett, *Records*, IV, 205–206.

40. [Newport First Baptist Church] "Book of Records . . ." (MS, Newport Historical Society), 23, 230, 232, 234, 238, 242.

41. An attested copy of the will is in Middletown Town Council records (MS, town clerk's office, Middletown, R.I.), Vol. III, pp. 248A–254A.

42. Newport Town Council records (MS, Newport Historical Society), III, 242; V, 13, 17.

43. Bartlett, *Records*, IV, 207–210.

44. Newport Town Council records, IV, 27, 28, 31, 41, 45; V, 4–5, 18, 27, 88–94, 109, 123, 133, 136, 137, 144, 146, 150, 174; Rhode Island Colony Records, IV, 272–274.

45. Colony law drew a distinction between town lands and town jurisdiction in 1696/7 (Proceedings in the General Assembly, V, 217–218). In Portsmouth the common lands became town property, pursuant to colony law and town decision (Rhode Island Colony Records, II, 109; [Portsmouth] *Early Records*, 225–229, 231–232, 252–255).

46. On Newport, see Middletown Proprietors' records (MS, town clerk's office, Middletown, R.I.), *passim*; on Westerly, Records of the Misquamicut Purchasers (MS, Westerly Public Library, Westerly, R.I.), II (covering 1707–1714); on Westconnaug, [Providence] *Early Records*, XVII, 223, 227–228, 239–240, and Rhode Island Historical Society *Collections*, XXV, 126–128; XXVI, 26–36, 94–98; on Jamestown, [copy of?] Samuel Cranston to committee of Conanicut proprietors, 12 April 1710, in H. W. Greene Papers (MS, Rhode Island Historical Society, Providence), 51, and Francis Brinley, "A Briefe Accot of Mr Samll Cranstons proceedings to gaine Bridget Sanfords Land, yt was Originally laid out by John Greene as pr the draught may be seene" (MS, Newport Historical Society, Box 117, folder 1).

47. Bartlett, *Records*, IV, 72, 83.

48. Brinley, "Briefe Accot of Mr Samll Cranstons proceedings."

49. The only case in which a land syndicate appeared in court as a collectivity was in 1722, when Andrew Harris brought suit as "one of the Proprietors of ye lands of Pautuxet . . . in behalf of himselfe & partners the rest of the proprietors of the sd Lands of Pautuxet." The defendant's attorney disputed Harris's representative character in a plea in abatement, which was overruled by the court. Tacitly the court may have accepted Harris's role — there is nothing to show whether there was further argument over it after the issue had been joined — but ruled against his claim in the end. (Andrew Harris v. William Randall, file papers, Box September 1722, General Court of Trials files, Superior Court clerk's office, Newport, R.I.). The same dispute was decided in the same way on strictly individual claims later ([Rhode Island] Superior Court records, Vol. I, 433, and file papers for Toleration Harris v. John Randall, in Box 1732, Superior Court clerk's office, Newport). Shortly before 1720 Andrew Harris had been involved in an even more complex dispute which the same syndicate of proprietors apparently made no effort to resolve (arbitration award and associated papers, Andrew Harris v. Jacob Clarke, General Court of Trials papers, Boxes 1716 & 1717, 1719). The other cases known to have been fought by proprietors' groups appeared as strictly individual matters in court records — e.g., Noah Whipple v. John Whipple (Providence Inferior Court of Common Pleas records, Vol. II, 476; cf. R.I. Historical Society manuscript collection M–Pl, P).

50. E.g., Rhode Island Historical Society Manuscripts, II, 53; XI, 25.

51. E.g., Westerly Land Evidences (MS, town clerk's office, Westerly, R.I.), Vol. II, 41, 82–89, for a complete set of deeds from colony to twelve purchasers and their quit-claim deeds to one another.

52. Rhode Island Colony Records, Vol. VI, 79; George C. Mason (ed.), *Annals of the Redwood Library and Athenæum* (Newport, R.I., 1891), pp. 38–39.

53. Rhode Island Colony Records, VI, 79; Newport Land Evidences (MS, City Clerk's office, Newport, R.I.), Vol. XXXIV, 524–527.

54. Herbert Kaplan, *The First Partition of Poland* (New York, 1962), *passim*.

Notes to Chapter 7.

1. V. O. Key, Jr., and Frank Munger, "Social Determinism and Electoral Decision: the Case of Indiana," in Eugene Burdick and Arthur J. Brodbeck, eds., *American Voting Behavior* (Glencoe, Ill., 1959), pp. 281–299.

2. V. O. Key, Jr., *A Primer of Statistics for Political Scientists* (New York, 1954), pp. 120–123.

3. See in particular the illuminating discussion by Erwin K. Scheuch, "Cross-National Comparisons Using Aggregate Data: Some Substantive and Methodological Problems," in Richard L. Merritt and Stein Rokkan, eds., *Comparing Nations* (New Haven, 1966), pp. 131–167; Austin Ranney, "The Utility and Limitations of Aggregate Data in the Study of Electoral Behavior," in A. Ranney, ed., *Essays in the Behavioral Study of Politics* (Urbana, 1962), pp. 91–102; and Nils Diedrich, *Empirische Wahlforschung* (Köln, 1965), esp. pp. 16–60.

4. These computations are based on the Republican percentage of the two-party vote by state, with some exceptions. For analytical purposes the combined Republican-Progressive percentage of the three-party vote is used for 1912, and the Republican percentage of the four-party vote for 1948. The 1892 election presents perplexing choices; here the Republican percentage of the two-party vote was used, except in Alabama, Florida, and Mississippi, where the local political situation made a combined Republican-Populist percentage of the three-party vote the most reasonable selection. For the first three pairs, $N = 38$; for the fourth, $N = 44$; for the fifth to seventh, $N = 45$; for the eighth, $N = 46$; for the ninth to twentieth, $N = 48$; for the twenty-first, $N = 50$.

5. See, e.g., Walter Dean Burnham, "The Changing Shape of the American Political Universe," *American Political Science Review* Vol. LIX (1965), 7–28.

6. Stanley Kelley, Jr., "The Presidential Campaign," in Milton C. Cummings, ed., *The National Election of 1964* (Washington, 1966), pp. 42–81. In a more journalistic vein, see Theodore H. White, *The Making of the President 1964* (New York, 1965), pp. 325–345; Robert D. Novak, *The Agony of the GOP 1964* (New York, 1965), pp. 439–464.

7. Kelley, "The Presidential Campaign," pp. 47–58; White, *Making of the President*, p. 346.

8. For discussions of these properties, see V. O. Key, Jr., "A Theory of Critical Elections," *Journal of Politics*, Vol. XVII (1955), 3–18; Walter

Dean Burnham, "The Alabama Senatorial Election of 1962: Return of Inter-party Competition," *Journal of Politics*, Vol. XXIV (1964), 798–824.

9. The convention data for 1896–1952 are found in Richard Bain, *Convention Decisions and Voting Records* (Washington, 1960), and for 1964 in *Congressional Quarterly Weekly Report* (July 17, 1964), 1482.

10. E. E. Schattschneider, *The Semi-Sovereign People* (New York, 1960), pp. 78–85.

11. For a useful discussion of this statistical method, see Murray B. Spiegel, *Theory and Problems of Statistics* (New York, 1961), pp. 73, 85–86. For this particular case, the formula is $Z = \dfrac{\% \text{ deviation } (1964) \text{ from mean } (1932\text{–}1960)}{\text{standard deviation } (1932\text{–}1960)}$.

12. For purposes of correlation, the raw Z scores have been converted here into points on a scale ranging from 0 to 100 (maximum negative to maximum positive).

13. Thus we find very low and sometimes negative correlations between 1964 Z and such sectionally structured elections as 1904, 1920, and 1924, since the sectional ordering among the states (especially as between the Far West and the Northeast) was wholly different from that found in such elections as 1896, 1916, or 1932.

14. For a discussion of this measure, see Robert R. Alford, *Party and Society* (Chicago, 1963), pp. 79–86. The data supporting the statement in the text are found here on p. 352. Averaging the index of class voting in elections for which there are more than one sample provides the following figures: 1936, 15.5; 1940, 25; 1944, 18; 1948, 30; 1952, 20; 1956, 14.5; 1960, 14.5.

15. For a preliminary discussion of the five party systems which have existed in American history at the national level, see my chap. X in William N. Chambers and Walter Dean Burnham, eds., *The American Party Systems: Stages of Political Development* (New York, 1967).

16. The *locus classicus* for this observation in the American context is V. O. Key, Jr., *Southern Politics in State and Nation* (New York, 1949), pp. 298–311.

17. Schattschneider, *Semi-Sovereign People*; see also his article, "United States: the Functional Approach to Party Government," in Sigmund Neumann, ed., *Modern Political Parties* (Chicago, 1956), pp. 194–215.

18. It should be noted that the stratification differentials in the three regions lumped together under "Rest of U.S." — Midwest, West, and South — were, in terms of this sample, extremely small.

19. This radical pro-Democratic movement among higher-status voters in the Northeast was not matched by a corresponding shift among lower-status voters, except for Negroes. There is good reason to suppose that Goldwater's *relatively* good showing among lower-status whites in the cities, as compared with Nixon's 1960 appeal among the same strata, was at least partly influenced by "backlash" factors. On the whole, however, the net effect was not a Republican gain but a near-duplication of the already lopsidedly pro-Democratic 1960 percentages.

20. See Alford, *Party and Society*, pp. 79–86. Because the SRC study for

1964 was seriously far off the mark, especially in the South, it is probable that the "real" index of class voting in 1964 was considerably less than 18 for the nation as a whole.

21. V. O. Key, Jr., "Interpreting the Election Results," in Paul T. David, ed., *The Presidential Election and Transition 1960–1961* (Washington, 1961), pp. 150–175. The formula may be expressed as $DR = \dfrac{x - y}{x} \cdot 100$, where x represents a given party's percentage of the two-party vote in one election, and y represents its vote in the following election. Obviously, if y is greater than x, the resultant figure represents accretion rather than defection. Although in some parts of the country the 1960–1964 defection ratio may be somewhat inflated because of the special religious-group factors in 1960, this appears not to have been a major factor either in New England or New York.

22. Negro jurisdictions throughout the country showed a very distinctively heavy Republican defection ratio. In St. Louis, for example, eight predominantly Negro wards swung from 19.9% Republican in 1960 to 3.3% Republican in 1964, with a Republican defection ratio of 83.4. Among the remaining twenty wards, on the other hand, the Republican percentages declined from 38.2% to 29.6%, a defection ratio of only 22.5.

23. The defection ratio for the state as a whole was 34.0. It is perhaps worth noting in passing that, of the four residential boroughs of New York City, only one (Queens) had as large an absolute Democratic percentage of the two-party vote in 1964 as in 1936, despite the much higher statewide Democratic percentage in 1964. Twenty-six of the sixty-five assembly districts in the city (40.0%) had defection ratios below the national average of 22.4, and forty of the sixty-five districts (61.5%) fell below the state ratio.

24. These are computed on a wholly geographical basis, i.e., without any attempt to weight the county units in terms of population proportions. The variances in Table 7 are based on Republican percentage of the two-party vote by county.

25. Although there is no easily derived set of quantitative scales for correlating regionalism with 1964 Z scores, a correlation between state percentage urban in 1960 and 1964 Z scores yields a r of +0.30, "explaining" 9% of the variance. Comparison of Tables 8 and 9 indicates that the positive relationship between region and 1964 Z is far higher.

26. In New York, for example, fourteen upstate counties had a variation from the 1932–1960 mean of less than one-half the national variation. All of them are heavily Republican and have been so since 1856. Of the 217 counties in the Middle Atlantic and New England states — most of them also traditionally Republican — Goldwater won just five.

27. The basic data for the 1845 New York census are taken from L. Holley, ed., *The New York State Register for 1845–6*, (New York, 1846), 1846 Supplement, p. 123. See also *Census of the State of New York for 1855* (Albany, 1857), esp. pp. 168–177. Counties with more than 10% of their 1845 native-stock population born in New England were included in the "Yankee" and Pennsylvania column in Table 10, except for counties (Clinton and Franklin)

in which the foreign-stock population was more than 20% of the total. To this group were added seven counties in western New York which had less than 10% New England stock, but were also at least as heavily populated by other out-of-state elements, mostly from the northern tier of Pennsylvania. The remaining nonmetropolitan counties were classified as "Yorker and mixed."

28. Madison County was the home of the prominent abolitionist leader Gerritt Smith. See Lee Benson, *The Concept of Jacksonian Democracy* (Princeton, 1961), p. 113. St. Lawrence County, known in the nineteenth century as "little Vermont," had originally been a Democratic bulwark before 1854 and was the home of Silas Wright, a leader of the more "radical," free-soil wing of the state Democratic party in the 1840's. In 1852 the Democrats won 48.4% of the total vote in the county, but only 15.0% in 1856. Thereafter its partisan alignments closely resembled Vermont's, as did its 1964 displacement.

29. See, e.g., Dixon R. Fox, *The Decline of Aristocracy in the Politics of New York* (New York, 1919); Benson, *Jacksonian Democracy*, for the period culminating in the 1844 election; and H. D. A. Donovan, *The Barnburners* (New York, 1925), for a study of the political forces leading to the 1848 Democratic schism and eventually to the realignments of the 1850's.

30. The definitive account of this unique area and its movements is Whitney R. Cross, *The Burned-Over District* (Ithaca, 1950).

31. A document which is particularly revealing of these antagonistic attitudes of New York City leaders to upstate rule after 1854 is Mayor Fernando Wood's proposal of 1861 for the secession of New York City from the state and the union. See Henry S. Commager, ed., *Documents of American History*, 5th ed. (New York, 1949), pp. 374–376. New York County gave Lincoln 34.8% of the vote in 1860, contrasting with 61.8% in the dominantly "Yankee" counties north and west of Albany.

32. County data for the 1860 referendum are found in *Tribune Almanac for 1861*, p. 41. One of the counties (Orange) failed to make a return in this referendum, so that for all computations involving it, $N = 59$.

33. Ralph A. Straetz and Frank Munger, *New York Politics* (New York, 1960), pp. 55–67.

34. *Ibid.*, pp. 39–41.

35. See, e.g., Charles M. Snyder, *The Jacksonian Heritage: Pennsylvania Politics, 1833–1848* (Harrisburg, Pa., 1958). German antagonism to the free school law of 1834 was so intense that it materially contributed to a split in the Democratic party which caused Governor Wolf's defeat in 1835. See pp. 50–67.

36. Bernard Berelson *et al.*, *Voting* (Chicago, 1954), pp. 100–101. In the absence of systematic comparative community studies involving survey methods, of course, speculations involving this "atmosphere" can only be highly suggestive rather than definitive. See Peter H. Rossi, "Four Landmarks in Voting Research," reprinted in Frank Munger and Douglas Price, eds., *Readings in Political Parties and Pressure Groups* (New York, 1964), pp. 343–344.

37. Angus Campbell *et al.*, *The American Voter* (New York, 1960), pp. 346–350.

38. Angus Campbell *et al.*, *Elections and the Political Order* (New York, 1966), pp. 109–111.

39. See Ruth C. Silva, *Rum, Religion and Votes: 1928 Re-Examined* (University Park, Pa., 1962). In this study, which is based on aggregate data at the state level only, Professor Silva argues forcefully — though not, in my opinion, persuasively — that neither religion nor attitudes toward prohibition were significant correlates of Al Smith's strength in 1928. The difficulty here seems to involve a level-of-analysis problem of the sort discussed by Scheuch (see Note 3). Such a view of 1928 seems difficult to square with the reactivation mechanisms discussed by Converse for 1960.

40. See, e.g., Daniel J. Elazar, *American Federalism: A View from the States*, (New York, 1966), pp. 79–140, for a good preliminary discussion of this concept.

41. Benson, *Jacksonian Democracy*, pp. 270–382.

42. Aage R. Clausen, "Response Validity: Vote Report," unpublished Survey Research Center paper (January 1967).

43. *Ibid.*, pp. 36–37. This explanation, which has considerable plausibility, raised the intriguing possibility that a considerable autogenerated error, concentrated among the most marginal, "know-nothing" parts of the electorate, infects not only the 1964 study but others as well. What effect, if any, this discovery may have on the substantive conclusions drawn from these studies about the properties of the American electorate remains unclear.

44. It is sometimes considered bad form to attempt regional partitions of a nationwide probability sample. Leaving aside the fact that this was done in Angus Campbell, et al., *The Voter Decides* (Evanston, Ill., 1954), the justification for making the attempt here is the existence of major discrepancies involving one major region of the country: the Northeast so far as the distribution of the vote is concerned, and the South so far as overreporting of the Democratic proportion of the vote is concerned.

45. It is difficult to disagree with Rossi's conclusion in light of the findings of this study. "As research findings accumulate from sample surveys, knowledge about the major correlates of the phenomenon grows at the same time that the problems from research become more specific. In short, as more is learned the questions to be put to empirical test tend to become more pointed. Enough is learned about the crucial populations most suitable for settling such problems. The representative sample survey at this stage often becomes an inefficient design. What may be needed most at such stages in the history of research on a given problem are a number of small, pointedly designed studies of crucial populations, rather than 'shotgun' designs." Munger and Price, *Readings*, p. 339.

46. Indeed, this precise point emerges from Survey Research Center work which undertakes to compare political perceptions in one congressional district dominated by the visceral race issue and perceptions in the country as a whole during the 1958 election. See Warren E. Miller and Donald E. Stokes,

"Constituency Influence in Congress," *American Political Science Review,* Vol. LVII (1963), 45–56.

47. The Democratic candidate for governor in 1966 campaigned far more explicitly for the "white backlash vote" than Goldwater himself had done in 1964, and with some success. In Baltimore City the Democratic defection ratio, measured between the 1962 and 1966 gubernatorial elections, was 4.2 in white wards with a median 1960 income of $4,000 to $5,999, 27.5 in white wards with median income above $6,000, and 79.1 in Negro wards. The citywide ratio was 32.0.

48. Donald E. Stokes, "Spatial Models of Party Competition," reprinted in Angus Campbell *et al., Elections and the Political Order,* pp. 161–179.

49. V. O. Key, Jr., *Politics, Parties and Pressure Groups,* 5th ed. (New York, 1964), pp. 222–227.

50. See, e.g., Robert A. Dahl's discussion of this point in R. A. Dahl, ed., *Political Oppositions in Western Democracies* (New Haven, 1966), pp. 34–69.

Notes to Chapter 8.

1. Karl Marx, *The Eighteenth Brumaire of Louis Bonaparte* (New York, n.d.), p. 22.

2. Irving Bernstein, *The Lean Years: A History of the American Worker,* 1920–1933 (Boston, 1966), p. 58.

3. Stanley Lebergott, *Manpower in Economic Growth: The United States Record Since 1800* (New York, 1964), pp. 187, 227–228.

4. S. M. Lipset and Reinhard Bendix, *Social Mobility in Industrial Society* (Berkeley, Cal., 1959); S. M. Miller, "Comparative Social Mobility: A Trend Report and Bibliography," *Current Sociology,* IX (1960).

5. Stephan Thernstrom, "Poverty in Historical Perspective," in Daniel P. Moynihan (ed.), *On Understanding Poverty: Perspectives from the Social Sciences* (New York, 1959); Thernstrom, "On Black Power," *Partisan Review,* XXXV (1968), 225–228. For a fascinating discussion of changing English attitudes toward social inequality since 1918 and their failure to correspond to changes in social reality, see W. G. Runciman, *Relative Deprivation and Social Injustice* (London, 1966).

6. Philip Dawson and Gilbert Shapiro, "Social Mobility and Political Radicalism: The Case of the French Revolution of 1789," unpublished paper delivered at the American Sociological Association meetings, August 1967.

7. E. P. Thompson, *The Making of the English Working Class* (London, 1964), p. 194.

8. Clark Kerr and A. J. Siegel, "The Interindustry Propensity to Strike — An International Comparison," in Kerr, *Labor and Management in Industrial Society* (Anchor paperback edition, Garden City, New York, 1964), pp. 105–147.

9. This material is exhaustively analyzed in Simon Kuznets, Dorothy S.

Thomas et al., *Population Redistribution and Economic Growth in the United States, 1870–1950*, 3 vols., (Philadelphia, 1957–1964).

10. James C. Malin, "The Turnover of the Farm Population in Kansas," *Kansas Historical Quarterly*, IV (1935), 339–371.

11. Merle Curti et al., *The Making of an American Community: A Case Study of Democracy in a Frontier County* (Stanford, Cal., 1959). For comparable data on an Iowa farming county in the same period, see Mildred Throne, "A Population Study of an Iowa County in 1850," *Iowa Journal of History*, LVII (1959), 306–330.

12. Blake McKelvey, *Rochester, The Flower City, 1855–1890* (Cambridge, Mass., 1949), p. 3; Stephan Thernstrom, *Poverty and Progress: Social Mobility in a Nineteenth Century City* (Cambridge, Mass., 1964), pp. 84–90, 167–168; Robert Doherty, "Social Change in Northampton, Massachusetts 1800–1850," unpublished paper for the Yale Conference on Nineteenth Century Cities, 1968.

13. Ray Ginger, "Labor in a Massachusetts Cotton Mill, 1853–1860," *The Business History Review*, XXVIII (1954), 67–91.

14. E. A. Wrigley (ed.), *An Introduction to English Historical Demography* (London, 1966), pp. 165–166; Lawrence Wylie, "Demographic Change in Rousillon," in Julian Pitt-Rivers (ed.), *Mediterranean Countrymen* (Paris, 1963), pp. 215–236.

15. Joan W. Scott, "Les Verriers de Carmaux," in Thernstrom and Sennett, *Nineteenth Century Cities*. Cf. the observations on itinerant English workingmen of the same period in Eric Hobsbawm's "The Tramping Artisan," in *Labouring Men: Studies in the History of Labor* (London, 1964), pp. 34–63.

16. The literature on the American business elite is conveniently reviewed in Lipset and Bendix, *Social Mobility*, chap. iv.

17. For a lengthy critique of the view that the opportunity structure in the United States today is less favorable than in the past and that poverty is accordingly "a permanent way of life" for the so-called "new poor," see my "Poverty in Historical Perspective," in Moynihan, *On Understanding Poverty*.

18. Hobsbawm, "The Labour Aristocracy in Nineteenth Century Britain," in *Labouring Men*, pp. 272–315; Royden Harrison, *Before the Socialists: Studies in Labour and Politics, 1861 to 1881* (London, 1965), pp. 26–33.

19. For citations to this literature as of 1964, see Thernstrom, *Poverty and Progress*, chap. viii; for a review of more recent findings, see Peter Blau and Otis Dudley Duncan, *The American Occupational Structure* (New York, 1967).

20. See the papers by these authors in Thernstrom and Sennett, *Nineteenth Century Cities*.

21. Cf. Gerhard Lenski, *The Religious Factor* (Garden City, N.Y., 1961), chap. iii. In this analysis of residents of Detroit, Lenski emphasized that Catholic rates of upward occupational mobility were lower than those for Protestants, but his own tables reveal more strikingly the pattern which prevailed in Boston — higher rates of *downward* mobility for Catholics who

began their careers in the middle class. Whatever the influence of religion upon mobility patterns in the past, however, national survey data collected in the 1960's suggests that today Catholics are not at all handicapped in this respect, and may, indeed, be more successful than Protestants as a group; see Andrew M. Greeley and Peter H. Rossi, *The Education of Catholic Americans* (Chicago, 1966), ch. vi, and Andrew M. Greeley, *Religion and Career: A Study of College Graduates* (New York, 1963).

22. Herbert G. Gutman, "Labor in the Land of Lincoln: Coal Miners on the Prairie," unpublished manuscript, 1967, p. 39.

23. Harrison, *Before the Socialists*, p. 30.

INDEX

Albee, Edward, 54
American Voter, The, 44, 212
Ardant, Gabriel: on geographical concentration of French fiscal revolts, 153
Arendt, Hannah, 164
Aydelotte, William: on generalization, 44–45

Bagehot, Walter, 71; *Physics and Politics,* 9
Baron, Hans, 78
Baxter, Richard, 132
Beard, Charles, 5
Beer, Samuel H.: Richter on, 3, 8–14, 18, 28–29, 36; his method of *Verstehen* vs. empirical generalization, 36, 46–57, 72–73; on limited generalization (dogma of universality), 41–46, 58–59, 70–73; on Popper, 41, 43, 67, 72; on Hempel, 41–42, 43; on Hume, 42; on Aydelotte, 44–45; on Bloch, 45, 59; on Nagel, 47, 68; on Wittgenstein, 47–48; on Max Weber, 48, 52, 53–54, 66; on Cobden and Bright, 51; on Dray, 52–53; on Snyder, 53; on Albee and Freud, 54; on history as past behavior, 58–60; on Lyell, 58; on Burnham, 59–60; on Tilly, 60; on history as duration, 60–65; on Lipset and Dahl, 64; on history as development, 65–73; on Durkheim and MacIver, 66; on Alfred Weber, 67; on Mill, Dewey, and Rustow, 68; on Santayana and Bell, 70; on Trilling, 71; biographical notes on, 256; *British Politics in the Collectivist Age,* 14, 21

Bell, Daniel: on assumptions of general education, 4, 70
Bendix, Reinhard: on relation of industry and social mobility, 222
Benedict, Ruth: *Patterns of Culture,* 9
Benson, Lee, 213
Bentham, Jeremy, 130
Birnbaum, Norman, 13–14, 37
Bloch, Marc, 59; *Feudal Society,* 45
Blumin, Stuart, 235
Bright, John, 51
Brinton, Crane, 140
Burke, Edmund: Richter on, 15; Epstein on, 106, 107, 109, 110, 112; on progress of French liberty, 115–116; Paine on, 121; Walzer on, 128, 268n1; *Reflections on the Revolution in France,* 112
Burnham, Walter Dean: Richter on, 28–29, 30, 33–34; Beer on, 59–60; on Munger, 186; on Key, 186–187, 193, 197, 219; on importance of party identification, 186; on his research focus, 187; on 1964 sectional alignment factors, 187–196, 217; on Goldwater campaign, 189–190, 197–198, 200, 202, 211, 215; on similarities of 1964 and 1896 elections, 190–193, 205; on Schattschneider, 193; on concepts of sectionalism, 196–197; on Northeast's party defection ratio, 197–198, 200; on New York's county deviations, 198–199, 201–206, 209, 210; on within-state variances, 198–201; on relationships of 1964 and 1856 elections, 204–205, 209; on Pennsylvania's county deviations, 206–209, 210; on

"Republican atmosphere," 209–211; on phenomenon of multiple latent voting cleavages, 211–213; on Converse, 212; on Benson, 213; on techniques of voting behavior study, 213–216; on Clausen, 214–216; on Rossi, 216; on continuity and change in American voting behavior, 216–220; on Stokes, 218; biographical notes on, 256

Chambers, William Nisbet, 18, 28–29; *Political Parties in a New Nation*, 21
Chicago, University of: theory and practice of general education at, 3–4, 8, 20
Clausen, Aage R., 214–216
Cobden, Richard, 51
Columbia University: theory and practice of general education at, 3–4, 8
Comparative method: Richter on, 24–29, 36, 79–80, 87–90, 101, 259n20; Tilly on, 141; Burnham on, 213; Thernstrom on, 223
Comte, Auguste, 25
Conant, James Bryant, 3–5 *passim*
Converse, Philip: on party preference gradients, 212
Cranston, Samuel, 178–182
Croce, Benedetto: *History as the Story of Liberty*, 8–9
Curti, Merle, 226, 229

Dahl, Robert, 64, 98
Dawson, Philip: on bourgeois social mobility, 223–224
Dewey, John: on causation, 68
Doherty, Robert, 226, 235
Dray, William, 52–53
Durkheim, Émile, 25, 66

Eliot, Charles William, 4
Eliot, T. S., 4
Engels, Friedrich, 30, 162
Epstein, Klaus: Richter on, 27–28, 30–31; on forces creating eighteenth-century European conservative movement, 103–105; on purpose of German conservatism, 105; on definitions of conservatism, 105–106; on Burke, 106, 107, 109, 110, 112, 115–116, 121; on Ruggiero, 106; on reform conservatives, 107, 108–110, 116–118, 120–121; on reactionaries, 107, 108, 110–111, 116, 120; on status quo conservatives, 107–108, 110, 116, 120; on recurring core of conservative argument, 111–120; on Catholic conservatives,

118; on characteristics of conservatism, 120–121; biographical notes on, 256; on revolutionary conservatives, 266–267n7
Erikson, Erik, 15

Federalist Papers, 89
Ferguson, Adam, 98–99
Freeman, E. A., 25
Freud, Sigmund, 15, 54; *Civilization and its Discontents*, 125–126

General Education in a Free Society/ General Education Report of 1945, see Harvard University
Gerth, Hans, 12
Ginger, Ray, 226
Gitelman, Howard, 235
Goldwater, Barry: campaign of 1964, 189–190, 197–198, 200, 202, 211, 215
Gossez, Rémi, 154, 155
Griffen, Clyde, 235
Gutman, Herbert, 235, 236

Halévy, Elie, 15, 96
Harrington, James, 94, 98
Harrison, Frederic, 236–237; *Order and Progress*, 236
Harrison, Royden, 231–232, 236
Hartz, Louis, 21, 32, 167–168, 184; *The Liberal Tradition*, 59
Harvard University: Social Sciences 2 at, 1–3, 8–23, 29, 32, 37; General Education Report of 1945 (*General Education in a Free Society*; "Redbook"), 3–5, 7–9, 13; Social Relations Department at, 12
Hempel, Carl, 41–42, 43, 75
Henderson, A. M., 12
History and Theory, 29
Hobbes, Thomas, 15, 127
Hobsbawm, Eric, 228, 231–232
Hume, David, 15, 42

James, Sydney V.: Richter on, 24, 32–33, 36, 37; on Hartz, 32, 167–168, 184; on Palmer, 32–33, 166–168; on Weber, 165, 170; on government and social order in colonial America, 165, 167–168, 170, 171; on role of central governments, 165–166; on Paine, 168; on corporative (Old Regime) vs. feudal social order, 168–171; on Lousse, 168–170; on early social order in Rhode Island, 171–172, 176; on colony's early government framework, 172–173, 176; on town government

framework, 173–174; on proprietors' organizations, 174–176, 180–182; on Rhode Island's role in Dominion of New England, 177–178; on Cranston's role in legal rationalization, 178–182; on significant features of Rhode Island's legal rationalization, 182–185; on corporative vs. rationalized social order, 185; biographical notes on, 256
Johnson, Chalmers, 140–141

Kafka, Franz: *The Castle*, 73
Kerr, Clark, 224–225
Key, V. O., Jr., 186–187, 193, 197, 219; *A Primer of Statistics for Political Scientists*, 186
King, Martin Luther, 164
Kluckhohn, Clyde, 12
Knights, Peter, 235

Langer, William, 162
Lenin, Nikolai, 99, 127, 128
Lenski, Gerhard, 236
Liberty League, 195
Lindsay, A. D., 13
Lipset, S. M., 64, 222
Literary Digest, 195
Locke, John, 15, 130, 136
Lousse, Émile, 168–170
Lovejoy, A. O., 25
Luther, Martin, 124
Lyell, Sir Charles, 58

Machiavelli, Niccolò, 94; *Discourses*, 86
MacIver, Robert, 66
McKelvey, Blake, 226
McLennan, J. F., 25
Malin, James C.: "The Turn-over of the Farm Population in Kansas," 226
Mandeville, Bernard, 96
Mandrou, Robert, 150–151
Mannheim, Karl, 30
Marcuse, Herbert, 21
Marx, Karl: Richter on, 13–14, 18, 30, 99; Walzer on, 124; Tilly on, 159, 162; on French urban rebellions, 161; Thernstrom on, 221
Meuvret, Jean, 150
Michels, Robert, 98
Michigan University Survey Research Center's 1964 election study, 187, 197, 212, 214
Mill, John Stuart: Richter on, 25; defines cause, 68; on Tocqueville, 74, 76, 78

Millar, John, 98–99
Miller, S. M., 222
Mills, C. Wright, 12
Milton, John, 125, 126
Montesquieu, Charles-Louis de Secondat, Baron de: on French spirit, 16–17; his use of comparative method, 26–27, 36, 79–80; influences Tocqueville, 74–103; his concept of democracy, 78–79; his belief in effect of physical and moral factors on society, 80–83, 91; his theory of functional equivalence, 81–83, 84, 100–101; his categories of government, 83–87; his inconsistency, 84–85, 102; his civic humanism, 95–101 *passim*; *Spirit of the Laws*, 80, 85, 86, 95
Moore, Barrington, 140–141
Mosca, Gaetano, 98
Mousnier, Roland, 150–151
Müller, Max, 25
Munger, Frank, 186
Murray, Henry, 12

Nadel, George, 29
Nagel, Ernest, 47, 68
Nietzsche, Friedrich, 15

Ostrogorski, M., 98

Paine, Thomas, 121, 168
Palmer, R. R., 32–33, 166–168
Pareto, Vilfredo, 13, 98
Parsons, Talcott, 12, 13, 15, 21; *The Structure of Social Action*, 13
Pascal, Blaise, 75
Pierson, George Wilson, 74, 76–78; *Tocqueville and Beaumont in America*, 74
Pocock, J. G. A., 93–94, 98
Ponteil, Félix: on geographical concentration of French tax rebellions, 153–154
Popper, Karl, 29; on causal explanation, 41, 43, 67, 72
Porchnev, Boris, 150–151
Pouthas, Charles, 159

"Redbook," *see* Harvard University
Richter, Melvin: on Social Sciences 2, 1–3, 8–23, 29, 32, 37; on Beer, 3, 8–14, 18, 28–29, 36; on Harvard General Education Report, 3–5, 7–9, 13; on factors affecting American attitudes toward higher education, 4–7; on Weber, 12–18 *passim*, 24, 26–27, 80,

86; on Lindsay, 13; on Marx, 13–14, 18, 30, 99; on Walzer, 14–15, 17, 19, 31, 37; on Rousseau, 15, 75, 96; on Tilly, 17–18, 29–30, 32, 33, 36; on Chambers, 18, 28–29; on James, 24, 32–33, 36, 37; on comparative method, 24–29, 36, 79–80, 87–90, 101, 259n20; on Freeman, Müller, McLennan, Lovejoy, Spencer, Comte, and Durkheim, 25; on Mill, 25, 74, 76, 78; on Roth, 26–27; on Epstein, 27–28, 30–31; on Burnham, 28–29, 30, 33–34; on Thernstrom, 30, 33, 34–36; on Montesquieu and Tocqueville, 36, 74–103; on Royer-Collard, 74; on Pierson, 74, 76–78; on Hempel and Whitehead, 75; on Pocock, 93–95, 98; on civic humanism, 93–102; biographical notes on, 257; *The Politics of Conscience: T. H. Green and His Age,* 21. *See also* Montesquieu, Baron de; Tocqueville, Alexis de

Rossi, Peter H., 216

Roth, Guenther, 26–27

Rousseau, Jean Jacques: Richter on, 15, 75, 96; Walzer on, 127, 132, 136

Royer-Collard, Pierre, 74

Rudé, George: on French rebellions, 162

Ruggiero, Guido de, 106

Rustow, Dankwart, 68

St. Just, Louis de, 125, 129

Sartori, Giovanni, 98

Sartre, Jean-Paul, 126

Schattschneider, E. E., 193

Schumpeter, Joseph A., 98

Scott, Joan, 228

Sennett, Richard, 235

Sewell, William H., Jr., 223, 230, 232

Shapiro, Gilbert: on bourgeois social mobility, 223–224

Smelser, Neil: *Theory of Collective Behavior,* 140

Smith, Adam, 98–99, 130

Snyder, Richard: on game theory, 53

Soboul, Albert, 162

Spencer, Herbert, 25

Stokes, Donald E., 218

Thernstrom, Stephan: Richter on, 30, 33, 34–36; on Marx, 221; on relation of mobility to collective industrial protests, 221, 224–225; on Bendix, Lipset, and Miller, 222–223; on Sewell, 223, 230, 232; on comparative analysis, 223; on Dawson and Shapiro, 223–224; on Thompson, 224; on Kerr, 224–225; on geographical mobility related to class identification, 224–229; on Malin, McKelvey, and Ginger, 226; on Curti, 226, 229; on Doherty, 226, 235; on his Newburyport study, 226–227, 229–231, 235–238; on his Boston study, 226–237; on Laslett, Wrigley, Scott, and Wylie, 228; on Hobsbawm, 228, 231–232; on occupational mobility, 229–232; on Royden Harrison, 231–232, 236; on relation of migration and occupational mobility, 232–235; on Blumin, Knights, Sennett, Gitelman, and Griffen, 235; on Gutman, 235, 236; on Weber, 235–236; on Lenski, 236; on Frederic Harrison, 236–237; on relation of occupational to property mobility, 236–238; biographical notes on, 257

Thompson, Edward: on working-class development, 224

Tilly, Charles: Richter on, 17–18, 29–30, 32, 33, 36; Beer on, 60; on relation of collective violence to French nineteenth-century modernization, 139–142, 162–164; on relation of changing French politics to collective violence, 139–145, 156–159, 161–164; on Brinton and Smelser, 140; on Johnson and Moore, 140–141; on use of comparative method, 141; on classifications of French collective violence, 145–146; on primitive disturbances, 146; on food riots, 146, 147–150, 157; on tax rebellions, 146, 150–155; on modern disturbances, 146–147; on reactionary disturbances, 146–156; on Porchnev, Mousnier, and Mandrou, 150–151; on Gossez, 154, 155; on urban rebellions, 156–158, 161; on modern forms of French disturbance, 158–164; on Marx, 159, 162; on Tocqueville, 161; on Engels, Langer, Soboul, and Rudé, 162; on Arendt and King, 164; biographical notes on, 257; *The Vendée,* 21

Tocqueville, Alexis de: his use of comparative method, 26–27, 36, 79, 87–90, 101; Mill on, 74, 76, 78; Pierson on, 74, 76–78; influenced by Montesquieu, 74–103; his inconsistency, 75, 85, 90, 102; Yale Collection of, 77, 87; his interpretation of factors affecting society, 83, 87, 89–93; his concept

of civic humanism (virtue), 84, 95–101 *passim*; defines *moeurs*, 90–91; on American morality, 130; *Democracy in America*, 74, 75, 77, 78, 89, 96, 100; *Old Regime and the Revolution*, 92, 97
Trevelyan, G. M., 52
Trilling, Lionel: on classical novel's field of research, 71
Troeltsch, Ernst, 22

Vigier, Philippe: on French politics, 140
Voting, 209

Walzer, Michael: Richter on, 14–15, 17, 19, 31, 37; on state terrorism, 122, 123–125, 127–129 *passim*, 268n3; on repression as form of revolutionary radicalism, 122–123, 125–129; on Puritan repression, 122–123, 127–128, 130–135; on Marx, 124; on Freud, 125–126; on Rousseau, 127, 132, 136; on Lenin, 127, 128; on Burke, 128, 268n1; on Tocqueville, 130; on routinization of terrorism, 130, 135–136; on Locke, 130, 136; on Smith and Bentham, 130; on Baxter, 132; on Jacobin repression, 132; on relation of self-government to repression, 136; biographical notes on, 257; *The Revolution of the Saints*, 14, 21
Weber, Alfred, 67
Weber, Max: Richter on, 12–18 *passim*, 24, 26–27, 80, 86; Roth on, 26–27; on use of comparative method, 27; Beer on, 48, 52, 53–54, 66; James on, 165, 170; Thernstrom on, 235–236; *Historismus*, 26; *Economy and Society*, 26
White, Paul Lambert, 77
Whitehead, Alfred, 75
Wilde, Oscar, 131
Williams, Roger, 171, 174
Wittgenstein, Ludwig, 47–48
Wylie, Laurence, 228

Yale University: Tocqueville collection at, 77, 87